The United Kingdom cereal market

David Colman

The United Kingdom cereal market

An econometric investigation into the effects of pricing policies

Manchester University Press

Published by
Manchester University Press
316-324 Oxford Road
Manchester MI3 9NR

ISBN 0 7190 0479 9

Printed in Great Britain
by William Clowes & Sons Ltd
London, Colchester and Beccles

Contents

Tables

Figures

Preface

Much recent research in agricultural economics has been of the econometric type. That is, attempts have been made to statistically identify economic and technical relationships within agriculture, principally with a view to gaining insights into the effectiveness of existing government policies towards agriculture and of learning something about the industry which might assist in the development of more suitable policies. It is acknowledged that the statistical estimates obtained are not always sufficiently acceptable to permit the attainment of these objectives. Nevertheless, it was felt at the outset of this study that insufficient attention had been paid to the problems of statistically identifying the appropriate economic relationships governing supply and demand responses within British agriculture, and that there was a need for work in this direction.

Rather than tackling the whole agricultural industry at once it was decided to try and identify the important relationships within the cereal sector of British agriculture, with a view to assessing the effectiveness of the two main arms of current government policy towards cereals, the deficiency payment scheme, and the minimum import price scheme. In order to accomplish this it was felt to be necessary to statistically estimate a model containing three sets of structures for (a) cereal supply, (b) cereal demand, and (c) livestock numbers. This latter is required because livestock numbers are presumed to greatly affect cereal demand, and at the same time to be influenced by the price of cereal feed.

Before attempting to estimate the functions of the model it has been necessary to gain a thorough knowledge of a number of areas, (a) the way in which cereal price policies are administered, and have developed, (b) the nature and economics of the cereal production process, and of the relationship between cereals and the other major enterprises in British agriculture, and (c) the nature of cereal demand outlets and their changing nature. A chapter is devoted to each of these three topic areas.

The empirical results are presented in three chapters, one chapter being devoted to each of the three basic sets of relationships in the model. These are followed by a chapter in which various tests are applied to the estimated functions of the model in order to examine (a) the predictive abilities of the model, and (b) the implications of the model for the application and effectiveness of cereal price policies. Basic conclusions of the study are then presented in the final chapter along with an evaluation of the role of the type of research performed. The basic conclusions include that there appear to be severe limitations on the extent to which cereal deficiency payments can be used to influence total cereal supply, but that there is considerable potential for using this policy to modify the proportions in which the various cereals are produced, and that imposing minimum import prices appears likely to cause an appreciable reduction in livestock numbers.

This study is based on a Ph.D. thesis presented at Manchester University, which in its original form covered only the period 1954 to 1967. Work after completion of the thesis indicated a superior alternative to the original supply model. In preparing the revision of this part of the econometric model, the analysis has been extended to cover the additional period 1967-8 to 1969-70 inclusive. There appeared to be no comparable reasons to alter the structure of the cereal demand and livestock inventory parts of the model, and consequently these are presented in their originally estimated form for the period 1954-5 to 1966-7.

Acknowledgements

First and foremost I should like to acknowledge the debt of gratitude owed to the late Mr. David Bugg. His kindly advice and friendship have been greatly missed since his most untimely death.

For their constructive criticisms, advice and encouragement I would like to express particular thanks to Professor Wat Thomas, Dr. John McInerney and Dr. John Bridge. The helpful views and assistance of many colleagues have also been of considerable value, and in this regard mention must be made of Mr. John Stewart and Mr. Dennis Leech.

Mrs. Kaylene Dhanda provided full-time clerical assistance on this project for twelve months, and her diligent and cheerful co-operation is greatly appreciated. A grant to finance this valuable clerical assistance was negotiated by Professor D. K. Britton via the Home-Grown Cereals Authority from the Agricultural Marketing and Development Corporation, and I wish to express my gratitude to all those concerned in this complex arrangement.

Finally I should like to thank all the many people at the Ministry of Agriculture, Fisheries and Food who undertook additional work to furnish data which were not available from published sources, and also to those professionally involved in the cereals market with whom the author had a number of very informative discussions.

1

Introduction

A. The central position of cereals in U.K. agriculture

Cereals occupy a key role in the agricultural industry of the United Kindgom. In terms of final agricultural sales, cereals contribute more to the gross incomes of U.K. farmers than any other crop, and on this score alone they rank as the premier crop. This, however, does less than justice to their contribution, for it is as feed inputs in livestock production that domestically produced cereals find their major outlet, large quantities being used as feed directly on the farms of origin.

Livestock and livestock product sales in recent years have contributed around 70 per cent of the value of final agricultural sales. The basic operation of livestock production is the conversion of feedingstuffs by animals into forms more readily digestible by human beings. Thus, feedingstuffs are a basic raw material of the livestock economy, and make up as much as 70 per cent of the variable costs of production in pig and poultry enterprises. Of the non-forage feedingstuffs consumed, cereals are undoubtedly the most important–80·7 per cent by weight of all concentrate feeds in 1968-9 were cereal grains or cereal offals. It is also clear that cereals are nutritionally more important in feeding the U.K's domestic livestock than are the forage products of grassland.[1] This being so it can be seen that cereals are basic to the livestock economy, and that between direct sales and the contribution to livestock production they are responsible for a major proportion of the productive output of the U.K. Agricultural industry. It is thus evident that cereal policies, which operate largely through the manipulation of cereal prices, have important implications for the livestock sector which comprises the bulk of the United Kingdom agricultural industry.

[1] In the absence of any published statistics on the aggregate value of grassland production, this assertion can only be supported by a rough estimate: In 1968-9, 38·37 per cent of livestock and livestock product sales were of pig and poultry products; roughly 70 per cent of their variable costs of production is for feedingstuffs, most of which (about 90 per cent) are cereal based. Cost studies indicate that grassland and cereals provided approximately equal contributions to dairy rations; dairying provided 31·82 per cent of livestock and livestock product sales in 1968-9, feed accounting for approximately 50 per cent of production costs. Output of fat cattle and calves in the same year was valued at 22·46 per cent of livestock and livestock product sales, and the contribution of cereals and grassland in these enterprises is roughly in a ratio of 35 : 55, with 60 per cent of variable costs attributed to feedingstuffs. In spite of grassland's greater contribution in cattle meat production, and that it provides about 90 per cent of the nutritional requirements of sheep (output valued at 7·4 per cent of 1968-9 livestock and livestock product sales), the clear implication of these figures is that the production value of cereal feedingstuffs used exceeds that of grassland.

B. Cereal imports

Substantial quantities of cereals and cereal products are imported into the U.K. From 1954 to 1969 the value of these averaged £224 million per annum, and the yearly level remained fairly constant. The volume of imports however exhibited a marked decline from the peak level in 1958-9 up to 1966-7, after which it has shown an upturn. That this decline occurred in the face of a considerable increase in total cereal utilisation in the U.K.—total cereal utilisation, excluding rice and cereal products other than wheat flour, rose steadily from 15·7 million tons in 1954-5 to 20·4 and 21·5 million tons in 1966-7 and 1968-9 respectively—implies not only that most of the growth in the U.K. market for cereals has been satisfied by home production, but that there has in addition been a measure of substitution for imports. It is the considerable expansion of domestic barley production, and to a lesser extent wheat production which has brought this situation about. Indeed, U.K. barley output increased prodigiously from 2·2 million tons in 1954-5 to 8·6 and 8·1 million tons in 1966-7 and 1968-9 respectively, and was sufficient to enable considerable exports of barley in the years from 1965-6 to 1967-8. In consequence the total value of cereal and cereal product exports rose to £41·6 and £40·5 millions respectively in these two years, which was approximately double the average value of exports in the previous six years.

The decline in cereal imports which has occurred since the late 1950's, has been largely due to a continuous reduction in barley and wheat imports; oats imports have also declined steadily but are not a significant proportion of the total. In the case of barley imports this reduction is clearly the result of substitution by domestically produced barley. The fall in wheat imports is also due partially to substitution, but is to some extent the result of a decline in wheat demand for food and industrial uses. There has also been some measure of substitution of home-grown cereals for imported maize. Maize imports reached a peak in 1961-3 and have fallen subsequently to a fairly stable level. Examination of the breakdown of maize utilisation since 1961-63 reveals that animal feed utilisation has declined slightly despite the considerable increased demand for cereal feedingstuffs as a whole, which implies some displacement by domestic grains, while the food and industrial demand for maize has continued to grow.

The current composition of cereal imports is such as to suggest that the potential for further import substitution is less than it formerly was. Most of the imports are now accounted for by maize and by hard wheat for flour milling, both of which are crops not readily replaceable by home-grown cereals. It is however evident that there has been a considerable cereal import saving potential in the past, and that there is limited room for further substitution. It is certainly clear that any change in domestic cereal output has implications for the cereal import bill. The Government has been keenly aware of this during the recent foreign exchange crisis, and its concern has been reflected in its economic policy towards the cereal sector.

C. Some general objectives of cereal policy

The major post-war instrument of U.K. agricultural policy has been the deficiency payment scheme, whereby farmers have received supplementary payments for their produce in addition to the returns generated by the open market. Manipulation of the size of these deficiency payments has been effected in pursuance of a number of policy goals.

One major aim of paying producers in excess of market prices has been to ensure 'proper remuneration and living conditions for farmers and workers and an adequate return on capital invested in the industry'.[2] This aspect of policy is largely motivated by social and political considerations. However, there does exist a rationale for blanket protection for agriculture, such as in the more efficient investment pattern which is stated to occur in the absence of price uncertainty.

A second basic policy objective which has received varying degrees of emphasis throughout the post-war period, is the contribution to the balance of payments. Implementation of cereals policy has certainly reflected this concern. For example, the 1957 Annual Price Review White Paper[3] states that, 'The major objective . . . calls for a selective expansion of net output with the main emphasis on the substitution of home-grown feedingstuffs, including grass, for imports . . .'. This objective was still being emphasised in 1968 with the recognition that the desired 'expansion of livestock production would increase considerably the demand for cereal feed and that, consistent with our international obligations, a substantial part of this additional requirement should be produced in this country'.[4]

The deficiency payments scheme has also been used to influence the relative rates of growth of different crop and livestock enterprises. To take the case of cereals; by changing the relative sizes of the guaranteed prices per hundredweight of different cereals, governments have sought to change relative cereal returns so as to adjust the cereal output mix to bring it more into line with the needs of the market. For example, for the 1957-58 harvest the guaranteed price of wheat was reduced by 1*s.* 2*d.* per hundredweight, while those of barley and oats were increased by 6*d.* and 2*s.* 8*d.* per hundredweight respectively. By contrast, in 1961-2 there was no change in the wheat guarantee, while barley growers received 1*s.* 2*d*. less per hundredweight and oats producers 3*d.* more. Many of these price changes are relatively small—a 3*d.* change in the price of oats is a change of less than 1 per cent—and since they are effected with a view to inducing changes in the cereal acreage, they would seem to imply that the policy

[2] Agriculture Bill 1946 (Cmnd. 6996).
[3] Cmnd. 109, para. 9.
[4] Cmnd. 3558, para. 45.

makers assume a fairly sensitive response of output to marginal changes in returns. It is thus of both importance and interest to estimate the elasticities of cereal acreage response to changes in (guaranteed) cereal prices.

A major development in cereals policy occurred in 1964 with the introduction, along with other measures, of minimum import prices for cereals and cereal products—oats, rye and rice being excluded. This had the objective to 'prevent unduly low-priced imports from undermining the market. The new guarantee arrangements will also bring the cost of the support system under better control, while maintaining the advantages of the present system . . .'.[5] The imposition of minimum import prices and their enforcement by means of levies represents a considerable departure in policy, and through the potential to raise the market price of all cereals it has serious implications for all cereal users, the largest of whom is the agricultural industry.

There are also a number of subsidiary goals in cereals policy such as that of ensuring orderly marketing throughout the year. Instruments aimed at securing this objective include the payment of wheat deficiency payments according to a seasonal scale, the seasonal incentive scheme for barley, and the forward contract bonus cheme operated by the Home-Grown Cereals Authority. Due, however, to the analytical restrictions imposed by data problems upon the ensuing study, it will not be possible to accommodate any analysis of the operations of these policy tools.

D. Aims of the study

In the light of the background information contained in the preceding sections, the aims of the study will now be defined.

The principal objective is to develop and empirically estimate a set of structural relationships, which explain, at an aggregate level, the operation of the cereals market in the United Kingdom, and which will permit evaluation of the impact of cereals policy upon cereal production, consumption and imports. Drawing upon the background of the previous sections it appears that an appropriate model would have to consist of at least (1) a set of cereal supply functions (with one function for each domestically produced cereal), (2) a set of cereal demand functions (with a function for each cereal in each of its major uses), and (3) a set of functions to explain the determination of the numbers of each major class of livestock in the U.K.

An appropriately specified model containing these three sets of elements will enable the impact of certain policy measures upon the cereals market to be evaluated along the following lines:

(1) The estimated supply structures should enable assessment of the effectiveness of the guaranteed or minimum import price policies in

(a) controlling the aggregate home-grown cereal supply, and

[5] Cmnd. 3215, para. 23.

(b) in effecting changes in the composition of home-grown cereal production.

(2) The demand and livestock inventory structures together should permit some assessment of the potential influence of the minimum import price scheme upon the domestic demand for cereals. The demand structures will enable some prediction of the direct influence of increased market prices for cereals upon the demand for them. It is, however, anticipated that changes in livestock numbers will be a major factor in explaining cereal demand changes. It is also anticipated that livestock numbers will be affected by changes in cereal prices, and thus it is expected that there will be an additional indirect effect upon cereal demand as a result of these changes. Hence, in order to fully evaluate the effects of changed market prices for cereals (resulting from increased minimum import prices) upon cereal demand it is felt desirable to consider the influence of cereal prices upon livestock numbers.

(3) In view of the importance of the balance-of-payments objective a model which would have practical importance should permit assessment of the effects of different cereal policies upon the volume of cereal imports and exports. As the intention is to design and estimate a model capable of explaining both the supply and demand for cereals, it should be possible to estimate the imports or exports of each cereal as the difference between them. Thus, the balance-of-payments effect of policy-induced price changes which influence either supply or demand will be reflected in changes in the size of the difference between total cereal demand and supply.

(4) A further objective of U.K. cereals policy is to substitute domestically produced feedgrains for imported ones. Appropriate construction of cereal feed demand functions to yield cross elasticities of demand with respect to other cereal prices will give insight into the feasibility of substitution—the greater the cross elasticities the greater the potential for substitution between cereals.

An empirical study such as the one proposed is also capable of satisfying a number of broader aims: the process of systematically testing hypotheses will hopefully lead to improved insight into the operation of the cereals market. Also, the success or otherwise in identifying important relationships between variables may suggest more effective means of accomplishing certain policy objectives. These broader aims are particularly important in view of the considerable importance of cereals in the U.K. agricultural economy and of the relevant paucity of empirical research in this area hitherto.

Having thus stated the aims of the study, it seems appropriate to digress and comment upon the title of the study. From statements already made it will be evident that, because of the close relationship between the cereals and livestock sectors, it is felt necessary to specify and estimate relationships to explain livestock numbers. It is not, however, considered that this incursion into the analysis of the livestock economy necessitates any change of title such as to suggest that this is a study of the cereal-livestock economy. For, firstly, there is to be no examination of the determinants of either livestock product demand or production, nor, secondly, is there to be any evaluation of the outcome of changes in livestock policy. Indeed, analysis of the livestock sector is only carried as far as is considered necessary to permit a thorough evaluation of the effects of cereal policy changes, and thus it seems appropriate to signify that this is a study of the cereals market only.

E. A review of some relevant literature

Relatively few econometric supply and demand studies have so far been performed for the U.K. agricultural economy, and much insight into the difficulties and techniques of estimation is provided by studies of agriculture in the U.S.A. which have been fairly numerous. Because of the central position of cereals in the agricultural economy many of these American studies have estimated cereal supply and demand functions either in general models of the agricultural sector or more restricted feed-livestock models.

One of the earliest feed-livestock models was the four-equation model estimated by Foote in 1953 by means of ordinary least squares.[6] Later models were more elaborate, and both Hildreth and Jarrett's[7] livestock-feed model of 1955 and Cromarty's[8] 1958 model of U.S.A. agriculture used limited information estimation procedures to estimate the multi-equation models simultaneously. These models have been further elaborated in Cromarty's[9] 1962 model of the wheat and feed-livestock sectors and by Feltner[10] in his development of the Hildreth-Jarrett model. While it is of no immediate relevance to this study to review the results of these studies in detail, it is important to note that in all except Foote's early model, the various equations of the models have been deemed to require simultaneous estimation. Particular emphasis has been placed upon the simultaneous interrelationships between cereal feed demand and the supply and demand for livestock and livestock products.

It is with regard to this simultaneity of determination that the current study departs from the American studies, for it will be assumed that no price variables need be treated as endogenous in considering U.K. agriculture. This basic difference of assumptions arises as a result of major differences

[6] Foote, R. J., *Statistical Analyses Relating to the Feed-Livestock Economy:* U.S.D.A., Tech. Bul. 1070, June 1953.

[7] Hildreth, C. J., and F. G. Jarrett, *A Statistical Study of Livestock Production and Marketing,* Cowles Commission Monograph No. 15, 1955.

[8] Cromarty, W. A., 'An Econometric Model for United States Agriculture', *J. Am. Statist. Ass.,* Vol. 54, pp. 556-574, 1959.

[9] Cromarty, W. A., *Predicting the Impact of Alternative Government Programs on the Wheat and Feed-Livestock Economies:* Michigan State U., Tech. Bul. 286, 1962.

[10] Feltner, R. L., 'Alternative Models of the Feed-Livestock Economy', Unpublished Ph.D. thesis, North Carolina State U., 1964.

in the markets for agricultural products in the U.K. and the U.S.A. In the first place, in marked contrast with U.K. conditions, the U.S.A. has a closed market with embargos or strict quotas on the import of all major temperate agricultural products. In consequence of this, price formation is almost solely the result of forces acting within the U.S.A. market. Secondly, in the U.S.A. the scope of government intervention in the market is much less, being confined to grains and cotton, and this is operated in a different manner. The Commodity Credit Corporation (C.C.C.) is empowered to purchase grain in the open market at a government-fixed support price, and to sell stocks if prices rise to the statutory minimum price 5 per cent in excess of the support price. Thus the C.C.C. adjusts cereal and cotton supply and demand in order to maintain prices within the limits laid down. Cereal and cotton prices can hence be viewed either as endogenous, with a powerful market force institutionalised to control prices, or as exogenous, given that government policy effectively restricts these prices within a narrow band. In consequence, cereal prices may be treated as exogenous, as in Feltner's study; but a simultaneous system is nevertheless required for the joint estimation of feed demand, livestock demand and livestock supply equations because livestock prices are free to vary, and these will be influenced by cereal prices, and in turn will affect the level of cereal demand.

No complete models of U.K. agriculture have been statistically tested, and econometric studies in this country have tended to concentrate on either supply or demand. As far as cereal supply in the post-war period is concerned there have been a number of studies and in chronological order these have been by Gardner,[11] Jones,[12] Hill,[13] Rachel Dardis[14] and Josling.[15] The only statistical studies of U.K. cereal demand are in Josling's study and another by Thomas,[16] this latter being confined to considering feed demand.

In their supply studies Jones and Hill have dealt with total grain acreage response, Rachel Dardis with total grain production, and only Gardner and Josling have tackled the problem of the acreage response of individual cereals (although Jones presents individual cereal acreage response functions estimated for the pre-war period). The approach to cereal supply in this

[11] Gardner, T. W., 'A Note on Cereal Prices and Acreages', *J. Agric. Econ.* Vol. 12, No. 3, pp. 361-370, June 1957.

[12] Jones, G. T., 'The Response of the Supply of Agricultural Products in the United Kingdom to Price, Part II', *Fm Economist.* Vol. 10, No. 1, pp. 1-15, 1962.

[13] Hill, B., 'Supply Responses in Grain Production in England and Wales, 1952-1963', *J. Agric. Econ.,* Vol. 16, No. 3, p. 416, June 1965.

[14] Dardis, Rachel, 'The Welfare Cost of Grain Protection in the United Kingdom', *J. Fm Econ.,* Vol. 49, No. 3, pp. 597-609, August 1967.

[15] Josling, T.E., *The United Kingdom Grains Agreement* (*1964*): *An Economic Analysis,* Institute of International Agriculture, Michigan State University, 1968.

[16] Thomas, W.J., the section concerning the U.K. in *The Stabilisation of World Trade in Coarse Grains: A Consideration of the Underlying Economic Issues,* F.A.O., Commodity Policy Studies No. 14, 1963.

study differs in essential respects from all of these. The principal distinctive feature is the development of an interrelated set of individual cereal acreage response equations involving both simultaneous and recursive relationship between equations. As a consequence of this development some of the estimational problems encountered by those who have attempted to estimate individual cereal acreage functions separately (Gardner, Josling and Jones) appear to have been overcome, in that the information conveyed by the model developed here seems to accord more closely to a prior expectations. Some of the equations in the system incorporate the orthodox Nerlove partial adjustment mechanism, a feature shared with the work of Hill, Jones and Josling.

In terms of period and area covered there is a great deal of overlap between this study and that of Josling, who estimated U.K. cereal supply and demand functions for the time period 1954-5 to 1965-6 (as opposed to 1955-6 to 1969-70 for this study). However, the current work also considers livestock-feed relationships; and the cereal supply, and many of the cereal demand functions to be specified differ considerably from those estimated by Josling. Only Jones and McClements appear to have tackled the problems of estimating livestock inventory equations for the U.K. In his first study, Jones[17] presents annual time series results for a number of livestock aggregates, excluding all cattle, fattening pigs or broiler fowls, for a variety of periods within the range of 1906 to 1958. All of the estimates are performed using Nerlove-type distributed lag models. The success of his results are varied with some negative adjustment coefficients being implied, but on the whole they suggest a negative response of livestock numbers to feed prices and a positive response to own product prices. Jones' second study[18] estimates a variety of functions for livestock inventories, disappearance and inflow, again using distributed lag models, but with six-monthly data for the period 1955 to 1964. The study does not attempt comprehensive explanation of all livestock numbers, and does not examine either fat cattle or fattening-pig inventories; examination of fowl production is by means of explaining chick placements rather than fowl numbers. The results obtained confirm those of the earlier study with respect to the negative influence of feed prices upon livestock inventories.

As far as livestock inventories are concerned, Jones has concentrated upon breeding livestock numbers and has not considered fattening livestock numbers in either study. Hence there is no examination of the relationship of breeding to fattening livestock. This failure to consider the determination of inventory numbers for all classes of livestock means that Jones' results cannot be used to fully evaluate the effect of cereal prices upon the livestock economy, and hence there is a need to develop the appropriate livestock inventory equations in the current study.

[17] Jones, G. T., op. cit.

[18] Jones, G. T., 'The Influence of Price on Livestock Population over the Last Decade', *J. Agric. Econ.*, Vol. 16, pp. 500-526, Dec. 1965.

The quarterly model to be used in explaining pig numbers is based directly on the successful model developed by McClements[19] in his investigation of the Northern Ireland pig economy. Details of this work will be presented in the section of Chapter 7 concerned with the specification of livestock inventory models.

F. The time period of the analysis

Controls upon agricultural production and marketing were imposed during World War II. The last of these which had important effects for the cereals market was not finally lifted until 1954, when concentrate (including cereals) feed rationing for livestock was abolished. It is thus from 1954 that the current analysis begins, and, although the basic coverage of the study runs up to 1967, for reasons explained in the preface the supply model is estimated up to 1969.

The basic economic model is set up for estimation with annual time series. Cereal production is on the basis of one sowing and one harvest per year and therefore annual time series is clearly appropriate for this part of the model. The annual period to be considered however is not a calendar year, but is the harvest year running from 1 July to 30 June; a year thus defined covers the period of influence of a given cereal harvest.

Cereal demand is in reality a continuous flow process, and the choice of a discrete time period over which to aggregate demand data is an arbitrary one. Because of data shortages it has proved difficult to calculate cereal demands over periods shorter than one year, so that an annual model has been dictated here as well. Fortunately the published annual demand data are also on a harvest year basis so that the demand and supply results fit conveniently together.

Livestock production is also a continuous process and the inventory of livestock can in principle be measured at any point in time. In fact quarterly census data are available which has enabled both annual and quarterly models to be estimated. It was decided to go to the lengths of estimating quarterly livestock functions because the technical production lags can be more accurately accommodated by this means.

[19] McClements, L. D., 'A Model of Pig Supply', *J. Agric. Econ.*, Vol. 20, pp. 241-250, May 1969.

2

Cereals legislation

Any model of the economic structure of U.K. agriculture, or of a sector of it, must necessarily reflect the impact of government policies for supporting agricultural prices. The effects of the deficiency payment system of support are particularly far reaching, in that the prices which farmers receive for a given commodity are greater than those paid for it by consumers. Hence in the case of cereals, which are simultaneously outputs and inputs (in livestock production) of agriculture, farmers' supply and demand decisions are based on different prices for the same commodity.[1] This differential is created by virtue of the fact that the amount of the deficiency payment is equal to the difference between a guaranteed price to producers of cereals and the price determined by market forces, although modifications of the system of payments have been devised so that producers receive some minimal indication of the signals generated by the market. Livestock producers, on the other hand, insofar as they purchase home-grown cereals, pay the market price (plus distributive margins), which will roughly correspond to the final price paid for imported cereals.

This system of support, coupled with the important fact that the U.K. is not self-sufficient in cereals, results in fundamental differences between the economic structures appropriate to a study of the U.K. cereals economy and those which have been proposed for the U.S.A., where, to date, most empirical studies in this area have been performed. For this reason, it appears germane to present a brief statement of the way in which U.K. cereals policies operate, with notes on their historical development.

A. A brief history and outline of U.K. cereal price support policy

The earliest Corn Laws dating back to 1361 were primarily designed to protect the interests of the consumer by preventing the export of corn and thus preventing the price of corn from rising too high.[2] In fact the Corn Laws from 1555 to 1663 specified price levels for wheat above which no corn exports would be permitted.

It wasn't until the Corn Laws of 1670, that cereals policy was designed to raise the prices received by British farmers. Under these Laws corn exports were permitted whatever the price of wheat, and at the same time a sliding scale of payments was introduced to be levied against wheat

[1] This is a difference over and above that which is due to the lag in the response of supply to price changes.

[2] This and ensuing details of the Corn Laws are taken from Lipson, E, *The Economic History of England, Vol. II*, pp. 448-464. A. & C. Black Ltd., 1934.

imported at less than 80 shillings a quarter. These measures to encourage domestic corn production and protect British agriculture from foreign competition were reinforced by the Corn Bounty Act of 1688. Under this Act merchants received export subsidies of five shillings per quarter for wheat, and lesser amounts for the other cereals. The bounties were abolished under the Corn Laws of 1773, which also considerably reduced the level of import duties. High protection policies were revived in 1815 with the prohibition of corn imports until the price of wheat exceeded 80 shillings a quarter, 'a terrible price in the money values of that day'.[3] However Lord Ernle claims after examining the economic conditions in the period before 1815, that '. . . down to 1815, they (the Corn Laws) exercised little or no influence on prices'.[4] This was not the position after 1815, when a shortage of domestic grain supplies, coupled with potential cheaper supply from overseas meant that the measures of 1815 were highly effective. Ultimately the burden imposed upon the consumer, and principally upon the emergent urban working class proved excessive, and the interests of the landowners were overcome with the repeal of the Corn Laws in 1846.

A free market in cereals then existed until the enactment of the Corn Production Act of 1917. This short-lived Act, which was designed to encourage the production of corn, empowered the Board of Agriculture and Fisheries to pay a deficiency payment per acre of wheat and oats in the event that the average price of these cereals fell below the minimum prices established by the Act. However, these measures proved too costly to the Exchequer and were repealed in the Corn Production Acts (Repeal) Act of 1921.

No further governmental support for agricultural prices was given until after the Agricultural Marketing Act of 1931. It was this Act which laid down the basic provisions for the establishment of Producer Marketing Boards, and which created the foundations for the development of the agricultural support policies operating today. Following in the wake of this Act, the Wheat Act was passed in 1932. Its principal provision was to empower the Wheat Commission to make payments to registered growers if the average price of home-grown millable wheat fell below an established standard price. The payments made for each hundredweight of wheat grown, were equal to the difference between the market prices and standard prices, but were subject to proportional downward adjustment if the actual supply of home-grown millable wheat exceeded the anticipated supply. This last provision was a loosely formulated precursor of the 'standard quantity' restriction upon payments, which was introduced into cereals legislation in 1964.

[3] Trevelyan, G. M., *British History in the Nineteenth Century,* p. 152. Longmans, Green and Co., 1922.

[4] Lord Ernle, *English Farming, Past and Present,* p. 270. Longmans, Green and Co., 1922.

Similar measures to those already in force for wheat were introduced, in the Agriculture Act of 1937, for barley and oats. In the case of these crops, the Minister was empowered to make payments to farmers in the event that prices were more than fivepence less than eight shillings per hundredweight (i.e. if prices fell below *7s. 7d.*). For each acre, growers of oats were to receive six times the difference between the price per hundredweight and eight shillings, or £1 per ton, whichever was the lesser and barley growers were to receive four times this price difference for each acre. Payments for both crops were made subject to 'standard acreage' provisions. By enabling their classification as oats or barely crops, mixed crops containing more than certain minimum proportions of either oats or barley became eligible for support.

Despite the fact that all purchases of cereals and other major agricultural commodities were controlled by the government from the outbreak of hostilities in October 1939 and not relaxed until November 1953, the Agriculture Act of 1947 reiterated and extended the policy provisions of pre-war Agriculture Acts. Support was extended to include rye, potatoes, sugar beet, milk, cattle, sheep, pigs and eggs. A number of methods of price support were created under this Act; 'The price may be a guaranteed fixed price; a rate of deficiency; a subsidy; or a price calculated in accordance with a formula, of which, for example the price of feeding-stuffs might be the basis'. From the date of this Act, all the major agricultural commodities produced in the U.K., with the exception of poultry meat and horticultural crops came under the umbrella of government support. This meant that with the abandonment of Government trading after the War the relative prices received by agricultural producers for different commodities were still not subjected to free market forces, but were stabilised and fixed annually to conform with governmental long-term planning objectives. This long-term stability was assured under the Act by the requirement that minimum prices for livestock and livestock products should be fixed on alternate years for the third and fourth years ahead.[5] For cereals, livestock and livestock products, guaranteed prices were established (at levels above the minimum price) for the twelve months subsequent to the annual March price review.

Agricultural price stability was further strengthened by measures introduced in the Agriculture Act of 1957. The Government undertook not to reduce guaranteed product prices for a given commodity by more than 4 per cent in any one year or by more than 9 per cent over three years, and not to reduce total guarantees by more than $2\frac{1}{2}$ per cent in any given year. As a result of the long-term nature of these assurances, the practice of announcing guaranteed prices for livestock and livestock products for up to four years in advance was discontinued.

Important modifications of the support arrangements for cereals were

[5] Thus in 1953 minimum prices were announced for 1955-6 and 1956-7, and in 1955 minimum prices were to have been announced for 1957-8 and 1958-9.

introduced in the Agriculture Act of 1964, following the conclusion of an agreement with the U.K.'s principal cereal suppliers, Argentina, Australia, Canada and the U.S.A.[6] The objectives of the agreement reached with these countries were to assure supplies of cereals, cereal products, and by-products at equitable and stable prices, to provide acceptable conditions of access to the U.K. market for cereals exporters, and to create greater stability in the international prices of these commodities. To achieve these objectives the Government undertook, 'first to restrain financial assistance so as to discourage the increase of domestic cereals production above a level consistent with these objectives and second to operate, in co-operation with their principal overseas suppliers, a system of minimum import prices for the main cereals, cereal products, and by-products'.[7] In compliance with the first half of this undertaking standard quantities of 3·3 million tons for wheat and 6·5 million tons for barley were imposed for the 1964-5 harvest.[8] The cereals price support scheme was modified so that if production exceeded these levels, the subsidy was calculated only on the standard quantity, thus reducing the deficiency payment per ton in proportion to the excess. Target indicator price provisions were added to the standard quantity provisions in order to strengthen the measures to limit Exchequer liability to wheat and barley growers. These target indicator prices were to be linked directly to the proposed minimum import prices and were to be lower than the minimum import price by a margin covering the 'recognised handling differentials, quality differences and present market conditions'.

The new measures were to be operated as follows: If production of a crop were to exceed the standard quantity and the average market price were to fall below the target indicator price, then the average deficiency payment (*Pd*) was to be equal to the difference between the guaranteed price (*Pg*) and the target indicator price (*Pt*) reduced by the proportion of the standard quantity (*sq*) to the quantity actually produced (*aq*). Hence

$$(2.1) \qquad Pd = (Pg - Pt)\frac{sq}{aq} \qquad sq < aq$$

Complementary provisions were made to increase the average payment in the case where production was less than the standard quantity and where the average market price fell below the target indicator price. In this case formula (2.1) would apply with $sq > aq$. Given that the average market

[6] For a full discussion of the conditions under which this agreement was reached, and of its economic implications see Josling, T. E., *The United Kindgom Grains Agreement (1964); An Economic Analysis,* Institute of International Agriculture, Michigan State University, 1968.

[7] *Cereals,* Exchange of Letters and Notes, Cmnd. 2339, Note 1, para. 5, 1964.

[8] No standard quantity for wheat was announced in the 1968 Price Review, and that for barley has been removed since the 1969 Review.

price (*Pm*) did not fall below the target indicator price the average deficiency payment would be given by

$$Pd = (Pg - Pm)\,\frac{sq}{aq} \qquad sq \lesseqgtr aq \tag{2.2}$$

The other half of the 1964 package was the imposition of minimum import prices for cereals, which was to be made effective by the imposition of levies.[9] This had two aims. Firstly to place an effective floor on market prices thus limiting Exchequer liability in the event that formula (2.2) above was operative. Secondly, viewed in the light of the objective to assure markets to the regular, major exporters of cereals, this can be seen as a means of preventing the erosion of this market by 'dumping' tactics on the part of those countries which might find themselves with a temporary surplus of grain.

In 1965 the Cereals Marketing Act was passed, setting up the Home-Grown Cereals Authority, with its main task of establishing forward contract schemes for the sale of domestically produced wheat and barley. Under these schemes, bonuses are paid to producers entering into contracts for the forward sale of their cereals. These seasonal payments are additional to those paid to barley growers under the Barley Incentive Scheme and to wheat growers under the adjusted Seasonal Scale of deficiency payments, both of which have been operated since the 1961-2 harvest year under Price Review arrangements. The cereals price supporting effects of these schemes are indirect and result from the creation of more orderly marketing—evening out the flow of cereal sales throughout the year, elimination of some of the uncertainty as to the prices to be received for later sales, and the prevention of unforeseen collapses in prices.

From this brief summary of events it can be seen that the price-support policies for cereals have evolved in a continuous way since 1952. The basis of this development has been the deficiency payment system, of making up the payments which farmers receive to a target level, whilst leaving the prices determined on the open market to respond to domestic and international market forces. (Prices of grains at U.K. ports are commonly used as indicators of world prices[10]). Since 1947 similar policies have also been adopted for all the other major agricultural (but not horticultural) commodities produced in the U.K., with the exception of milk and eggs

[9] The levy arrangements distinguish between imports from countries which have concluded agreements with the U.K. (co-operating countries) and those which have not (non-co-operating countries). A general levy is applied to cereal imports from non-co-operating countries to raise the general offer price to the minimum import price. Country levies may be applied to imports from any co-operating country to raise their prices to the required level. There are also provisions for consignment levies which can be imposed when required on individual parcels of imported grain.

[10] For a full discussion of the relationship between domestic and international cereal prices, see Appendix 1.

which are subsidised under a different system, and a relatively stable environment for the planning of farm enterprises has been created.

In principle, the imposition of minimum import prices for cereals in 1965 marks a distinct change of policy, in that U.K. market prices are protected from international pressures which would push them below the minimum level, and thus cannot be regarded as world prices in the event that they are forced to this level. However, this policy has not been prosecuted with much vigour thus far. The minimum import prices imposed in 1964-5 remained unchanged for four years at levels which only required the imposition of small levies.[11] Since July 1968, import levies of up to £3 a ton have occasionally been required to raise the price of imported barley to the minimum levels laid down. But these occasions have not been frequent enough to require modification of the assumption that the U.K. is an open market for cereals.

In summary, there are two major arms of policy affecting the cereals market. On the one hand guaranteed prices are used to influence cereal supply, and on the other minimum import price legislation exists which enables the U.K. market price for cereals to be raised, and which is therefore capable of influencing the cereal demand (and also has implications for the livestock sector). Thus because the econometric investigation to be pursued has as its prime aim an assessment of the effects of these policies, it is clear that estimation of the effects of guaranteed and market prices upon cereal supply and demand assumes central importance in this study.

One thing that has emerged from this discussion of cereal policy is that cereal prices may be considered to be exogenously determined. The prices which farmers receive for cereals are guaranteed prices (since 1964-5 the payments to producers have been modified slightly in line with the standard quantity provisions) which are established at the Annual Price Review. The prices paid by cereal users may also be assumed to be exogenously determined. If the minimum import prices, which have operated since 1964-5 are used to raise imported (and hence U.K. market) prices for cereals, then user prices are clearly exogenously determined. As has been seen, however, the m.i.p. policy has thus far had little effect upon prices, but even without this it may be assumed, because the U.K. cereal market is an open one, that domestic market prices for cereals are exogenously determined by the international market. (Appendix 1 is concerned with the validation of this assumption.) Given, then, that both the U.K. producer and user prices for grain are exogenously determined, price variables will enter only as explanatory variables into the supply and demand functions to be estimated.

[11] As stated by Josling, T. E. op. cit., p. 113, 'The minima (minimum import prices) that were set were well below the prevailing prices (1963-6). Strong demand has kept world prices up until recently, and there is no evidence that import prices would in general have dropped in the absence of U.K. policy.'

3

Production decisions in U.K. agriculture and factors affecting their outcome

There are many explanatory economic, technical, institutional and social variables other than prices which influence cereal supply, cereal demand and the number of livestock. If structural relationships are to be specified, which permit identification of the effects of prices subject to policy control upon the relevant outcome variables, it is necessary that these other explanatory factors and their influence should be allowed for. With this objective in view the present chapter is devoted to describing the factors which influence the supply decisions of U.K. farmers, and to examining the environment in which these decisions are taken.

Section A of the chapter states the general nature of the problem facing agricultural producers with respect to their choice of enterprise mix. Examination of this basic situation results in the suggestion of a number of theoretical features which should be incorporated in the structural equations to be specified. There are also implications for the size of the expected parameters in these relationships.

Section B presents data designed to illustrate the relative profitabilities of the major enterprises in British agriculture. This has as its main objective the identification of those enterprises which are the principal competitors with cereals, and thus will facilitate the specification of the appropriate aggregate supply function for cereals. The information should also assist in formulating livestock inventory (supply) functions.

In Section C attention is focussed upon factors which may be expected to influence the choice between different cereals, and which seem likely to determine the supply of individual cereals. This information has implications for the specification of supply functions of the individual cereals.

Because of the considerable influence which weather conditions exert upon agricultural production, Section D of the chapter is confined to an examination of the ways in which weather affects the supply of cereals and to some of the problems of compiling suitable weather variables.

A. The limited range of 'feasible solutions' in farm production decisions

The objective of the argument developed below is to try and show that for most farms the decision-making process is so tightly constrained that, in the short run, only limited output responses to relative changes of input and output prices are likely to occur. It is also suggested that a large part of the expansion of farm enterprises which does occur is due not so much to the contraction of other enterprises as to improvements in technical efficiency, which reduce the influence of certain physical and technical constraints upon the feasible output mixes.

Consideration of these farm-level decision-making problems is pursued under the assumption that knowledge about the operating characteristics of the micro-units will lead to some generalisations about behaviour of the agricultural sector as a whole, and particularly about aggregate cereal supply response. In discussing these problems it has seemed appropriate to lapse into the jargon of linear programming despite the fact that there is no application of such techniques in this study. Rather, the following farm-level approach is considered to provide the most suitable point for the development of an aggregate cereal supply model suitable for estimation from time series data.

(1) *Constraints imposed by nature*

For any particular farm location, nature is likely to constrain the set of feasible production alternatives which can be considered. Where natural conditions are most favourable the constraints imposed enable a wide range of alternatives to be feasible, while unfavourable conditions will exist when choice is restricted amongst a small set of low-return alternatives.

The main natural features which impose limitations upon production are (a) climatological, (b) those concerning soil type, (c) relief, which is closely connected with climate, and (d) the incidence of diseases and pests of various types. Information on the effects of the first three of these factors upon agricultural production in England and Wales has been extensively documented by Coppock in a series of maps.[*1] The evidence he presents shows that in England and Wales a clear relationship exists between these three factors, in that the west of the country tends to have higher rainfall and relief, and less of the best land and sunshine than the east. In consequence, arable production is largely concentrated in the east of the country whilst dairying and livestock rearing dominate the agriculture of the western counties. The existence within broadly homogeneous regions of small areas whose geological, climatological or geographical characteristics differ substantially from the surrounding region, and which therefore exhibit a markedly different pattern of agricultural production from the region as a whole, only serves to underline the importance of the constraints which nature places upon agriculture. One such area is the south Lancashire plain where the reclaimed alluvial soils provide for the most intensive area of arable cultivation in the west of the country, which contrasts markedly with the dairying area which surrounds it.

Regional differences in the workability of the soil, its fertility, of climatic variations, and of incidence of disease give rise to typical crop rotation and livestock production patterns which differ from region to region.[2] While it is true that the rigid requirement of rotational husbandry is less inflexible than it was, the existence of these requirements still inevitably leads to a certain inelasticity of supply, since the enterprise mix

[*1] Coppock, J. T., *An Agricultural Atlas of England and Wales,* Faber, 1964.

[2] Ibid., pp. 102 and 193.

will often be determined largely by husbandry requirements, and the influence of changing relative prices may be only marginal. Hence, some inelasticity of supply will result from limitation of the set of feasible enterprises, and a further source of inelasticity will be caused by husbandry constraints upon the proportions in which the feasible enterprises may be combined.

(2) *Institutional constraints*

The institutional constraints upon agricultural production which may be of particular importance are those concerning the location of specialised product markets and processing plants. A two-way relationship occurs here, insofar as institutions of this nature tend to become sited in areas of specialised production. This confers further productive advantages on these areas while at the same time creating a comparative disadvantage for producers on small areas of suitable land elsewhere who are sited at some distance from the main producing centres, and who would thus incur high transport costs in conveying their produce to the main centres. For example, only two out of 17 sugar factories are situated outside East Anglia, Lincolnshire and Yorkshire, which means that producers with suitable land in other parts of the country are at a severe disadvantage in the growing of sugar beet. Similar locational advantages will occur with respect to other specialised facilities, the capacity and placing of which will impose limitations on the supply response to price changes.

(3) *Fixed factors in agricultural production*

An asset may be considered as fixed 'if the cost incurred in changing the quantity used of a given asset is greater than the benefits derived therefrom'.[3] This definition covers the case of the benefits and costs of scrapping capital as well as those of acquiring more of it. To the extent that there exists a range between the salvage and acquisition prices of capital there is a set of output and variable factor prices which will provide returns to fixed assets such that there is no inducement to either sell or acquire more of them.

Salvage prices of many forms of agricultural capital such as farm buildings and specialised equipment may be low. Indeed it is characteristic of many farms that their capital assets, including land of specific qualities, may have low opportunity costs with respect to their current uses. Hence under normal conditions farmers are reluctant to scrap parts of their capital stock. Also, many farmers are short of liquid assets and are disinclined to borrow large sums, so that farmers may exhibit a marked reluctance to enlarge their capital stock in the short run.

As Edwards points out, '. . . for small product price changes, most assets subject to fixity will remain fixed at existing levels and one would expect an inelastic supply response'[4] assuming diminishing marginal returns to the variable factors. For large price increases it becomes profitable to

[3] Edwards, C. 'Resource Fixity and Farm Organisation', *J. Fm Econ.*, Vol. 41, p. 749, 1959.

[4] Ibid., p. 755.

enlarge the stock of certain assets and the supply curve will be elastic. Both Edwards and Heady,[5] however, state that the supply elasticity of response to falling prices is very low in view of the low salvage values for existing assets, and that the supply curve is irreversible. If this is the case it has important implications for the estimation of linear supply functions from aggregate data. Ideally, two separate functions should be fitted, one for increases and one for falls in price. Unfortunately the amount of data available in the present study does not permit this, but inspection of the residuals of regressions might indicate the existence of differential responses to upward and downward price changes.

An important factor conditioning supply response is the rapid improvement of agricultural technology, which causes the supply function to shift markedly to the right. This has certainly occurred in cereals production in the U.K. in recent years, where the increase in cereal yields has enabled returns per acre to grow in spite of the steady decline in prices per ton of cereals. Hence, it has been possible for producers to expand cereals output without an equiproportional increase in the stock of fixed inputs. Such rapid technological advance in particular lines of production would also enable producers with a fixed stock of assets to expand output of one product without having to reduce the output of other products. This is because many technological advances have come in the form of improved variable factors of production such as seeds, herbicides and so forth.

The effects of rapid technological advance may well reinforce the fixed asset effect upon the irreversibility of product supply functions; in times of declining prices output can be profitably maintained by adopting the new techniques, while in times of increasing prices strong incentives may exist for the adoption of the new methods.

If innovation is rapid its effects may well dominate those of prices in determining supply response and the enterprise structure of agriculture. It will therefore be of the utmost importance in estimating supply and derived demand relations to specify functions which take account of the effects of technological improvement.

(4) *Uncertainty and imperfect knowledge*

The constraints discussed so far are essentially of a static nature in that they state a set of conditions which producer's decisions must comply with at all times. In a linear programming sense they define a set of feasible solutions which may be considered constant through time for any given set of production coefficients. In standard linear programming problems it is assumed that, in response to a change in relative factor or product prices, farms will move from one optimum solution in the feasible set to another. In such problems no assumption is made concerning the time path of adjustment between the two static equilibrium positions, and the transition is assumed to be instantaneous or timeless. However, instantaneous

[5] Heady, E. O., *Economics of Agricultural Production and Resource Use*, p. 700, Prentice-Hall, 1952.

adjustment does not reflect the decision-making situation in agriculture. In particular, the existence of uncertainty about future conditions causes farmers to adopt conservative strategies in changing their pattern of output. In the absence of certain knowledge about future prices it is generally accepted that producers make plans on the basis of expected prices.[6] But as Day points out, 'In a linear programming model with a finite number of alternatives, predictions of aggregative behaviour could be grossly unstable if only this (the price expectations) part of the hypothesis were included. In some agricultural regions certain rather specialised alternatives, even at discounted prices, are relatively more profitable than others, and usually by substantial margins. Consequently unless explicit upper and lower bounds are set to reflect uncertainty, a programming model will predict much greater specialisation for a given year than is commonly observed . . .'.[7] The rationale for the inclusion of these upper and lower bounds is not strong, but in Henderson's study they were used to describe the influence of uncertainty, imperfect knowledge and quasi-fixed factors.[8] Two other justifications for their use might be added. One of these is the influence of a crop rotation which, should it be adhered to strictly, would permit farmers only partial adjustment to the maximising position consistent with their price expectations. The other justification is that while the best farmers may quickly adjust their system to maximise profits subject to their price expectations it is widely accepted that many farmers merely follow the lead of those whose judgement they accept as good. As this involves a time lag it inevitably means that the response of the 'follower' farmers to price expectation changes is slower than optimal.

One way in which these limitations on the adjustment path may be incorporated into programming models is to use Day's recursive system, in which plans in one period are dependant upon those of the preceding period, and where the adjustment of output and input levels between periods is constrained by upper and lower bound restrictions, the so-called flexibility constraints.

The implications of the above discussion for the estimation of supply and derived demand functions are that dynamic features of price expectations and adjustment lags should be allowed for in the theoretical models: use of the Nerlove adaptive expectations and partial adjustment models is discussed in Chapter 5.

B. Production choice in U.K. agriculture

The list of operative constraints considered above is not exhaustive, and the area of feasible choice may be further limited by such factors as the

[6] See in paticular Nerlove, M., *The Dynamics of Supply*, pp. 46-59. Johns Hopkins Press, 1958.

[7] Day, R. H., 'An Approach to Production Response', *Agric. Econ. Res.*, Vol. 14, No. 4, U.S.D.A., p. 138, 1962.

[8] Henderson, R. M. 'The Utilization of Agricultural Land: A Theoretical and Empirical Enquiry', *Rev. Econ. and Statis.* Vol. 41, No. 3, pp. 242-259, 1959.

tenancy system of a farm or by its size. Nevertheless it is clear that there are a number of important constraints, and that for many U.K. farmers the feasible range of production choice is narrowly defined. As a result of this it seems likely that competition between enterprises is more restricted than is often thought to be the case.

It is instructive to look at the figures for average gross margins per acre for major agricultural products as presented in the N.A.A.S. Farm Management Handbook 1967 and Table 1 below. A gross margin per acre is

Table 1: Average gross margins per acre for agricultural products, 1967

Crop enterprise	*£/Acre*
Maincrop potatoes	73
Early potatoes	64
Sugar beet	57·4
Vining peas	55
Winter wheat	33·8
Spring wheat	28·9
Oats	28·0
Barley	27·5
Livestock enterprise	*£/Forage acre*
Dairying–Freisians and Channel Is.	47
Dairying–other	41
Beef–single suckled calves	10-27*
Fattening store cattle–winter	21
Dairy followers–Freisian	20
Beef store cattle rearing	(–)3·5-14*
Fattening store cattle–summer	12·5
Fat lamb production	12·5

Source: N.A.A.S. *Farm Management Handbook 1967,* M.A.F.F.
* Different systems.

calculated as the value of gross output per acre minus the variable costs of production. As such, gross margins can be interpreted as indicating the profit which can be obtained by increasing output of a particular product by one acre, in circumstances where it is not necessary to increase the stock of fixed assets. Because farm sizes may be, in general, assumed to be fixed, marginal increases in one land-using enterprise entail a corresponding reduction in the size of other enterprises. The comparison of gross margins indicates the change in returns which could be achieved by switching land from one use to another where this is technically feasible and where no additional capital is required. To the extent that the figures presented are averages for the country as a whole they should indicate the marginal competitiveness of the various agricultural enterprises at a national level. Table 1 indicates that, using this limited profit criterion and ignoring intensive market garden crops, for any given capital stock potatoes then sugar beet and vining peas are likely to be grown at the maximum permissible acreages, in order to maximise profits. Dairying and cereals appear to be the next most profitable enterprises for marginal expansion, with livestock production from cattle and sheep for meat presenting the least attractive alternatives.

Because of the husbandry and disease constraints discussed earlier it is not possible for farmers to grow maincrop potatoes and nothing else; they must choose some mixed husbandry system. The returns to mixed husbandry farms which specialise in particular types of production are summarised in Table 2.

It will be noted that the ranking of specialised farming systems by net income per acre, is consistent with the ranking of the gross margins of the major products. Farms specialising in pigs and poultry in fact head the ranking by virtue of yielding a higher net output per acre than other groups of farms. This is misleading, for usually pig and poultry enterprises are not directly land using, but are supplementary enterprises on many farms and use the land of other farms in the form of purchased feeding stuffs. (This is shown to be the case by Table 3 which indicates that tenant's capital on specialist pig and poultry farms averages roughly twice that of any other type of farm, and that returns per £100 tenant's capital are exceeded by general cropping farms). Of the remaining types of farm, cropping farms producing potatoes, sugar beet and other crops, are the most productive. These are followed closely by (2) specialised dairy farms, (3) mainly dairy farms, with a tie in places (4) and (5) between cropping farms with mainly cereals and mixed farms. Lagging behind in productivity are (6) cattle and sheep farms and (7) sheep farms; these two types of farming are generally pursued on land which severely restricts the production of cereals, milk or vegetable crops.

Net income per acre does not however enable comparison of the true profitability of these farm types since it represents the return to farmers' labour, and also to tenant's capital; the extent of these stocks of capital and unpaid labour will vary considerably between farming systems. Available data does permit variations of tenant's capital to be taken into account, and this is done in Table 3.

In fact as Table 3 indicates, the average tenant's capital per acre on specialist dairy farms is higher than on general cropping farms so that the higher profitability of general cropping than dairying becomes even more marked when the index of profitability is returns on tenant's capital rather than net income per acre. The position of specialist pig and poultry farms has already been discussed and returns to tenant's capital indicate that this form of farming is the second most profitable behind general

Table 2: The output of specialised farms in England and Wales

	450-599 standard man days		*600-1,999 standard man days*	
	1965	*1965*	*1965*	*1965*
Specialist dairy farms				
Av. Acreage	121	122	205	206
Net output per acre (£)	41	42	44	44
Net income per acre (£)	17	17	15	14
Mainly dairy				
Av. Acreage	100	100	146	147
Net output per acre (£)	29	29	36	36
Net income per acre (£)	11	10	13	11
Mostly sheep				
Av. Acreage	262	262	525	524
Net output per acre (£)	7	7	7	6
Net income per acre (£)	2	2	5	5
Livestock, cattle and sheep				
Av. Acreage	186	188	283	288
Net output per acre (£)	18	17	19	19
Net income per acre (£)	6	4	5	5
Cropping, mostly cereals				
Av. Acreage	200	199	306	310
Net output per acre (£)	34	30	35	34
Net income per acre (£)	10	7	10	8
General cropping				
Av. Acreage	83	81	147	150
Net output per acre (£)	51	55	54	57
Net income per acre (£)	15	18	16	18
Mixed farms				
Av. Acreage	118	118	186	187
Net output per acre (£)	28	28	32	32
Net income per acre (£)	9	9	9	9
Pigs and poultry				
Av. Acreage	*a*	*a*	69	69
Net output per acre (£)	*a*	*a*	87	96
Net income per acre (£)	*a*	*a*	31	36

Source: Farm Incomes in England and Wales, 1966, M.A.F.F.

a Data not given.

N.B. Net Output is gross output minus the costs of feed, seed and livestock.

Net Income represents the return to the farmer and his wife for their own manual labour and for their management and interest on all farming capital excluding land and buildings.

cropping and ahead of dairying. The remaining classes of farming, mixed, cattle and sheep, all demonstrate a low level of return on tenant's capital, thus confirming the impression given by the gross margin data. Unfortunately, the Farm Income 'Blue Book' does not give the capitalisation figure for cropping farms with mainly cereals, but the figure may be expected to lie below that for general cropping farms. In this case cereal farms would be more profitable than mixed farms, and would in all probability be highly competitive in returns with the group of 'mainly dairy' farms, for which the tenant capital figure is also missing.

Table 3: Estimated tenant's capital and returns to it, 1966

Type of farming	*Tenant's capital £/Farm*	*Tenant's capital £/Acre*	*Net farm Income*	*Net farm income/£100 tenant's capl*
Dairy	7,223	56·0	1,408	19·5
Livestock, mostly sheep	5,968	12·9	760	12·7
Livestock, cattle and sheep	8,614	32·2	1,128	13·1
General cropping	13,191	50·3	3,528	26·7
Mixed	12,114	55·4	2,038	16·8
Pigs and poultry	9,298	118·4	2,135	23·0
All types	**9,234**	**47·6**	–	–

Source: Farm Incomes in England and Wales, 1966, M.A.F.F.

What basically emerges is this: The most profitable agricultural products in the U.K. are potatoes and sugar beet. These crops are highly demanding of growing conditions, labour at peak periods, and management quality. All constraints permitting, they will be the first choices of producers, and in suitable areas the farming system will be built around them. In the east of the country, where potato and sugar-beet production is chiefly concentrated, their production is backed up by the production of other arable crops, principally cereals. In wetter conditions, such as on the heavier soils of North Cheshire, potatoes combine with dairying as the basic farming system.

Dairying appears to be the next most profitable enterprise, but because of its very rigid labour requirements many farmers prefer to select the second best alternatives of cereal or cereal-livestock production, since these provide an easier way of life, less tying of working time. As it is, larger farms can produce an adequate living from cereals without the managerial strain imposed by dairying, and it is worthy of note that in 1966 the average cropping, mainly cereals, farm was 332 acres, whilst the average specialist dairy farm was only 100 acres. Smaller farms require more intensive production to provide an adequate living to their occupiers, and hence are not likely to be devoted to the second-best alternative. In some areas cereals may be a poor alternative to dairying, for in wetter areas the cultivation of arable crops may be difficult, especially on heavy soils in the west. In other areas, particularly in the more favourable growing conditions in eastern counties, the higher than average yields of cereals may make them a more profitable proposition than dairying.

Beef and sheep production are generally inferior alternatives to the other enterprises, and pigs and poultry are mainly supplementary or highly specialised in large units independent of farming. There is competition for resources between all of the enterprises mentioned, but the main competitive area would appear to be between dairying and cereals, which of all the land using enterprises are alternatives over a fairly wide range of farm situations. Hence in studying cereal supply, conditions in dairy production might be expected to have more influence than those of other products, and provision should be made for this competition in the structural relationships to be tested. (In this country agricultural price-support arrangements limit the direct relationship between the cereal and livestock enterprises at the farm decision-making level–see Chapter 2).

In studying the demand for cereals for livestock feed it is argued later, in Chapter 4, that the number of livestock units will be the main determinant of demand. Because of the divorce between the livestock and cereal economies caused by the price-support arrangements, and because of the limited competitiveness of pig, poultry, sheep and beef cattle enterprises with other products, the conditions of demand for these other products may be expected to only weakly influence livestock supply decisions and hence the feed demand for cereals.

C. The choice between cereals

Table 1 indicated that the profitability ranking of cereals on the basis of gross margins is winter wheat, spring wheat, oats and then barley. The ordering of the last of these two is highly suspect, as most Provincial Agricultural Economic Survey Reports indicate higher gross margins to barley than to oats; certainly the returns per acre figures generated later in this study indicate that returns per acre of barley have been generally higher than those of oats, but less than those of wheat, during the period since 1954. In the case of wheat and barley, yields have risen rapidly, and, despite decreases in the price (including subsidy) of these cereals, returns per acre have increased. Oats yields have increased more slowly, but the price including subsidy has increased; nevertheless, on average, wheat and barely have been more profitable alternatives than oats.

While, over the period since 1954, winter wheat would appear to be the producers' most profitable crop, followed by spring wheat, barley and oats, the wheat acreage remained at roughly the same level while the barley acreage trebled and the oat acreage declined by more than half. This suggests some fairly stringent constraints upon the decision-making situation.

The principal constraints operating appear to be the varying disease susceptibilities of the different crops and the soil conditions which the crops will tolerate. With wheat, it is considered that continuous growing leads to a rapid build up of disease in the soil, with a consequent significant depression of yields.[10] This has meant the continuance of rotational husbandry, and the apparent imposition of a ceiling on the area which farmers can devote to wheat. In contrast, continuous barley growing is now practised in many areas (despite the voices frequently heard stating that the disease problem is becoming acute), and it is the relative freedom from disease, enabling continuous growing, which has facilitated the enormous expansion of the barley acreage. The expansion has been at the expense of oats which are less profitable, and of grassland, and it has also been facilitated by a large decline in the potato acreage. Oats thrive better than the other cereals on acid soils, and can also ripen in wetter, colder conditions. This accounts for the concentration of oat production in Scotland, where the crop seems a better alternative than barley or wheat.

Recent breeding experiments have produced new varieties of oats which seem likely to produce yields comparable to those of barley. This being so, and coupled with the probable increase in the disease problems of continuous barley growing, a resurgence of oats may be expected; in fact in 1967 the oats acreage increased and the barley acreage declined for the first time since 1954, a pattern of development which has persisted in subsequent years.

D. The influence of weather in cereals production[11]

The outcome of agricultural production decisions are affected by a number of exogenous factors such as weather conditions, outbreaks of disease and the depradations of pests. The effects of these will be felt in both livestock and arable production. With forage-consuming livestock, weather may influence the length of the grazing season and the amount of forage growth, and will thus affect the relative proportions of cereals and forage used in achieving a given amount of livestock output. Relatively little work has been done on the measurement of aggregate livestock-weather relationships, and attempts by the author to discover measurable relationships between feed demand and weather conditions have drawn a blank. Hence, no discussion of such relationships is attempted here. Similarly, it is very difficult to quantify the effects of disease and pest incidence upon aggregate agricultural output, and discussion of these is likewise omitted.

[10] Wallace, D. B., 'Cereal Production in the U.K. and Cereal Imports over the Years', *Ceres*, No. 1, p. 5, 1968.

[11] This part of the chapter is based on a paper by the author which has been contributed to Britton, D. K., *Cereals in the United Kingdom*, pp. 94-99. Pergamon, 1969. With permission from Pergamon Press Ltd.

The effects of variations in weather conditions upon the output of arable crops are, however, quantifiable, and are of considerable importance. In view of the subject of this study, the effects of weather on cereal output are of crucial interest, and the rest of this chapter will be devoted to these and their measurement.

There are three major areas of influence of weather on cereals output. They are on (1) the preparation of the seedbed and sowing of the crop, (2) the course of plant growth, and (3) the conditions at harvest. In other countries, additional influences may be of significance; for example there is the 'winter effect' in French cereal production, which is the name given by Oury to the killing of winter cereals by periods of extreme cold.[12]

(1) *Weather effects on soil preparation and sowing*

Weather conditions for the autumn sowing of winter wheat have proved highly variable over a period of recent years. In general, the position has been that in those years when rainfall has been relatively high during the months of August to November the acreage of winter wheat sown has been depressed. This can be clearly seen by reference to Figure 1. Here it is indicated that in years of high rainfall the acreage of wheat sown by December was low, and that the converse happened in years of low rainfall. There are two aspects to the way in which rainfall influences the winter wheat acreages. One is that high rainfall during August and September delays the harvest and thus reduces the opportunity to get on to the land before winter sets in. The other aspect is that, heavy rain during this period makes cultivation and sowing difficult, even when a late harvest does not present a constraint to these operations. Adverse conditions for planting may also be caused by extremely dry weather baking the ground to an unworkable condition. This state of affairs has been rare in the U.K., but there are reports that in the autumn of 1955 dry conditions held up soil cultivations until November.

Examination of Figure 1 reveals that the pattern of winter wheat sowings is almost the converse of that of autumn rainfall. It is true that there are one or two years in which the changes of the magnitudes of both variables are of the same sign, but any large change in rainfall can be seen to be accompanied by large changes of opposite sign in winter wheat plantings. It can also be seen from the same figure that the June wheat acreage closely follows the pattern set by wheat plantings at the previous December, although the absolute sizes of the variations in the June acreage are less than those at December. From this it can be inferred that the level of spring wheat sowings compensates to some extent for those before December, being larger in years when the December acreage is low, but that spring sowings are never sufficiently large to compensate fully for poor performance the previous autumn.

[12] Oury, B., *A Production Model for Wheat and Feedgrains in France (1946-1961)*. North Holland Publishing Company, 1966.

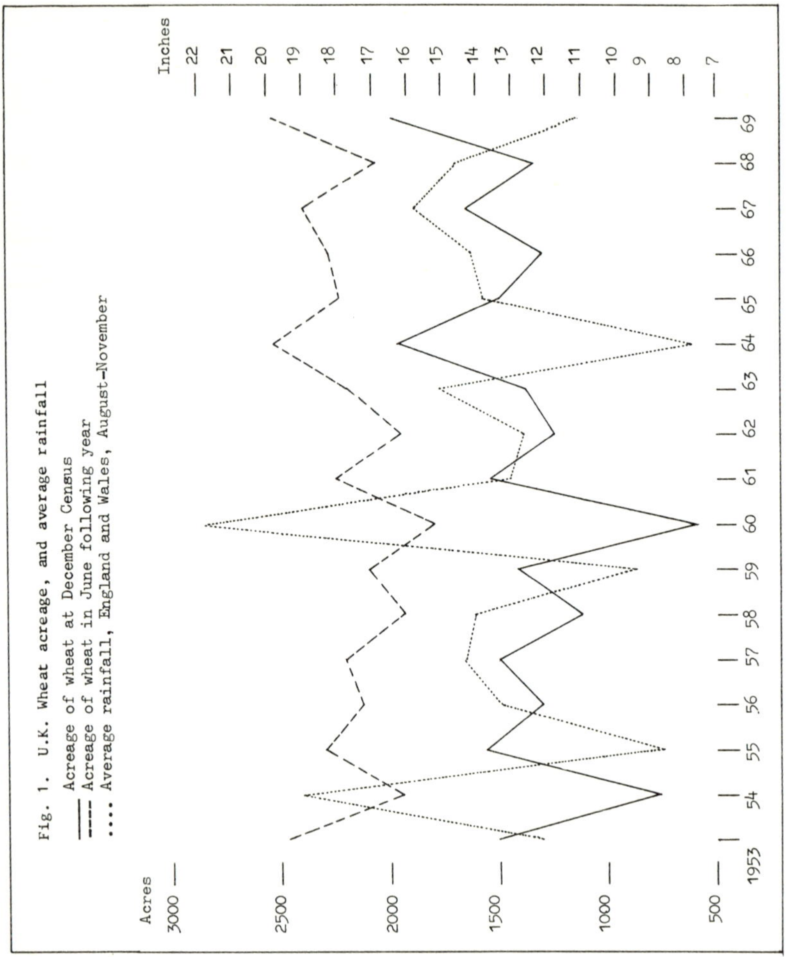

Fig. 1. U.K. Wheat acreage, and average rainfall

A further link in the causal chain set up in cereals growing by fluctuation in autumn rainfall is illustrated by Figure 2. This shows that the percentage by which the barley acreage has increased has been less in the years when the wheat acreage was large.[13] In other words the proportionate changes in the barley acreage during the period 1954-1970 demonstrated a pattern which is the converse of that shown by the wheat acreage; the only year out of line in this case was 1965, when barley exhibited a large acreage increase despite a large rise in the wheat acreage.

The existence of this complementary set of patterns suggests a strong interrelationship between the acreages of wheat and barley. Given that wheat is generally sown before barley this casual expiricism suggests that poor weather causes reduced wheat sowings which is adjusted for in turn by the barley acreage. This is potentially most important, and also appears to hold true when the combined acreage of late-sown cereals is substituted for barley. For, as Figure 2 shows, the pattern of change in the combined acreage of all cereals other than wheat is a muted version of the barley acreage pattern.

Poor weather conditions may also interfere with the establishment of spring crops of cereals, but due to the length of time available to farmers for spring cultivation there is every reason to assume that even in years of adverse spring weather farmers are able to establish their planned acreages, though yields may be affected. Certainly, it has not proved possible to measure the effects of adverse conditions upon spring planting of cereals by simple correlation.

(2) *Weather effects in the growing period*

What is important here is the weather conditions required for optimum plant growth and the effects of deviations from these. As a result of agronomic experiments it has been determined that there are optimal conditions for seed germination, tillering, and ripening and for all the stages of plant development. These conditions are produced by the existence of a correct balance between such weather factors as moisture availability, temperature, solar radiation, and air movement—factors affecting evapotranspiration and photosynthesis—plus a complex of factors to do with soil structure and the availability of plant nutrients.

To produce a single index measure of the weather conditions affecting plant growth is difficult, especially when the yield to be explained is of a crop which is dispersed over a wide area. The host of problems involved has been discussed at length elsewhere,[14] but some of the major problems are briefly treated below.

[13] The barley acreage expanded rapidly until 1967. Hence the 13·6 per cent increase in 1966 (+735,000 acres) is absolutely much larger than the increase of 12·9 per cent in 1956 (+299,000 acres.)

[14] See for example Shaw, L. H., 'The Effect of Weather on Agricultural Output: A Look At Methodology', *J. Fm Econ.*, Vol. 64, 1964, pp. 218-230.

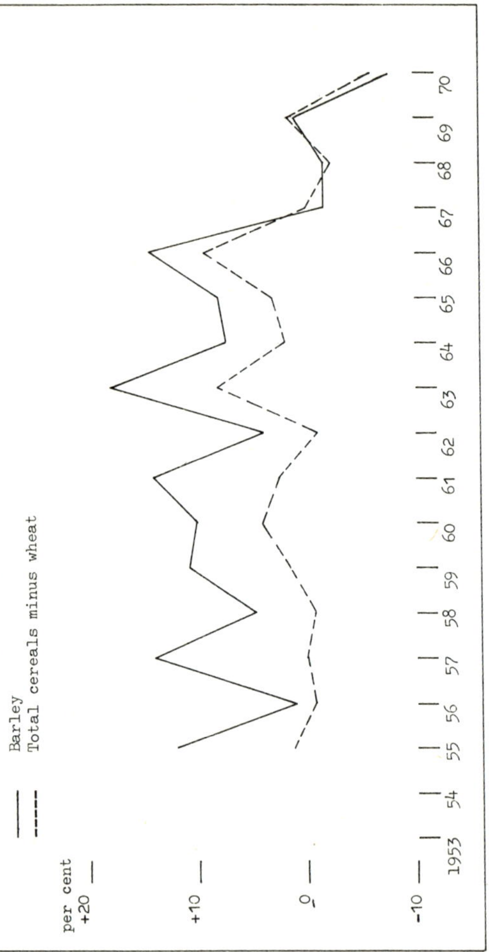

Fig. 2. Change in the barley acreage, and the total cereals minus wheat acreage - percentage of previous year's acreage

The optimal weather requirements may differ for different stages of physiological developments, so that aggregation of weather data over time may obscure the effects of extreme conditions which might occur at some limited and critical period for plant growth. There are important problems in aggregating meteorological and crop data over a wide geographical area, since the weighting given to meteorological observations at different points should correspond to the importance of the crop being studied at the same points. In fact, in a relatively small area such as the U.K. summers tend to be either 'bad' or 'good' over the whole country, so that the aggregation problem may not be so serious. Oury found, in his work on cereal production response in France, that a weather index constructed for conditions at one central point, provided just as good an explanation of output as a weighted index of data for all regions.[15] Data availability also creates problems, in that while experiments may determine the importance of a number of interacting weather variables, nationwide data on all but rainfall and temperature is rarely available. Weather indices constructed to take account only of temperature and rainfall have been extensively used in Oury's study. Similar indices are used in the later econometric measurement of the impact of weather on U.K. cereal yields, but it has been found that changes in the rainfall level dominate the values of the index, and thus only rainfall data are presented in Figure 4.

Testing with a number of formulations of the weather variable has revealed that variations in weather conditions during June, July and August give a better explanation of cereal yields than variables for any other period. Coincidentally, the graph of the average June to August rainfall in England and Wales for the period 1954-1966 shows a basic two-year cyclical pattern with rainfall in alternate years being higher and then lower than in the previous years. Cereal yields over the same period have risen steadily due to the continuous adoption of higher-yielding varieties, increased fertiliser application, and the generally expanded use of improved 'technology'. Around this rising trend however, yields from year to year have usually varied in the opposing direction to rainfall. The correlation is not a perfect one, but as Figure 3 shows, after the trend is considered, wheat yields have shown a pattern which is approximately the converse of that of June to August rainfall. Barley and oats yields have followed the pattern slightly less closely, but it is clear that an important relationship exists between grain yields and rainfall during the ripening period.

(3) *Weather effects on harvest*

The effects of weather on harvesting are less easy to quantify than the effects previously indicated, for no easily defined indicator is available to measure the outcome of fluctuating rainfall conditions at harvest. That harvesting costs may be greatly increased by heavy and prolonged periods of rain or high winds in the harvesting period is self evident, and can be documented by reference to N.A.A.S. Crop Husbandry records. A catalogue

[15] Oury, B., op. cit.

Fig. 3. Average U.K. cereals yields

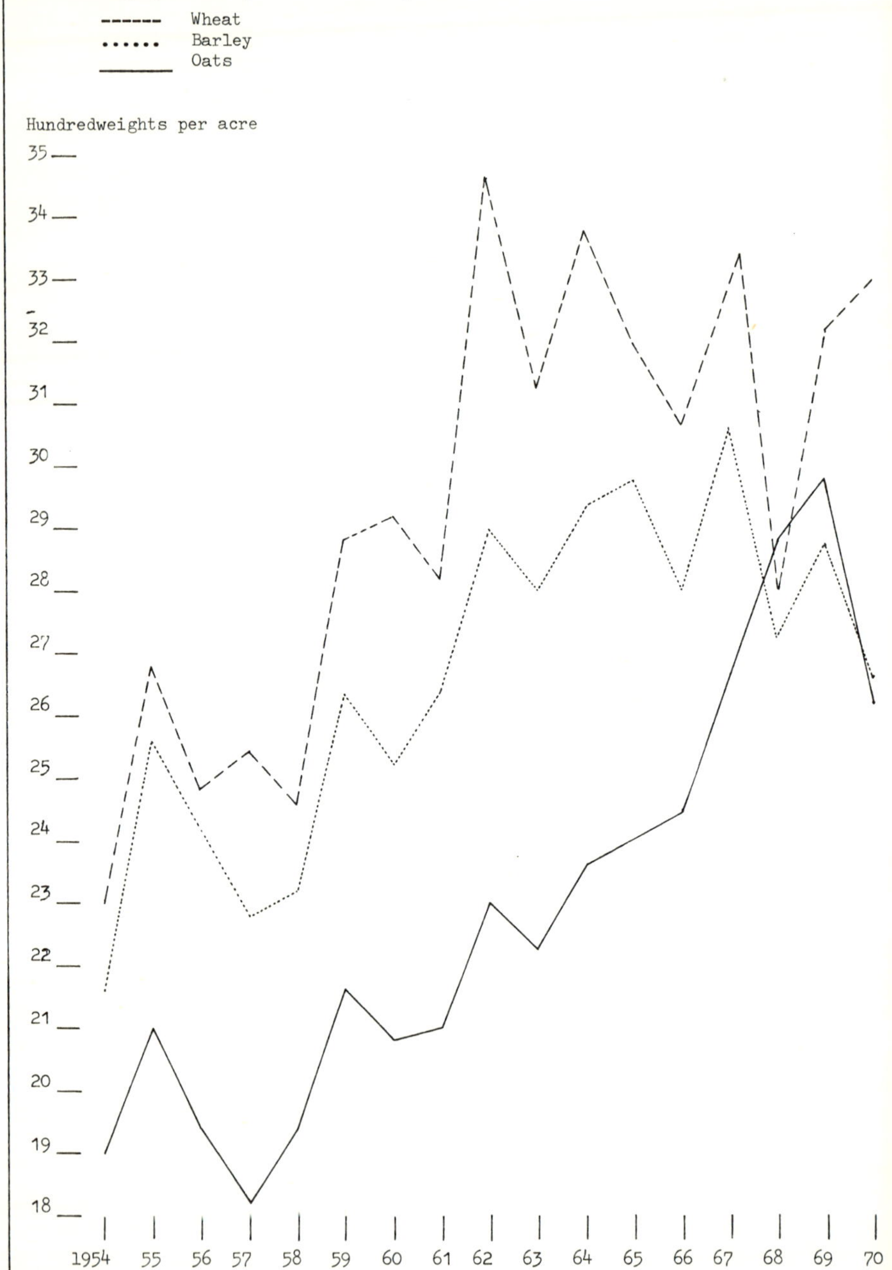

of effects attributed to poor harvesting conditions would include lodging of the grain, sprouting of grain in the ear, green ears in the ripe crop, some loss of grain, and the delaying of autumn preparation of the land. One of the most important of these effects is that poor weather late in the season may adversely affect the quality of the harvested crop, so that in years of bad conditions a relatively smaller proportion of the crop is eligible for human and industrial use and has to be diverted to the lower-paying animal food market.

(4) *Summary*

From the data presented it is evident that fluctuations in weather conditions have had significant effects upon the variations in annual acreages

Fig. 4. Average rainfall in England and Wales in the months, June, July and August

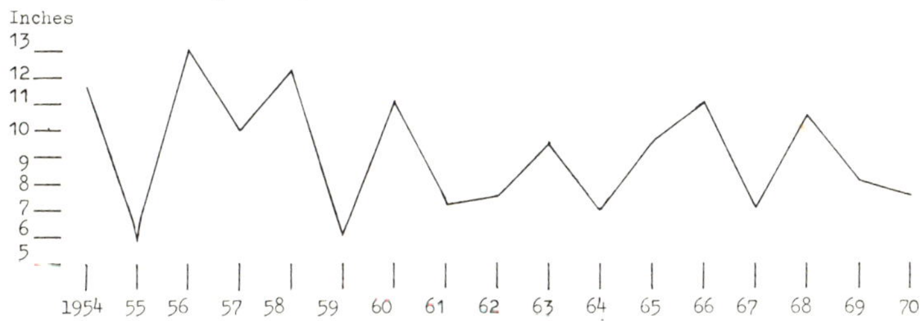

of wheat and barley planted (oats to a minor extent), and upon the yields of these crops, while the costs of harvesting have undoubtedly also been affected in a number of years. If these weather effects were cumulatively good or bad in any given years then the economic implications could be considerable. As it is, much of the year-to-year variation in the U.K. cereals output must be attributed to the vagaries of nature and not to producer's intentions, and in postulating relationships to describe cereal supply response suitable provision should be made for the effects of weather upon planted acreage and yields. Weather is of course not the sole factor influencing cereal production and it is clear from the graphs presented that there have been underlying changes in cereal acreages and yields which are unrelated to variations in the weather. All that has been attempted at this stage has been the identification of the way in which weather influences cereal production in order to aid formulation of the functions of the cereal supply model.

4

Factors affecting demand for cereals

Before statistically estimating demand functions for any commodity it is necessary to identify those market features which make the appropriate specification of the functions differ from those of a 'standard' abstract commodity. In the case of cereals these technical and institutional factors are sufficient to warrant a complete chapter. Particular emphasis is given to the (changing) relationship between livestock and their feed requirements, the problems this poses for the formulation of feed input demand functions, and the way in which these problems have been approached.

A. Animal feed demand

(1) *Types of feed*

There are three major types of feed for agricultural livestock. These are (1) forage and preserved forage, which are consumed only by herbivores (cattle, sheep and horses), (2) high-energy feeds, which are mainly the cereal grains, and (3) high-protein content feeds such as oilseed residues, and fish and meat meals. The last two of these groups are known as concentrate feeds.[1] All three types of feed supply both carbohydrates and amino acids (protein) and hence their classification is to some extent arbitrary. However although forage is the cheapest form of energy supply for herbivores,[2] high levels of output per animal require that a certain proportion of the nutrient requirements be obtained in a less bulky form; thus the forage intake of herbivores is limited and concentrated sources of nutrients are required. (In the case of sheep the demand for concentrate feed is restricted to short periods of time such as lambing, and they mainly subsist on forage. Hence sheep will be omitted when considering demand for concentrate feeds.) In general feeds with high-protein content cost more per unit of weight than do feeds, such as cereals, with low-protein contents, and for this reason, plus the fact that the two types of feed play different nutritional roles, it is useful to distinguish between them. Clearly the distinction between the two feed types must be somewhat arbitrary, and for the purposes of this study the dividing line has been set at 13 per cent digestible crude protein,[3] since this appears to fit the classification of

[1] For a very full classification of livestock feeds into these categories see Hildreth, C. J. and F. G. Jarrett, *A Statistical Study of Livestock Production and Marketing*, Cowles Commission Monograph No. 15, 1955.

[2] See section by Thomas, W. J. in F.A.O., Commodity Policy Studies No. 14, *The Stabilisation of World Trade in Course Grains: A Consideration of the Underlying Economic Issues*, 1963.

[3] The digestible crude protein coefficients have been taken from McDonald, P., R. A. Edwards, and J. F. D. Greenhalgh, *Animal Nutrition*, Oliver and Boyd, 1966.

Hildreth and Jarrett. Thus protein feeds are defined to have more than 13 per cent D.C.P., and high-energy feeds to have less.

Because of the generally high price of protein feeds and the requirements of minimum cost production, it is necessary that inputs of these feeds be restricted to the minimum levels consistent with the amino-acid requirements of livestock. For this reason it seems possible that there may exist a complementary relationship between high energy and protein feed demand. Despite the fact that cereals do not fall into the class of protein feeds, this hypothesis is important enough in the context of cereal feed demand to warrant testing by means of estimating demand functions for both types of concentrate.

Similarly it may also be true that in the diets of herbivores there exists complementarity between forage and concentrate usage. Unfortunately due to the inadequacy of the forage supply data it will not be possible to test this hypothesis in the same way as for the two concentrate feed classes.

(2) *Livestock–feed relationships*

(a) *Complementarity between livestock and feed.* Livestock may be viewed as a rather peculiar type of capital equipment. In producing off-spring, eggs and milk they process feed into a specific range of products. In meat production animals assimilate feed in order to augment themselves to the point where the costs of further assimilation of feed and use of attendant inputs outweigh further gains in the value of the animal. In both these types of process livestock may be viewed as short-run (or even long-run in the case of dairy cows) capital equipment, which requires only one raw material input, feed, plus a number of service flows in the production process.

Livestock are singularly different from other forms of capital in other respects. Most types of capital may deteriorate slightly if not in use, but livestock deteriorate completely (die) if not fed. If they do not die there will be a level of nutrition which, if not attained, may permanently affect their productive capacity. The costs incurred by not feeding livestock are therefore high, and it is probable that rather than feeding livestock at much reduced levels of nutrition they will be disposed of for slaughter. If the nutritional minimum is high relative to the full production ration, there is likely to be such a high degree of complementarity between feed and animal inputs that the demand for feed in the aggregate may be almost completely determined by the numbers of livestock. This is especially true since there are no grounds to assume that feed levels cannot be adjusted rapidly, in terms of annual observation periods, to optimal levels.

It thus seems reasonable to propose that the appropriate specification of feed demand functions will express feed demand in a given period as a function of numbers of livestock in the period, and feed, product and other factor prices during the period. However if there is a high degree of complementarity between total feed requirements and livestock numbers the short-run response of aggregate feed demand to changes in product and feed prices is likely to be small, given the number of livestock. The main effect of changes in feed, product and other input prices may instead be expected to operate indirectly through the effect on decisions about livestock inputs in production.[4] We may expect that increased feed prices will lead to reductions in livestock numbers, while increased livestock product prices will increase the numbers of breeding and producing animals, but cause a decrease in fattening livestock of slaughterable age. Converse reactions would be expected to decreases in these prices. Nevertheless, we may anticipate some short-run effects of changes in these prices upon aggregate feed demand, and may expect that they will operate through a raising or lowering of the plane of nutrition at which livestock are fed. But as mentioned previously the scope for modifications of this type would appear to be small. The preceding reasoning does not, of course, rule out the possibility of short-run substitution between different nutrient sources in response to changes in their relative prices, but as is discussed later there are institutional restrictions upon even this type of substitution.

Some casual evidence of the degree of complementarity between livestock numbers and feed demand is provided by Tables 4 and 5(i). It can be seen that over the period 1954 to 1968 livestock of all major classes increased; cattle by 13 per cent, pigs 18 per cent, fowls 53 per cent and sheep by 22 per cent. Over the corresponding period of time feed consumption also increased steadily. High-energy feed use, particularly of cereals, rose faster than livestock numbers in general, largely due no doubt to adoption of more capital intensive livestock production methods—an example of which is the change to indoor cattle fattening on grains in place of traditional finishing on pasture. Protein feed use rose by only 18 per cent over the 15-year period compared with 42 per cent growth for high-energy feeds, which might appear to belie complementarity between these two feed types. However if rates of feed usage are measured over the shorter period 1954-5 to 1965-6 they are 35 per cent for high-energy feed and 29 per cent for protein feed, a very close correspondence. Thus the divergence feed growth rates is mainly due to the last few years, and may be attributed in part to increased usage of synthetic amino acids in place of organic protein sources; a factor not accounted for in estimating protein feed consumption.

While there is this broad complementarity between livestock numbers and consumption of the broad feed aggregates, the same evidently does not hold between livestock and individual cereals as sources of annual nutrients. As shown in Table 5(ii) changes in cereal consumption for feed are dominated by the very large increase in the amount of barley fed to livestock. By comparison the usage of oats, mixed corn and wheat offals

[4] In order to test this hypothesis regressions have been performed to explain the numbers in different livestock classes as a function of feed price, product price and other variables.

has declined steadily, the latter resulting no doubt from the reduced quantity of wheat milled for flour over this period. Maize consumption increased until 1962-3 and then declined, whilst wheat consumption followed the pattern of U.K. wheat plantings, falling until 1961-2 and sharply increasing thereafter. This contrast between the steady increase in livestock numbers and the variable feed usage patterns of the different cereals suggests a fairly high degree of substitutability between these high-energy feeds.

Table 4: Livestock in the U.K.–at June census (thousands)

	Cattle calves	*Pigs*	*Fowls*	*Sheep*
1954	10,718	6,251	79,835	22,873
1955	10,668	5,843	83,420	22,949
1956	10,907	5,474	88,275	23,594
1957	10,881	5,974	90,699	24,796
1958	10,956	6,485	95,887	26,105
1959	11,291	5,984	102,263	27,612
1960	11,771	5,724	98,358	27,871
1961	11,936	6,043	108,392	28,967
1962	11,859	6,722	104,028	29,498
1963	11,716	6,859	106,834	29,344
1964	11,627	7,379	112,920	29,657
1965	11,943	7,979	112,115	29,911
1966	12,206	7,333	113,523	29,957
1967	12,342	7,107	120,148	28,885
1968	12,151	7,387	121,753	28,004
1969	12,374	7,783	125,624	26,604
Percent increase				
1954-1968	13·4	18·2	52·5	22·4

Sources: C.S.O. *Monthly Digest of Statistics,* and M.A.F.F. *Ag. Stats.* U.K.

However a rider should be introduced at this point, for there is evidence which demonstrates that certain cereals are preferred in the rations of particular livestock, and this must place some restriction on the substitutability of cereal feeds.

Most individual feeds have different nutrient values for different classes of livestock. For instance, the digestible crude protein content of wheat as a percentage of fresh weight is 10·3 if fed to ruminants, 10·6 for pigs, and 7·9 for poultry.[5] Hence, in view of the different amino-acid and energy

[5] McDonald, P., R. A. Edwards and J. F. D. Greenhalgh, *Animal Nutrition*, Appendices 1 to 3, Oliver and Boyd, 1966.

Table 5: Animal feed consumption (thousand tons)

(i) Consumption by aggregate feed classes

	High Energy Feed*	*Cereal Feed*	*Protein* Feed*
1954-5	10,833	8,459	2,113
1955-6	10,868	8,567	2,143
1956-7	11,054	8,590	2,185
1957-8	11,298	8,833	2,245
1958-9	12,678	10,087	2,529
1959-60	12,362	9,818	2,559
1960-1	12,663	10,072	2,656
1961-2	13,137	10,584	2,817
1962-3	14,190	11,774	2,677
1963-4	13,838	11,357	2,567
1964-5	14,419	12,064	2,805
1965-6	14,628	12,128	2,726
1966-7	14,252	11,835	2,406
1967-8	15,126	12,810	2,513
1968-9	15,328	12,889	2,500
Percent increase 1954-69	41·5	52·4	18·3

* For details of the calculation of these values see Appendix 2.

(ii) Usage for cereals for livestock feed (thousands tons)

	Wheat[a]	*Barley*[a]	*Oats*[a]	*Mixed cereals*[b]	*Maize*[a]	*Sorg-hums*[c]	*Wheat milling offals*[d]
1954-5	2,178	2,127	2,044	555	1,347	190	1,774
1955-6	1,728	2,215	2,362	510	1,281	468	1,676
1956-7	1,910	2,681	2,163	407	1,232	190	1,796
1957-8	1,807	2,966	1,950	325	1,592	188	1,867
1958-9	1,948	2,948	1,983	275	2,294	633	1,869
1959-60	1,540	3,162	1,874	259	2,425	557	1,769
1960-1	1,656	3,673	1,813	219	2,349	357	1,725
1961-2	1,457	3,783	1,589	169	3,034	548	1,668
1962-3	2,239	4,366	1,523	154	3,096	395	1,592
1963-4	1,836	5,470	1,261	118	2,412	259	1,735
1964-5	2,394	5,775	1,139	101	2,265	387	1,508
1965-6	2,383	5,759	1,043	91	2,337	512	1,507
1966-7	2,156	5,953	923	93	2,208	497	1,481
1967-8	2,369	6,478	1,072	117	2,645	124	1,380
1968-9	2,523	6,748	1,035	151	2,248	179	1,490
Percent 1954-5 to 1968-9	15·8	217·3	−49·4	−72·8	66·9	−5·8	−16·1

Sources: [a] Commonwealth Economic Committee, *Grain Crops Review*
[b] M.A.F.F., *Crop Utilisation Reports*
[c] C.S.O., *Overseas Trade Accounts of the U.K.*
[d] C.S.O. *Monthly Digest of Statistics*

requirements of various livestock, the ranking of feeds in order of nutritive value will vary between classes of livestock. Thus an increase in cattle numbers is not likely to cause an equal increase in demand for all types of high-energy or protein feed, but will affect the demand for some cereals or some oilseed residues more than others.

As far as the demand for cereals is concerned, the Report on the Feedingstuffs Practices Survey of 1957-59 produces figures which indicate the differences in the cereal composition of the diet of the principal classes of livestock. These are summarised in Table 6 and it can be seen that the principal cereal in cattle rations was oats, barley in pig rations and wheat for poultry.

Table 6: Percentage distribution of straights* by type, Oct. 1957-Sept. 1958

Home-grown straights	*Wheat*	*Barley*	*Oats*	*Mixed cereals*	*Pulse*	*Other*
All cattle	2·4	17·1	53·4	21·3	2·7	3·1
All pigs	6·9	66·3	15·5	9·9	1·2	0·2
All poultry	31·3	17·5	30·4	20·4	0·3	0·1
All livestock	9·1	30·5	38·8	18·0	1·8	1·8
Purchased straights						
All cattle	3·5	5·4	9·5	1·6	1·3	78·7
All pigs	13·3	32·8	3·1	–	–	50·8
All poultry	53·1	4·1	8·0	10·2	–	24·6
All livestock	21·9	14·6	6·8	3·9	–	52·8

Source: M.A.F.F., *A Report on the Feedingstuffs Practices Survey of 1957-59*, Table 9

* A straight feed is one which is acquired in an unprocessed form for mixing on the farm.

No doubt the situation has changed since 1957-59, but, unfortunately, no comparable survey results are available for a later period. It is to be expected, however that if such figures were available they would indicate a marked increase in the proportion of barley in cattle and pig rations, and a sizeable decline in the proportion of oats. The overall proportion of wheat in the ration is likely to have remained very much the same, but to be larger relative to the proportion of oats. The proportion of mixed cereals in livestock rations will have declined since 1957-59 as reflected in the much reduced mixed cereal acreage in the U.K.

It has already been indicated that there may be nutritional reasons for the preferences for a particular cereal in feeding a given type of livestock, but an additional reason may be the existence of pure tradition. The rotational crop husbandry patterns, mentioned in the previous chapter, have been allied to particular livestock production patterns. Hence, in some regions the production of fattening cattle may have been associated with the presence of oats in the typical local crop sequence. Feeding methods adopted for reasons associated with rotational husbandry may persist after the rotation has been abandoned. Whatever the reasons for these preferences it is clear that the feed demand for a particular cereal is going to depend more upon changes in the numbers of particular types of livestock than upon livestock numbers as a whole. As Tables 5 and 6 show for the period since 1954, most of the series giving the numbers of livestock and the series for the feed usage of particular cereals move uninterruptedly either upwards or downwards. This multicollinearity problem is further complicated by the fact that for this period the data series on cereal prices also show a secular decline over the period.

The above statement on livestock–feed complementarity has been developed at some length because of its important implications for the appropriate specification of feed demand functions, and also because it provides some *a priori* hypotheses concerning the size of the parameters of such functions.

It has been argued that it is the number of livestock on farms which largely determines the level of feed demand, and also that there is no difficulty in rapidly adjusting feed consumption to the optimum economic level. This being so, a static specification of the annual demand function appears appropriate, and we can anticipate that current livestock numbers will explain a high proportion of the variance of current feed demand.

If the assumption of complementarity is appropriate it may also be anticipated that the current period effects of feed and other relevant prices will be small, and that these will reflect the possibilities of adjusting the plane of nutrition at which livestock are fed. It may further be hypothesised that the main effects of feed and livestock prices upon feed demand operate not through adjustments of the plane of livestock nutrition but by causing adjustments in the numbers of livestock. In order to test this hypothesis, Chapter 7 is devoted to the estimation of the determinants of livestock inventories.

(b) *The changing feed requirements of livestock.* The discussion in the last section left out of account a major element of the relationship between livestock and feed which is that over time there has been a reduction in the amounts of feed required by particular types of livestock. This has resulted in part from the continuous breeding of new strains of livestock capable of more efficient conversion of feed into livestock products. In addition, progress in animal husbandry—associated particularly with controlled environment housing for livestock, increased awareness of the critical nutrients in livestock diets, and more adequate methods of disease control—has substantially improved the efficiency of livestock as feed convertors. For example, Ministry of Agriculture data indicates that, whereas an average of 8·4 pounds of concentrate feed was required to produce a dozen eggs in 1954-5, only 6·0 pounds were needed in 1966-7.[6] Improvements on a similar scale have been achieved in broiler fowl and pig production. These developments may fairly be classed as technical change, and their significant size suggests that account will have to be taken of them in formulating feed demand equations.

(c) *Construction of an aggregate livestock variable.* It will be evident from the preceding discussion that the major determinant of total feed demand is the numbers of livestock of different types, and also that different types of animals generate different feed demand functions, e.g. the feed demand function for a calf will differ markedly from that of a dairy cow or a fattening pig. Thus we can in principle distinguish total feed demand for a large number of different types of livestock. For reasons already stated, it may be assumed that the appropriate demand functions should have static specifications, so that using conventional input demand theory[7] we may represent the set of total feed demand functions as

$$FD_{it} = a_{0i} + a_{1it}L_{it} + a_{2i}PF_t + a_{3i}PO_{it} + a_{4i}PI_t + u_{it} \quad (4.1)$$

FD_i = total feed demand for livestock of class i
L_i = average number of livestock of class i on farms during the time interval over which feed demand is aggregated
PF = a price index of feeding stuffs–assumed for simplicity to be the same for all i
PO_i = a price index of the output of livestock type i
PI = a price index of other inputs employed in conjunction with feed–assumed to be the same for all i
u = a random disturbance term
i = $1, 2 \ldots, k, k+1, \ldots, m, m+1, \ldots, n$
i = $1, 2, \ldots, k$ are subclasses of the cattle population
i = $k+1, \ldots m$, are subclasses of the pig population
i = $m+1, \ldots, n$, are subclasses of the poultry population

(Sheep, turkeys, horses and goats have not been considered for the purposes of this study).

Notice that the coefficients, a_{1it}, of livestock numbers are explicitly recognised as changing with time. This is to take account of the large changes in the nutrient requirements of specific types of animal which were discussed in the last section.

Set of equations (4.1) cannot be estimated due to the absence of data on feed consumption by livestock types. Instead we have data on the total consumption of feed of certain types by all livestock. Let us therefore

[6] Source references for this and other feed conversion series are given in Appendix 2 in connection with the construction of appropriate livestock variables for inclusion into the feed demand functions.

[7] For a full statement of the relevant theory see Cowling, K., D. Metcalf and A. J. Rayner, *Resource Structure of Agriculture*, pp. 16-29. Pergamon Press, 1970, and Heady, E. O., and L. G. Tweeten, *Resource Demand and Structure of the Agricultural Industry*, pp. 50-55. Iowa State University Press, 1963.

assume that the dependent variable $\sum_{i=1}^{n} FD_{it}$ is available, and that we are forced to estimate the aggregate function.

$$(4.2) \qquad \sum_{i=1}^{n} FD_{it} = b_0 + b_1 \sum_{i=1}^{n} L_{it} + b_2 PF_t + b_3 \sum_{i=1}^{n} PO_{it} + b_4 PI_t + V_t$$

However the form of the set of individual livestock feed demand functions, (4.1), strictly requires that the aggregate relationship should be

$$(4.3) \qquad \sum_{i=1}^{n} FD_{it} = \sum_{i=1}^{n} a_{0i} + \sum_{i=1}^{n} a_{1it} L_{it} + \sum_{i=1}^{n} a_{2i} PF_t + \sum_{i=1}^{n} a_{3i} PO_{it} + \sum_{i=1}^{n} a_{4i} PI_t + \sum_{i=1}^{n} u_{it}$$

No aggregation problem exists with respect to the third and fifth terms on the right-hand sides of (4.2) and (4.3), because of the assumption that the variables PF_t and PI_t enter identically into all i equations (4.1). Thus it can be stated that b_2 in equation (4.2) equals $\sum_{i=1}^{n} a_{2i}$, that $b_4 = \sum_{i=1}^{n} a_{4i}$, and also that $b_0 = \sum_{i=1}^{n} a_{0i}$ and $V_t = \sum_{i=1}^{n} u_{it}$.

There is however an aggregation problem with respect to the remaining terms on the right-hand sides of equations (4.2) and (4.3). In the case of the fourth term on the right-hand side even if $b_3 = \sum_{i=1}^{n} a_{3i}$, it would still be true that $\sum_{i=1}^{n} a_{3i} \sum_{i=1}^{n} PO_{it} \neq \sum_{i=1}^{n} a_{3i} PO_{it}$.[8] The aggregate livestock term suffers from a similar difficulty, in that even if we could estimate $b_{1t} = \sum_{i=1}^{n} a_{1it}$ it would still be true that $\sum_{i=1}^{n} a_{1it} \sum_{i=1}^{n} L_{it} \neq \sum_{i=1}^{n} a_{1it} L_{it}$, but we are of course only able to estimate the constant b_1 and not b_{1t}.

It is possible to calculate a weighted output price index, $\sum_{i=1}^{n} W_i PO_{it}$, using total values of net output from livestock of type i as the weights, W_i. It will be assumed that the use of this variable, rather than $\sum_{i=1}^{n} PO_{it}$ in equation (4.3), will overcome the aggregation problem associated with this term.

The method proposed for deriving the aggregate livestock variable is to construct an approximation to the theoretically required variable $\sum_{i=1}^{n} a_{1it} L_{it}$, that is to express livestock numbers in terms of their technically determined feed requirement.

[8] For a discussion of this aggregation problem see Allen, R. G. D., *Mathematical Economics (2nd Edition)*, pp. 701 and 710. Macmillan, 1964

The basic procedure is to express the a_{1it} in terms of two separate coefficients, such that

$$a_{1it} = x_{1i} \cdot y_{1it} \qquad (4.4)$$

where x_{1i} is the technical feed equivalent (livestock unit equivalent) of an animal of class i in the base year for the statistical analysis, 1954-5, and where y_{1it} is an index of the change in the feed requirements of the given animal type which is set equal to one in the base year.

The livestock unit estimates, the x_{1i}, are basic estimates and have been taken from a National Agricultural Advisory Service publication.[9] Data for the y_{1it} have been obtained from a variety of sources;[10] and it should be noted that the appropriate method of computing these indices varies according to livestock type. For fattening animals the appropriate index is the feed-conversion index per pound of liveweight gain, given the assumption that average slaughter weights have not changed with time. For breeding animals other than dairy cows and poultry a similar index is appropriate. For laying fowls and dairy cows the product of two indices is required, the one being an index of output per animal, and the second an index of feed requirement per unit of output.

If as a result of the proposed procedure $\sum_{i=1}^{n} x_{1i} \cdot y_{1it} L_{it}$ were equal to $\sum_{i=1}^{n} a_{1it} L_{it}$ the statistically estimated coefficient of this variable in the total feed demand equation (4.2) should be one. Insofar as this equality is not achieved then b_1', the coefficient of the livestock index, should be equivalent to

$$b_1' = \frac{\sum_{i=1}^{n} a_{1it} L_{it}}{\sum_{i=1}^{n} x_{1i} \cdot y_{1it} L_{it}} \qquad (4.5)$$

In fact no total feed demand equation has been estimated in this study. What have been estimated are feed demand functions for 'high-energy feed', 'protein feed', 'total cereals' and for the major cereals individually. Nevertheless, in the absence of better alternatives, the same livestock variable designated as L_t and constructed on the principles outlined above will be employed in the total cereal, high-energy and protein feed demand relations.

However a supplementary system of weights will be employed in constructing livestock variables for the individual cereal feed demand equations. As indicated in Table 6 above, the relative importance of the different cereals in livestock rations depends upon the type of animal

[9] An 'Information Sheet', by J. R. Hopkins, West Midland Region of N.A.A.S., Wolverhampton, April 1967.

[10] For details of these sources see Appendix 2.

considered. This implies that the weighting of a particular livestock class in obtaining the aggregate livestock variable for, say, the barley feed demand equation should differ from that for the wheat feed demand equation. In the absence of any time series data on the changing cereal composition of livestock diets, the figures in Table 6 have furnished this supplementary set of weights. Thus in the barley feed demand equation the aggregate livestock variable is

$$LW_t = \sum_{i=1}^{n} k_{ib} \cdot x_{1i} \cdot y_{1it} L_{it} \tag{4.6}$$

where the k_{ib} is the proportion of barley in the concentrate diet of livestock of class i observed in 1957-1959.

3. *Increased importance of purchased feed–particularly compounds*

It is probable that the price elasticity of demand for individual feeds (as opposed to the three broad classes of feed) is affected by the form in which, and the method by which, producers acquire concentrate feeds. With respect to the second of these points; farmers may produce grains for consumption on their own farms. In this case the market is by-passed and it seems unlikely that changes in relative concentrate feed prices will substantially alter decisions to utilise home-grown grain on the farm. Hence this fraction of demand is likely to be price inelastic in the short run. The alternative is for farmers to purchase feed from off-farm sources, and it is to be expected that this part of demand will be more responsive to changes in relative prices. As Table 7 indicates, the quantity of grains consumed on farms of origin has remained basically stable over the period of study, while purchases from commercial sources (Column (4)) have increased substantially. Thus, on this evidence it might be expected that demand will have become more responsive to relative price changes.

There are two major forms in which producers acquire concentrates. They may purchase straights for on-farm mixing or they may purchase compounds. Compounds are mixed according to complicated formulae to ensure balanced rations to the various classes of livestock. In fact the larger compounders mix according to minimum-cost linear programs but with a considerable number of constraints governing the nutrient balance, maximum and minimum levels for the inclusion of individual feeds, and restrictions on the rate of change of the composition.[11] The extent of these constraints is such that only limited price substitutability of feeds is possible. While in principle home-mixed rations are produced according to similar restrictions and objectives, the complexity of the constraints considered and the strictness with which they are applied are less. Hence, it is likely that the higher the proportion of home-mixed rations to purchased compounds the higher will be the price elasticity of demand for individual feeds. But as Table 7 indicates the consumption of purchased compounds has increased more rapidly during the study period than the

[11] Thomas, W. J., *op. cit.*

consumption of straights. This increase in compound feed consumption reflects particularly the increase in poultry and pig numbers. Both of these classes of livestock are increasingly intensively housed and are not able, under current husbandry systems, to forage for feed. The complexity of their nutritional requirements has meant that many producers purchase all of their feed supplies in processed form. As a result of this increase in compound feed usage the price responsiveness of feed demand may have diminished during the study period.

Table 7. Concentrate feed consumption–type and source

	a. (1) Total feed consumption	*b.* (2) Estimated deliveries of compounds	*c.* (3) Non-compound feed consumption (Thousand tons)	*b.* (4) Total deliveries of concentrated feedingstuffs	*d.* (5) Feeds consumed on farm of origin
1955-56	13,011	6,992	6,019	10,111	2,900
1957-58	13,543	7,343	6,200	10,981	2,562
1959-60	14,921	8,473	6,448	12,068	2,853
1961-62	15,954	9,219	6,735	13,274	2,680
1963-64	16,405	9,111	7,294	13,063	3,342
1965-66	17,354	9,532	7,822	14,651	2,703
1967-68	17,639	9,907	7,732	14,152	3,487

Sources:

a. Basic estimate of the study. See Appendix 3 (High-energy feed + protein feed).

b. C.S.O., *Economic Trends*, No. 130, August 1964, Supplement, M.A.F.F., Aug. 1967, and private communication.

c. Includes straights, cereal livestock mixtures and processed cereals.

d. This is in effect a residual and represents the differences between estimated total feed consumption and the quantity of feed passing through recognised commercial channels.

(3) = (1) – (2)

(5) = (1) – (4)

B. Cereal demand for human and industrial uses

Whereas cereals are competitive in their uses as animal feeds, the demand for them for human and industrial purposes is generally as the basic raw material in some manufacturing process. Hence the principal use of wheat is in flour milling, barley for malting and brewing, maize for breakfast cereals, malting and glucose production, and oats is processed in porridge and oatmeal. There is some competition between barley and maize for malting, some between wheat, oats and maize in breakfast cereals, and some between oats, barley and wheat in biscuit preparation. However in general the substitution between cereals in most human consumption usages is minimal. Hence the demand for individual cereals in these uses is closely tied to the level of final demand, and is not influenced in the same way as cereal feed demand by changes in the relative prices of substitutes. It is possibly as a result of this that, during the study period, the changes in the food demand for cereals have been orderly. The major factors affecting final demand have moved secularly. Population and incomes have steadily increased, and the prices of processed items with a cereal base have also increased despite decreases in the prices of the cereal raw materials. In consequence as Table 8 indicates, the human and industrial demand for the individual cereals has either increased or decreased monotonically. Wheat demand has declined, largely reflecting the negative income elasticity of demand for bread; barley consumption has increased with the growth in beer and whisky demand; maize demand has risen sharply reflecting its increased competitiveness with barley for malting and general proliferation in the industrial uses for it; oats demand has declined

Table 8. Human and industrial consumption of cereals (Thousand tons)

	Wheat	*Barley*	*Oats*	*Maize*	*Rye*
1955-56	5,851	975	162	357	18
1957-58	5,753	1,030	165	500	20
1959-60	5,543	1,077	141	678	20
1961-62	5,520	1,172	136	765	19
1963-64	5,473	1,218	126	963	27
1965-66	5,485	1,342	129	1,081	26
1967-68	5,123	1,352	115	1,185	16
1968-69	5,256	1,397	115	1,250	26

Source: C.E.C., *Grain Reports*

as a result of the reduced demand for porridge and oatmeal products. It is noticeable that the changes in food demand are not as large as those in the feed demand for cereals, and thus the aggregate demand for cereals for all uses has been dominated by changes in feed demand.

The existence of separate feed and food markets for cereals underlines the important fact that wheat, barley and oats are not homogeneous commodities. Cereals for human and industrial consumption are of higher quality than those used in animal feed and they command higher prices. In fact there is a continuum of prices for cereals of different qualities, and theoretically a multiplicity of demand functions for cereals of different grades should be estimated. However data availability does not permit this and in the analysis which follows cereals are treated as if they are of two qualities only, feeding and for food. It must be acknowledged that this (necessary) approach masks certain distinctions which may be of importance from a policy point of view.

Food wheat, for example, is far from being a homogeneous commodity. It consists of hard wheats, principally from North America, which command the top prices, Australian filler wheats, and domestic soft wheats. The technical requirements of bread making are such that only a limited proportion of domestic soft wheats can be used for flour. Hence, when the U.K. wheat crop is large it does not necessarily have the effect of replacing imported bread wheats. Instead the price for millable domestic wheats is depressed until it becomes competitive with other feeding quality grains. Thus some of the inferences to be drawn from aggregate analysis based on assumptions of product homogeneity should be guarded against. There do, however, also appear to be well-defined limits to substitution between domestic and imported feedgrains, as can be seen from the fact that the recent large crops of barley have not led to the elimination of maize and sorghum feed imports, but have led instead to substantial exports of barley. Thus, all other things being equal, increased domestic wheat output would be expected to depress domestic wheat prices.

But all other things are not equal. Important changes have taken place in bread making, where adoption of the Chorley-Wood dough-making process is allowing a higher proportion of soft wheats to be used in the manufacture of bread.[12] For any domestic crop of wheat this should have the result of progressively decreasing the price differential between imported and domestic wheats. (See Appendix 1.)

A further development is that new varieties of wheat such as Maris Widgeon which are more suitable for flour milling are being introduced in this country. This underlines a further problem, which is, that in analysing the cereals market, we are dealing with a product which is changing physically as time progresses. For example the protein content of grains is being constantly increased, and other grain characteristics are either being bred out or bred in. If these changes were rapid the usefulness of time series analysis for such commodities might be seriously questioned. As it is the period used in this study is probably short enough for this not to constitute a serious problem.

C. Summary

This chapter has been the last of three whose purpose it has been to examine the factors which influence the cereals market. The process of examining these factors has led to many suggestions for features and variables which should be incorporated into the supply and demand functions to be specified. For example, amongst other things, it has emerged that it would seem appropriate to introduce some form of adjustment mechanism into the cereal supply equations. Examination of livestock–feed relationships revealed the conditions which should be satisfied by the livestock variables entering feed demand equations, and has led to the generation of a specific proposal as to how such variables should be constructed. In addition, to the extent that many of the factors considered have suggested rigidities in the supply and demand for cereals, various implications have emerged concerning the probable influence of prices in the cereal market.

[12] Greer, E. N., 'The Wheat Variety, Maris Widgeon,' *Ceres*, No. 1, p. 13.

5

Cereal supply—model specification and results

The approach adopted for the analysis of cereal supply is to examine separately the determinants of cereal acreages and yields. This seems justified in that land may be considered the key input in cereal production decisions, with such inputs as labour, machine time, seed and others being determined complementarily with acreage. An adequate explanation of planted cereal acreages corrected for random (weather) factors should reveal the reactions of cereal producers to the economic variables which interest us from a policy point of view. It is true that producers may adjust the application of yield-determining inputs, such as fertilisers and herbicides, in response to economic variables. However, it may be postulated that farmers employ these factors so as to maximise yield per acre, and that optimal practice varies little from year to year. In any case data on the application of fertiliser and herbicides to cereal crops are not available, so that it is not possible to incorporate these variables into the supply analysis. Estimating acreage and yield responses separately ensures that the misspecification errors associated with the absence of this data does not influence the acreage response part of the model, but is concentrated in the less-complex yield-response sector.

The first part of this chapter is devoted to the specification of theoretical structures to explain the U.K. supply of wheat, barley, oats and mixed cereals and to a statement of the assumptions upon which these specifications are based. Two different basic models will be proposed differing only with respect to the way in which barley acreage response is handled.

In presenting the various theoretical equations of these models each explanatory variable is prefaced by a positive or a negative sign. These are to denote the expected direction of influence of the relevant explanatory variables upon the dependent variable.

A convention of using capital letters to denote logarithmically transformed variables is adopted. Non-transformed variables are denoted by the same letters as their transforms but with the first letter in a lower case. All the theoretical structures are expressed in logarithmic variables to reflect the assumption that explanatory variables react multiplicatively together as opposed to simply additively. In presenting the results of estimation in the second part of the chapter however, some results will be given for untransformed variables. This will be done wherever statistical tests reveal it to be superior, but also where transformed and non-transformed data yield similar results and where the non-transformed results permit readier interpretation. Where logarithmically transformed variables are presented they are in natural logarithms to the base *e*.

Only one crop of each cereal is sown and harvested in a year, so that there is no difficulty in selecting annual time series as the most appropriate basis for analysis. The yearly period adopted for purposes of data measurement is a harvest year running from 1 July to the following 30 June. Data is available from the annual December census of wheat plantings up to that date (these are to be defined as the winter wheat acreage), and from the June census on the acreage of all cereals planted by that time. It is assumed that the relevant acreages registered by the censuses as having been sown during, say, 1955-6 (by the December 1955 and June 1956 censuses) are the acreages actually harvested in 1956-7, that is harvested during the period August and September 1956. This temporal classification of the available data gives the key to the time subscripts of the variables in the equations to be estimated.

A. Specification of cereal supply models

(1) *Acreage response*

Production theory based on a static technology implies that the supply of a commodity is determined as a function of its price per unit, the prices of alternative products and the prices of inputs. As an input, the acreage demanded for cereal growing will be dependent upon the same factors as cereal supply. However, as was suggested in Chapter 3 cereal production technology has not been static and as a consequence cereal yields (and crop yields generally) per acre have increased markedly over the study period. Hence prices alone have not been responsible for causing alterations in the profitability of alternative land uses, but yields have also played a major part and should be included in the list of explanatory variables. An initial specification of an acreage response function may thus be specified as:

$$(5.1) \qquad A_{it} = f((+)P'_{it}, (-)P'_{jt}, (+)Y_{it}, (-)Y_{jt}, (-)P'_{kt}, (-)Y_{kt}, (-)P_{nt}, u_t)$$

A = acreage harvested (measured at the June census in the previous harvest year)
Y = yield per acre
P' = price, including subsidy, per unit of output
P = price per unit
u = disturbance term
i = wheat, barley, oats or mixed corn
j = the set of cereals excluding the endogenous (ith) one
k = the set of alternative agricultural products
n = the set of agricultural inputs

The number of explanatory variables necessitated by such a specification is large and would result in the loss of a large number of degrees of statistical freedom. It is however possible to maintain the basic logic of equation (5.1), which is that the acreage devoted to cereal i is dependent upon the relative profitabilities of the various alternative uses of the land, while achieving a reduction in the number of explanatory terms on the right-hand side. Multiplication of appropriate crop prices (P'_i, P'_j, P'_k) by the yields per acre of these crops gives returns per acre (R_i, R_j, R_k). Similarly, in principle, input price data could be employed in conjunction with technological production data to produce cost per acre variables (C_i, C_j, C_k), to give the formulation.

$$(5.2) \qquad A_{it} = f(R_{it}, R_{jt}, R_{kt}, C_{it}, C_{jt}, C_{kt}, u_t)$$
$$R_i, R_j, R_k = Y_i \times P'_i, Y_j \times P'_j, Y_k \times P'_k$$

Unfortunately no reliable cost data are available for the estimation of such a specification as (5.2), which means that relative profitabilities per acre for different crops cannot be employed as explanatory variables. This may not be a major problem in the case of differences in profitability between different cereals, since the cost structures of cereal are similar, and a comparison of returns per acre may reliably indicate relative profitabilities. If however, we wish to consider an enterprise such as dairying as being competitive with cereals for the use of land, there are no comparable grounds for assuming that the ratio of barley returns per acre to returns per acre from dairying will reflect the relative profitability of land in these two uses.

In Chapter 3 it was also suggested that capital fixity in agriculture results in inability to quickly adjust output and input levels in response to price changes (although the response may be more difficult if expansion is indicated rather than if contraction is called for). For this reason it seems appropriate to introduce a Nerlove[1]-type partial adjustment mechanism into the specification, particularly since there are no cereal capital stock data which could be employed instead. An additional justification for the adoption of this procedure is to be found in the husbandry constraints which give rise to rotational systems of husbandry, since these also place constraints upon the rate at which enterprises can be adjusted.

The particular form of adjustment mechanism chosen imposes a geometrically declining response through time, something not specifically implied by the rationale for an adjustment process. Griliches[2] has taken up this point and has suggested alternative distributed response shapes, although his objections to the Nerlove adjustment process seem to apply more to quarterly than to annual data. The choice of a geometrically declining form of response is necessarily a somewhat arbitrary one. However, there are some justifications for this particular form. One of these stems from the fact that the degree of uncertainty about events increases the further into the future one looks. It is reasonable therefore to expect farmers' planned reactions to price changes to occur mainly in periods immediately following the price changes rather than in more distant periods. Assuming that the operation of the economic, technical and

[1] Nerlove, Marc, *The Dynamics of Supply*. The Johns Hopkins Press, 1958.
[2] Griliches, Zvi, 'Distributed Lags: A Survey', *Econometrica*, Vol. 35, 1967, pp. 24-33.

physical constraints permit such a pattern of response then a geometrically declining lag form would appear to be appropriate.

The general acreage response function can now be rewritten as

$$A_{it} = f(A_{it-1}, R_{it}, R_{jt}, R_{kt}, u_t) \qquad (5.3)$$

given that cost of production per acre data are not available.

Cereal production is subject to lags between the decision to produce a crop and the final realisation of that decision at harvest time. It is evident that production decisions of this nature must be based upon expectations about costs to be incurred, and the prices and yields to be obtained, rather than on the known values of these variables.

As was outlined in Chapter 2, the rules governing the administration of the deficiency payment scheme ensure that the degree of price uncertainty associated with the prices producers receive is small, and that expected gross prices approximately equal last period's prices. It is slightly more difficult to make a similar assertion about the yield component of returns in that weather factors cause crop yields to vary between years, so that farmers are likely to base yield expectations on a notional 'normal' yield. However, year-to-year variations in cereal yields have rarely exceeded 10 per cent so that expected normal yields are not likely to differ greatly from the previous year's yields. Under these circumstances it appears that a Nerlove-type adaptive returns expectation mechanism can be introduced into the model with the plausible assumption that the adaptive expectations coefficient equals one.[3] Introducing this mechanism causes all the returns variables on the right-hand side of equation (5.3) to enter with a one period lag. In addition to the variables already mentioned, acreage harvested will be influenced by factors which affect the realisation of production plans, such as weather which, if bad, may prevent cultivation and sowing of the land. The 'basic' set of acreage response equations thus becomes

$$A_{it} = f(A_{it-1}, R_{it-1}, R_{jt-1}, R_{kt-1}, X_{t-1}, u_t) \qquad (5.4)$$

X = other factors affecting ploughing and planting the crop.

(a) *Model 1.* Model 1 is comprised of a set of equations which explicitly explain the acreage of each of the cereals considered in the analysis.

It is proposed to explain the acreage of wheat by means of two separate equations, one for the winter wheat acreage and the other for spring wheat. This appears justified on two counts, one is that winter wheat varieties require a cold period for optimal germination, and are sown early, while spring wheat does not and is sown later. Sowings of the two crops are therefore influenced by different sets of weather conditions. Winter

[3] In the preparation of this study cereal price and returns variables were constructed using Nerlove's (op. cit) suggested scheme for different values for the adaptive expectations coefficient. These experiments failed to 'improve' upon the results which will be presented below.

wheat has higher yields than the spring varieties and has been consistently more profitable than spring wheat, so that the two crops are also influenced by different sets of economic factors.

There is some evidence to suggest that the economics of winter wheat growing are rather special. This special condition is that over the study period wheat prices have been sufficiently high to encourage winter wheat to be grown at the maximum technically possible level. In evidence of this, the East Midland N.A.A.S. Crop Husbandry Reports, state for quite a number of years that the maximum possible acreage of winter wheat was sown.[4] In the years for which such a statement was not made, autumn weather conditions were wet and appear to have hampered cultivation and sowing. If the hypothesised situation has existed then at no time have prices been low enough to discourage winter wheat production, and the acreage will be found to be unresponsive to wheat price changes. Inclusion in the relevant specification of returns per acre from wheat and barley will permit testing of the hypothesis that the acreage of winter wheat is not influenced by returns to the crop or by returns to barley as a competitive alternative.

A further implication of the economic optimum exceeding the technological one, is that the adjustment mechanism is redundant, since there is no question of adjusting towards any new optimum from the current position. Hence the lagged endogenous term is not included in the winter wheat acreage equation. It is however not true to say that the actual level of winter wheat plantings coincides with the 'desired' technological maximum, since weather factors frequently prevent this from being achieved, and hence an appropriate weather variable must be employed to take account of this

The specific nature of the 'technological maximum' acreage of winter wheat cannot be stated. It is undoubtedly a notional concept to some extent, in that farming practice conforms in a non-rigid way to the tenets of good husbandry. With winter wheat these notions include that the crop should be planted only after potatoes, or after temporary grassland. Given that the potato acreage has markedly declined it might therefore be felt that the technically feasible acreage of winter wheat has also declined. At the same time, the development of new winter wheat varieties and the adoption of more flexible attitudes by farmers may have lessened the binding character of notional husbandry constraints. Machine-power availability may also place restrictions upon the ability of producers to prepare wheat land in the interval between the cereal and potato harvests and the onset of winter. Machine power available on farms has steadily increased so that any constraint of this nature should have diminished.

[4] *Reports of the Regional Crop Husbandry Advisor, N.A.A.S., East Midland Region,* for the April to March years 1957-8, 1959-60 and 1961-2 all refer to the fact that the maximum acreage of winter wheat was drilled, and other reports refer to a full winter wheat acreage being sown.

Whatever the true nature of the 'technological constraint' on winter wheat growing it is evident that producers and their advisors accept its existence. It is however likely that the level of operation of this constraint has altered over the study period, although no firm expectation can be made as to whether this change has been up or down. To accommodate this possibility a trend variable is included in the resultant specification:

$$(5.5) \qquad AWW_t = f((+)RW_{t-1}, (-)RB_{t-1}, (-)W_{t-1}, (\pm)T, u_t)$$

AWW = acreage of winter wheat harvested
RW, RB = returns per acre, from wheat and barley respectively, including subsidy
W = a weather index for the period September, October and November
T = time

It may be assumed that farmers make some overall initial plan about the acreage of cereals, and about the allocation of this acreage between the different cereals. Subsumed in this is that a general plan is formed about the acreage to be planted to wheat in each year. Chapter 3 has provided evidence that the acreage of winter wheat, as defined in this study, is highly susceptible to bad autumn weather conditions. Thus if a target wheat acreage is to be achieved spring wheat sowings must compensate for plantings of the earlier wheat. Hence the spring wheat acreage function is set up to reflect the hypothesis that spring wheat sowings adjust inversely to changes in the current year's winter wheat acreage rather than to the previous year's spring wheat acreage.

Gross margin data suggests not only that spring wheat profitability has been lower than that for winter wheat, but that it has been similar to that for barley. Given that barley sowing typically follows immediately after that of spring wheat in areas where both are grown, it is possible that there is economic competition between these two crops, and this is allowed for in equation (5.6). As there is less time available for wheat sowing in spring than for either barley or oats, the weather may well interfere with realisation of the required acreage, which justifies the inclusion of the spring weather index in

$$(5.6) \qquad ASW_t = f((-)AWW_t, (+)RW_{t-1}, (-)RB_{t-1}, (-)WS_{t-1}, u_t)$$

ASW = acreage of spring wheat harvested
WS = a weather index for February, March and April

Mixed cereals, which are combinations of oats with other crops, principally barley, are used entirely for livestock feed on the farm of origin. A casual inspection of yield and acreage data for this crop reveals a very close relationship with those for oats. Therefore in the following discussion remarks about oats will also be considered to apply to mixed cereals.

During all but the last few years of the study period returns and profits per acre from oats have been less on average than those of barley. However the greater adaptability of oats than barley to wet and acid soils has assured that oats has retained a place in the farming system. More extensive liming of the land has reduced soil acidity in general, and this coupled with the development of hardier barley varieties has enabled barley to take over a substantial acreage from oats. Another factor which may have played a role in facilitating this change is the altered attitude to continuous barley growing. So long as farming opinion held that it was not 'right' to grow barley for more than two or three successive years oats was relied upon to follow barley to extend the period of continuous cereal growing. This role for oats has lessened as more farmers have considered it feasible to grow almost continuous barley.

These factors suggest that non-quantifiable technical and attitudinal changes have influenced the displacement of oats by barley, and that a trend term should be included in the oats acreage specification in addition to the returns variables for oats and barley. This trend term may also capture the influence of the decline in the number of horses upon oats production. Oats have always been a more important source of feed for horses than for other livestock, and the steady reduction in their number has undoubtedly reduced demand for oats, both on and off the farm.

Given that the partial adjustment mechanism is retained, the specification of the oats and mixed cereal acreage response functions are

$$(5.7) \qquad AO_t = f((+)AO_{t-1}, (+)RO_{t-1}, (-)RB_{t-1}, (\pm)T, u_t)$$

$$(5.8) \qquad AMC_t = f((+)AMC_{t-1}, (+)RO_{t-1}, (-)RB_{t-1}, (\pm)T, u_t)$$

AO, AMC = acreages of oats and mixed cereals harvested
RO = return per acre of oats

The discussion leading to the specification of equations (5.7) and (5.8) included consideration of the competitive relationship of barley and oats, and implies that returns to barley and oats should also enter the specification of the barley acreage response equation.

The argument of the effect of wheat acreage decisions and sowings upon the barley acreage needs to be pursued in several stages: It has already been hypothesised that an overall plan is made in each year of the total acreage for cereals and its allocation between the individual grains. The basis for assuming a target total cereal acreage is that grain harvesting, drying and storage capital can be used to handle any grains, and that installed capacity will be adjusted to the cereals acreage as a whole. At the same time on the basis of economic and technical factors some initial targets will be established for each cereal. For wheat the target acreage may be assumed to consist of the technological maximum for winter wheat under normal weather conditions plus the economically and technically optimal spring wheat acreage associated with this. Because of the extreme weather conditions which occur in autumn winter wheat sowings are frequently depressed and, despite compensation by spring wheat sowings, the wheat target may not be achieved. Barley is planted after spring wheat where both are grown, and its acreage can be increased from initially planned levels to compensate for reductions in wheat sowings in order that the target total cereal acreage is achieved. It is unlikely that any such compensation has been effected via the oats acreage, since in general oats has been an inferior alternative to barley, and barley can always be grown on wheat land. Therefore if it is assumed that the barley acreage may compensate the wheat acreage, the latter should be employed as an explanatory variable of the former. However, it has also been hypothesised that spring wheat is competitive with barley at the margin. Such competition based on returns expectations would be reflected in the barley plan, and would suggest that wheat returns should be included as an explanatory factor of the barley acreage. It might however be argued that the inclusion of both wheat returns and the wheat acreage as explanatory variables amounts to double counting since the former affects the latter. Since the compensation effect supersedes the planning effect the wheat acreage would appear to be the most appropriate of the two variables to introduce in equation (5.9) below.

On the basis of evidence presented in Chapter 3 it was concluded that the major competitive use for cereal land is in dairying. In the light of previous discussion on the competitive positions of wheat and oats it also seems likely that any adjustment of the cereal acreage to economic conditions in the dairy industry will be manifest in adjustments of the barley acreage. Hence returns per acre from dairying may be the most appropriate measure of opportunity cost to include in the barley acreage equation. (Ideally profit per acre from dairying would be used, but no suitable variable is available). A further implication of the preceding remarks is that if a strong market for cereals in general were to induce expansion of cereal production it would probably be the barley acreage which would increase in response. Stated differently, it may well be the case that high cereals returns in general, rather than just for barley, would result in an increased barley acreage. It is therefore proposed to examine the effects of including a weighted index of returns per acre of all cereals as an explanatory variable for the barley acreage.

One factor which may have assisted the expansion of the cereal (and hence barley) acreage is the decline which has taken place in the amount of land devoted to potato production. This has occurred because of the failure of potato demand to match the rate of increase in potato yields per acre. This has led to a reduction in the acreage quotas allocated by the Potato Marketing Board and has resulted in a steady release of good arable land for alternative uses. Because the sugar beet acreage is also controlled by quotas, the only arable enterprise capable of absorbing the quantity of land made available–about 400,000 acres between 1954 and 1969–has been cereals. It might therefore be appropriate to use the acreage of potatoes as a factor explaining the barley acreage. (Economic factors such as the price of potatoes would not serve the purpose because of the distorting effects of market intervention by the Potato Marketing Board.)

Taking into account the factors just discussed, and retaining the partial adjustment mechanism gives the specification:

$$AB_t = f((+)AB_{t-1}, (-)AW_t, (-)APO_t, (+)RB_{t-1}, (-)RO_{t-1}, (-)RM_{t-1}, (+)RG_{t-1}, (\pm)T, u_t) \quad (5.9)$$

AB = acreage of barley harvested
RM = returns per acre from dairying
RG = weighted returns per acre from cereals
APO = acreage of potatoes at June census $t-1$

(b) *Model 2.* This model varies from model 1 in only one major respect, which is that the barley acreage is determined indirectly as opposed to directly. This is accomplished by introducing a total cereal acreage response into the system of equations and determining the barley acreage as the difference between the total cereal acreage and the sum of the acreages of winter wheat, spring wheat, oats and mixed cereals. Thus we have

$$aB_t = aG_t - aWW_t - aSW_t - aO_t - aMC_t, \quad (5.10)$$

where aWW_t, aSW_t, aO_t and aMC_t are determined by equations (5.5), (5.6), (5.7) and (5.8) and where aG_t = acreage of all cereals harvested, excluding rye.

All the assumptions needed to justify this second model have already been stated. It will be recollected that model 1 assumed the formation of a total cereal acreage plan. Similarly, the justification for the inclusion of returns to cereals as a whole and dairying returns variables in equation (5.9) was the economic pressures for change in the overall level of cereal production would be reflected principally in increased barley production. It hence seems reasonable to postulate a total cereals acreage response function.

(5.11)

$$AG_t = f((+)AG_{t-1}, (+)RG_{t-1}, (-)RM_{t-1}, (-)WS_{t-1}, (-)W_{t-1}, u_t).$$

The two weather variables employed in previous equations are included because the planned total cereal acreage may not be achieved as a consequence of adverse weather conditions. It should be noted that the model incorporating equations (5.10) and (5.11) retains all the features assumed in the original model. All the cereals other than barley are generated as before, and changes in the barley acreage plan will be the main feature reflected in the total cereal acreage response equation. Establishing the barley acreage by (5.10) allows the wheat acreage compensation effect to be built into the model, and this too accords with model 1.

(2) *Yield response*

While a properly specified model of cereal yield response might be fairly complex, the absence of suitable data places strict limits upon the set of estimable functions. For example data is not available on the quantities of insecticides, herbicides or fungicides applied to cereal crops. Similarly there is no data for the quantities of fertilisers applied to cereals as a whole let alone to the individual cereals. There are, however, data for the total quantities of fertilisers by type delivered to farmers. These quantities will be assumed to be applied to the soil immediately, and will be employed to explain cereal yields. Evidently total fertiliser applications have largely reflected practices in grassland management, but to the extent that they do reflect fertiliser application to cereals they may prove to be better explanatory variables than simple trends.

Reliable data is available on various aspects of national average weather conditions throughout the year. This makes it possible to test various alternative hypotheses about the effect of weather during the growing period upon cereal yields, it being generally accepted that there is a strong relationship between them.

It is also possible that there may be diminishing marginal yields on less suitable land drawn into cereal production. In order to examine this hypothesis the acreage of the cereal whose yield is to be examined is proposed as an explanatory variable. Thus we have

$$Y_{it} = f((-)W_g, (+)F_{t-1}, (-)A_{it}, u_t) \tag{5.12}$$

Y_i = yield of cereal i
Wg = a weather index or indices for a suitable period during the growing period – primarily a measure of rainfall
F = total deliveries of all, or some particular type, of fertiliser during the crop year preceding that of the August-October harvest
A_i = acreage harvested of cereal i

B. Cereal supply results

It should be acknowledged at the outset that a considerable number of alternative regression equations have been examined in the course of this study, and that only a selected number are presented below. Such a selection procedure lays the study open to the accusation that results have been selected to support a specific line of reasoning, and that alternative results might have been presented which are consistent with an alternative set of hypotheses. It is not possible to simply rebut this charge But in defence it is argued that considerable attention has been given to the construction of a rational set of hypotheses about the generating processes of cereal acreages. To the extent that this set of structures, as specified in equations (5.5) to (5.11), is acceptable, it constitutes the sort of model which would serve as a basis for the examination of some of the effects of cereal pricing policies. In order that such an examination may be conducted quantitatively, rather than merely qualitatively, it is necessary to obtain numerical estimates of the structural relationships involved. But in presenting the results of estimation it is considered desirable to operate within the fairly tight framework of rationally derived hypothesis and to resist, as far as possible, the temptation to include statistically 'nice' results which do not fit into a convincingly arguable system.

Unless otherwise stated, the results have been obtained by ordinary least-squares multiple regression.

(1) *Cereal acreage response results 1955-6 to 1969-70*

Attention in this chapter is primarily focused on the properties of alternative estimates of the basic equations in the acreage response models. While this includes some mention of their forecasting ability, detailed examination of this will be deferred until Chapter 8.

(a) *Wheat acreage response.* Despite the deficiencies of the winter and spring wheat acreage results presented below, they are superior to any results obtained from experiments to explain the wheat acreage as a whole. Results of the latter, which are not presented, fail to explain as much of the variance in the wheat acreage as do the former, and they also suffer from the fact that the most appealing results, statistically speaking, lack for a convincing explanation. Experimentation with a large number of alternative wheat and barley return and price variables failed to generate any results in which the winter wheat acreage responded to prices in a way consistent with general economic theory. This is however consistent with the previously stated hypothesis that wheat prices have remained at a level sufficient to induce the maximum feasible winter wheat sowings. The most satisfactory result achieved is in fact the following

(5.13)
$$aWW_t = \underset{(206{\cdot}28)}{1964{\cdot}61} - \underset{(91{\cdot}91)}{452{\cdot}50}w_{t-1} + \underset{(12{\cdot}24)}{37{\cdot}57}t$$

$R^2 = 0{\cdot}72$ $\quad \bar{R}^2 = 0{\cdot}67$ Durbin-Watson (*D-W*) Statistic = 3·10

aWW = acreage of winter wheat harvested (1,000 acres), as measured at the December census in the previous year

w = a de Martonne aridity index for September, October and November constructed according to the formula

$$w = \frac{12}{n} \cdot \sum_{i=1}^{n} P_i \bigg/ \left(10 + \frac{1}{n} \cdot \sum_{i=1}^{n} H_i\right)$$

where $i = 1, 2, \ldots, n$ months, P_i is the monthly average rainfall in England and Wales, H_i is the monthly average of the daily mean air temperature at sea level in England and Wales, and 10 is an arbitrary constant. t = a linear time trend.

N.B. Numbers in parentheses are standard errors. Variables denoted with a lower-case first letter are not logarithmically transformed.

Although this result only explains about 70 per cent of the variance in winter wheat plantings it should be remembered that the total variance is very high (refer to Figure 1). It has previously been suggested that these movements in sowings are not induced by economic factors but are due to an inverse relationship between autumn rainfall and acreage. Indeed, as it turns out, the autumn aridity index is a powerful explanatory variable in equation (5.13).

No unequivocal interpretation can be placed on the statistically significant positive coefficient of the linear trend variable in (5.13). It might be interpreted as indicating that the technically determined maximum winter wheat acreage is increasing (fairly rapidly) with time, and this may be due to increased flexibility of attitudes with regard to husbandry constraints, or to an increase in mechanical power on farms.

A number of spring wheat acreage results are presented in order to illustrate the nature of the evidence on the responsiveness of the wheat acreage to cereal prices. All of the results share some common features, the principal of which is that there is a highly statistically significant (and stable) inverse relationship between the acreages of spring and winter wheat. This is consistent with the hypothesis that spring wheat sowings compensate any shortfall in winter sowings so as to achieve more nearly the target wheat acreage. A further common result is that spring wheat sowings are negatively correlated with a variable which principally reflects spring rainfall, suggesting that the period for spring wheat sowing may be rather inelastic. While the relevant coefficient for this relationship is only significant in the absence of the economic variables it exceeds its standard error in each case.

(5.14)

$$\underset{}{aSW_t} = \underset{(451{\cdot}54)}{1928{\cdot}09} - \underset{(0{\cdot}07)}{0{\cdot}51aWW_t} - \underset{(497{\cdot}06)}{302{\cdot}53(rB/rW)_{t-1}} - \underset{(72{\cdot}02)}{96{\cdot}94wS_{t-1}}$$

$$R^2 = 0{\cdot}82 \quad \overline{R}^2 = 0{\cdot}77 \quad D\text{-}W = 1{\cdot}53$$

aSW_t = acreage of spring wheat harvested (1,000 acres)
wS = de Martonne aridity index for February, March and April
rB, rW = returns per acre of barley and wheat respectively, including subsidy (£'s)

Result (5.14) corresponds exactly to the prior specification (5.6). The coefficient of the ratio of lagged barley to wheat returns can be seen to have the expected sign, indicating a positive spring wheat acreage response to wheat returns and a negative one to barley returns, but because the coefficient has a large standard error it must be interpreted with great circumspection. Nevertheless if this coefficient were treated as a 'good' estimate of the true parameter it would imply an own-price elasticity of 0·32 and an elasticity with respect to the price of barley of –0·32 (These and all other elasticities cited in this chapter are calculated using the appropriate values of the explanatory variables required to estimate the 1967-8 acreages; that is using 1966-7 prices.) Similar elasticity estimates are obtained from equation (5.15), in which the returns ratio variable has been replaced by the variable of their difference, and into which a linear trend variable has been introduced as this marginally improves the coefficient on the returns variable.

(5.15)

$$aSW_t = \underset{(169{\cdot}93)}{1746{\cdot}11} - \underset{(81{\cdot}04)}{169{\cdot}86}wS_{t-1} + \underset{(7{\cdot}09)}{10{\cdot}66}t + \underset{(10{\cdot}70)}{6{\cdot}42}(rW - rB)_{t-1} - \underset{(0{\cdot}08)}{0{\cdot}56}aWW_t$$

$$R^2 = 0{\cdot}86 \quad \bar{R}^2 = 0{\cdot}80 \quad D\text{-}W = 1{\cdot}79$$

With the same reservations as before this result implies that spring wheat sowings respond with elasticities of 0·29 to the price of wheat and –0·25 to the price of barley. The consistency of these estimates with those from equation (5.14) is achieved despite using markedly different specifications of the relative returns variable, and this possibly lends them greater credibility than is warranted on the grounds of statistical significance. *N.B.:* As no evidence has been found of price responsiveness in the winter wheat portion of the wheat acreage, the elasticities associated with equation (5.15) imply total wheat acreage elasticities of 0·11 and –0·10 respectively in response to changes in wheat and barley prices; these prices are defined to include deficiency payments.

In both of the previous two results the returns variables have played a weak role, and it is therefore interesting to consider the effect of dropping the returns variable from equation (5.15)

(5.16)

$$aSW_t = \underset{(161{\cdot}74)}{1762{\cdot}77} - \underset{(79{\cdot}11)}{162{\cdot}11}wS_{t-1} + \underset{(6{\cdot}90)}{10{\cdot}06}t - \underset{(0{\cdot}08)}{0{\cdot}56}aWW_t$$

$$R^2 = 0{\cdot}85 \quad \bar{R}^2 = 0{\cdot}81 \quad D\text{-}W = 1{\cdot}57$$

Comparison indicates that the shift from (5.15) to (5.16) has no significant influence on the coefficients of variables common to both equations or upon the variance explained. This suggests that the weak showing of the returns variable in equation (5.15) is due to a genuinely weak relationship between aSW_t and $(rW - rB)_{t-1}$; the simple correlation between them is in fact only –0·0026.

From the point of view of prediction equation (5.16) may well perform as satisfactorily as (5.15), but the latter may still retain some additional interest from the point of view of policy implications.

(b) *Oats and mixed cereal acreage response.* Because of the apparent similarity of behaviour of the oats and mixed cereal acreages, it has also been decided to present a set of results for the combined acreage response. Thus three sets of results will be presented in this section. A number of alternative specifications are presented in each set since there are a variety of ways in which the economic variables are able to enter the relationships and exert an appropriate (statistically significant) relationship.

Consider first the oats acreage response equations in Table 9. In equation (5.17) a high proportion of the variance in the oats acreage is explained by the lagged endogenous variable and the lagged relative returns of barley to oats, both of which exhibit highly significant influences. The short-run elasticities of response to the prices (including subsidy) of oats and barley implied are 0·64 and –0·70 respectively, and there are no grounds for considering these implausible, although they are possibly larger than is normally assumed to be the case. An unsatisfactory feature of this result is that the coefficient of the lagged endogenous variable exceeds one, which

Table 9: Oats acreage response

Equation	(5.17)	(5.18)	(5.19)	(5.20)
Intercept	–0·85	–0·86	0·49	8·90
	(0·49)	(1·06)	(0·85)	(2·81)
AO_{t-1}	1·12	1·12	0·96	0·49
	(0·07)	(0·14)	(0·11)	(0·19)
$(RB/RO)_{t-1}$	–0·67		–0·53	–0·26
	(0·27)		(0·26)	(0·23)
$(YB/YO)_{t-1}$		–0·61		
		(0·26)		
$(PB/PO)_{t-1}$		–0·74		
		(0·91)		
T			0·08	
			(0·04)	
AB_t				0·62
				(0·18)
Elasticity of response to *PO*	0·64	0·97	0·51	0·24
Elasticity of response to *PB*	–0·70	–0·80	–0·57	–0·27
R^2	0·98	0·98	0·98	0·99
$\bar{R}^2$	0·98	0·97	0·98	0·99
D-W	2·18	2·10	2·17	2·05

All the symbols for variables have already been basically explained, but note that $(RB/RO)_{t-1}$ is used to represent $\log_e (rB/rO)_t$; similar interpretations apply to the other ratio variables.

implies a negative adjustment coefficient. This is a meaningless result in terms of the assumptions of the partial adjustment model which were employed to justify the inclusion of the lagged endogenous term in the basic specification (5.7). It is not however surprising in a situation where the endogenous variable changes in a highly correlated way with time, as it does in this case. If this relationship is due to a set of exogenous variables which are not, or cannot like attitudes, be included in the estimated relationship, then the lagged endogenous variable, which will also be highly correlated with time, will pick up the effects of the omitted variables. This appears to be one of the inherent problems of Nerlove-type distributed lag models, and places a question mark over their estimates of the adjustment coefficient. These circumstances do not, however, necessarily mean that the short-run elasticity estimates are unreliable; indeed the lagged endogenous variable may be a useful device for capturing the effects of unquantifiable variables and thus preventing them from distorting the influences attributed to other included variables.

Given the preceding remarks it is interesting to note in equation (5.19) the effect of adding a time-trend variable into specification (5.17). This variable exhibits a significantly positive coefficient, and whilst not significantly affecting the other coefficients its inclusion does result in the estimated adjustment coefficient becoming positive, although the speed of adjustment actually implied by the coefficient ($\gamma = 1 - 0{\cdot}96$) is improbably slow. It is therefore of considerable interest to examine result (5.20) in which the current acreage of barley appears as an explanatory variable. The effect of the change is to generate an adjustment coefficient of 0·51 which implies that long-run elasticities are approximately only twice the short-run elasticities, which is much more acceptable. At the same time the inclusion of AB_t does markedly affect the coefficient of the $(RB/RO)_{t-1}$ variable, causing it to be nonsignificant. This is perhaps not surprising, since it can be argued that the inclusion of both of these variables amounts to double counting, and that only one variable to reflect competition with barley should be included. Defensively it can be argued that there are aspects of competition between the two crops which cannot be represented by RB/RO_{t-1}, such as the reduced on-farm demand for oats, and the decrease in soil acidity which favours increased barley production. It may be argued that the variable AB_t captures these effects. It must also be noted that, although the acreage response to price elasticities implied directly by (5.20) are lower than from the other equations, if AB_t responds positively to the variable $(RB/RO)_{t-1}$ then the true elasticities implied exceed those presented in Table 9. It could well be the case therefore that equation (5.20) is the most useful equation structurally and that it provides the most useful set of information for price policy evaluation purposes. However for forecasting purposes equation (5.19) is probably preferable in that it does not incur the difficulty of requiring a forecast of AB_t first.

Equation (5.18) indicates the outcome of re-estimating (5.17) with the returns variable split down into its two components for relative prices and yields of barley to oats. The change is seen to have virtually no effect on the intercept term or on the coefficient of AO_{t-1}. Despite the failure of the relative price variable to acquire a significant coefficient, it is interesting that the magnitude of this coefficient is similar to that of the relative yield variable. Since all the variables are logarithmically expressed this implies a similar acreage response elasticity to both relative prices and

Table 10: Mixed cereal acreage response

Equation	(5.21)	(5.22)	(5.23)	(5.24)	(5.25)	(5.26)
Intercept	0·19	–0·43	0·79	0·35	13·58	9·16
	(0·17)	(0·33)	(0·21)	(0·30)	(4·71)	(4·07)
AMC_{t-1}	1·00	1·10	0·91	0·99	0·46	0·69
	(0·04)	(0·06)	(0·04)	(0·06)	(0·19)	(0·18)
$(RB/RO)_{t-1}$	–1·74				–2·61	
	(0·26)				(0·37)	
$(YB/YO)_{t-1}$		–1·25				–1·89
		(0·28)				(0·36)
$(PB/PO)_{t-1}$		–3·24				–3·62
		(0·71)				(0·62)
$(RB - RO + 5)_{t-1}$			–0·19			
			(0·04)			
$(YB - YO + 2)_{t-1}$				–0·16		
				(0·04)		
$(PB - PO + 3)_{t-1}$				–0·13		
				(0·04)		
AB_t					–1·26	–0·89
					(0·44)	(0·38)
Elasticity of response to *PO*	1·57	4·37	0·91	10·35	2·54	4·96
Elasticity of response to *PB*	–1·91	–3·37	–0·91	–4·93	–2·70	–3·83
R^2	0·99	0·99	0·97	0·98	0·99	0·99
$\bar{R}^2$	0·99	0·99	0·97	0·97	0·99	0·99
D-W	2·44	2·99	1·55	2·41	2·63	2·43

AB, *AMC* = acreages of barley and mixed cereal harvested (1,000 acres). The variable $(RB - RO + 5)_{t-1}$ is used to represent $\log_e (rB - rO + 5)$, where 5 is an arbitrary constant to ensure that the variable always has a positive value. Similar interpretations should be accorded to the yield and price difference variables.

relative yields, which tends to justify the use of the combined variable $(RB/RO)_{t-1}$ in the other equations.

Much of the discussion of the oats acreage results also applies to those for mixed cereals in Table 10. Again there is the problem of coefficients of the lagged endogenous variable exceeding or being close to unity, except in the cases where AB_t is used as an explanatory variable (equations (5.25) and (5.26)).

One additional feature in these results is that introducing the returns variable in the form of the difference in returns per acre between barley and oats generates a statistically significant result. Indeed in this case it does not matter whether the price variables enter through the returns variables, or if these returns variables are split down into their yield and price components, the coefficients obtained are statistically significant in all cases. However the price response elasticities of mixed cereals implied by the equations in which prices and yields enter separately seem improbably high, especially in equation (5.24). That the elasticities for mixed cereals should be higher than those for oats is surprising in that mixed cereals are not usually traded in the market and might therefore not be expected to be very price responsive. On the other hand it might be argued that, as mixed cereals are grown and fed on the farm as an alternative to purchasing oats in the market, the market price of oats is a true measure of the value of mixed cereals to the producer. On the same basis it might be assumed that an increased barley price would induce a shift into barley production for sale.

One further contrast between the mixed cereal and oats results is that in the former the addition of the barley acreage to the set of explanatory variables does not reduce the effect attributed to the relative price or returns variables, but actually enhances it. In consequence equation (5.25) has the desirable property of a fairly large adjustment coefficient–desirable in that there are no grounds for assuming great technical inflexibility in switching between cereals other than wheat–while also having good statistical properties throughout. As there is no strong *a priori* evidence about the true price elasticities, although there is some predisposition towards accepting smaller rather than larger values, result (5.25) could be argued to have superior economic properties to (5.21) and (5.23) which would appear to be alternative candidates.

This problem of choosing equations for the final model can be simplified if it is accepted that the behaviour of the oats and mixed cereal acreages are sufficiently alike to permit them to be treated in combination. Doing so generates the results in Table 11, and it is perhaps not surprising in view of the much smaller size of the mixed cereal acreage than that of oats, that the results lie fairly close to the comparable ones in Table 9.

Separating the returns variables into their components ((5.28) and (5.30)) again yields higher price response elasticities than might have been anticipated, but the coefficients on which they are based are non-significant. Hence the choice of most satisfactory result would seem to lie between the three remaining equations and any choice between them must be somewhat arbitrary. The prime candidate, despite inclusion of the controversial AB_t explanatory variable, seems to be equation (5.31) which possesses a number of attractive qualities: (1) a plausible estimate of the short-run price elasticities of response–this in common with other equations, (2) a positive adjustment coefficient of a magnitude which indicates an acceptable degree of flexibility in shifting between oats or mixed cereals and other crops, and (3) a statistical fit which captures the recent upturn in the *AOMC* acreage. These last two features, which are not shared by the

Table 11: Oats plus mixed cereal acreage response

Equation	(5.27)	(5.28)	(5.29)	(5.30)	(5.31)
Intercept	–0·65	–0·95	0·03	–0·32	10·01
	(0·40)	(0·86)	(0·34)	(0·56)	(2·75)
$AOMC_{t-1}$	1·09	1·13	1·01	1·05	0·45
	(0·06)	(0·12)	(0·05)	(0·08)	(0·18)
$(RB/RO)_{t-1}$	–0·76				–0·47
	(0·23)				(0·18)
$(YB/YO)_{t-1}$		–0·68			
		(0·23)			
$(PB/PO)_{t-1}$		–1·12			
		(0·79)			
$(RB - RO + 5)_{t-1}$			–0·06		
			(0·03)		
$(YB - YO + 2)_{t-1}$				–0·06	
				(0·03)	
$(PB - PO + 3)_{t-1}$				–0·04	
				(0·03)	
AB_t					–0·71
					(0·19)
Elasticity of response to *PO*	0·68	1·48	0·29	3·33	0·43
Elasticity of response to *PB*	–0·68	–1·22	–0·34	–1·68	–0·53
R^2	0·98	0·98	0·98	0·98	0·99
$\bar{R}^2$	0·98	0·98	0·97	0·97	0·99
D-W	2·35	2·44	1·77	2·46	1·96

other results, might be construed as an indication that the full nature of the competitive relationship between oats or mixed cereals and barley cannot be adequately represented by conventional price and yield indicators; a fairly complex additional variable is required and simple trend terms are insufficient. As a consequence, in spite of the difficulty associated with the nature of the additional variable employed, equation (5.31) seems to exhibit the 'best' set of properties for examining the effects of cereal price policies.

(c) *Barley acreage response.* The problems posed by 'trend' in the barley acreage analysis are if anything more serious than those encountered with oats and mixed cereals. Firstly, there is a high degree of correlation between the barley acreage and time, with the consequence that the acreage and its value lagged one year has a simple correlation of 0·98. Also a number of the other explanatory variables in specification (5.9) move in a highly correlated way with time which gives rise to serious multicollinearity problems. This causes a certain amount of instability in the estimated coefficients, according to which variables are included in the estimated equation. A number of experiments were performed, such as deflating all variables by different trending variables in an attempt to overcome these problems, but it was found that the most acceptable results on *a priori* grounds were obtained using variants of the basic model (5.9), and a number of these are presented in Table 12.

Table 12: Barley acreage response

Equation	(5.32)	(5.33)	(5.34)	(5.35)	(5.36)	(5.37)	(5.38)
Intercept	2·79	2·32	2·53	10·68	9·59	10·04	13·88
	(0·96)	(1·03)	(0·87)	(1·60)	(1·48)	(6·68)	(7.09)
AB_{t-1}	1·09	1·02	1·08	0·45	0·46	1·05	0·97
	(0·05)	(0·04)	(0·05)	(0·10)	(0·06)	(0·05)	(0·08)
AW_t	−0·47	−0·30	−0·41	−0·31	−0·32	−0·46	−0·38
	(0·33)	(0·14)	(0·12)	(0·07)	(0·06)	(0·13)	(0·14)
$(RB/RO)_{t-1}$	0·61		0·44			0·59	0·72
	(0·33)		(0·15)			(0·20)	(0·22)
APO_t							−0·30
							(0·23)
$(RM/RG)_{t-1}$	0·09	−0·14		−0·026			
	(0·14)	(0·08)		(0·044)			
RG_{t-1}					0·20		
					(0·11)		
$AOMC_t$				−0·50	−0·45		
				(0·09)	(0·08)		
$APTGF_t$						−0·67	−0·89
						(0·61)	(0·61)
R^2	0·99	0·99	0·99	0·99	0·99	0·99	0·99
$\overline{R}^2$	0·99	0·99	0·99	0·99	0·99	0·99	0·99
D-W	2·26	2·38	2·37	2·12	1·88	2·31	2·20

The first equation presented in the Table adheres fairly closely to specification (5.9), except for the omission of the trend and potato acreage variables. Both these variables are omitted to reduce the problems of multicollinearity; the potato acreage because it is assumed to play a lesser role than the other included variables, and the trend variable because it is likely to react with other variables without it being possible to judge whether its inclusion creates more bias problems than its exclusion.

The unsatisfactory features of result (5.32) are revealed by comparison with equations (5.33) and (5.34). Whereas the relative returns of barley-to-oats variable is nonsignificant and the relative returns of dairying to cereals has the 'wrong' sign when both variables are considered together, excluding each of the two variables in turn causes $(RB/RO)_{t-1}$ to capture a highly significant effect in (5.33) and $(RM/RG)_{t-1}$ to achieve the appropriate sign and almost become significant in (5.34). Also in contrast with (5.32) the acreage of wheat appears to exert a significant negative influence on the barley acreage in both (5.33) and (5.34). However, since competition between barley and oats has already been indicated to exist, and as it is strongly felt that dairying and cereals are competitive, total exclusion of either one of these competitive effects would appear to represent a serious misspecification. What has therefore been attempted is to retain both competitive effects by, (a) replacing $(RB/RO)_{t-1}$ in (5.32) by the current acreage of oats plus mixed cereals (equations (5.35) and (5.36)) and (b) replacing $(RM/RG)_{t-1}$ by the current acreage of permanent and temporary grassland plus fodder crops, this acreage being used as a proxy for the land allocated to dairying (equations (5.37) and (5.38)).

Turning first to the equations in which competition from oats and mixed cereals is represented by the explanatory variable $AOMC_t$. This procedure is not strictly in line with that for representing competition from barley in the oats acreage response by means of simultaneously including the two explanatory variables AB_t and $(RB/RO)_{t-1}$. However the objective in the present situation is to see what effect will be attributed to $(RM/RG)_{t-1}$ if $(RB/RO)_{t-1}$ is replaced by some other variable to represent the same competitive forces. As can be seen from equation (5.35) the result of doing this is that $(RM/RG)_{t-1}$ collects only a very small coefficient of appropriate sign; in none of a variety of alternative specifications containing both this variable and one for oats competition was it possible to achieve any more satisfactory result. Some part of the weak showing of this variable may be due to the poor quality of the milk returns data. These doubts stem from the fact that the necessary data at national level were not available to convert the expression of U.K. average returns per cow to a per acre basis so that regional data had to be employed instead. Consequently, it is interesting to note from equation (5.36) that substituting weighted acreage cereal returns per acre for $(RM/RG)_{t-1}$ has a negligible effect on the coefficients of the other variables shared with (5.35) but does result in an almost significant coefficient on the cereal returns variable itself. Undoubtedly the increase which has taken place in per acre cereal returns (and profits) has been a major factor in encouraging the expansion of barley production. It has permitted farmers with satisficing income objectives to switch from less congenial, more intensive enterprises, such as dairying, to the less demanding production of cereals and still generate a 'satisfactory' level of income from smaller holdings; this despite the fact that more intensive enterprises would still yield higher net incomes per acre. Hence the absolute level of cereal returns may well be an important determinant of barley production and equation (5.36) may have good structural properties. Certainly the inclusion of $AOMC_t$ as an explanatory variable has resulted in an acceptable estimate of the adjustment coefficient, although the method of generating this result is open to criticisms already voiced.

However it is not possible to appraise equation (5.36) at its face value. This is due to the existence of interrelationships between the barley acreage response equations and the acreage equations for other cereals, such that the effect of a change in the barley price upon the barley acreage has to be assessed with the aid of a system of equations. Because of the very weak evidence supplied by equation (5.14) of the influence of barley prices on the wheat acreage, we will set aside any consideration of the effects of price changes operating through (5.14) upon the barley acreage. However the presence of $AOMC_t$ as an explanatory variable in equation (5.36) cannot be overlooked in view of its significant inverse relationship with the price of barley, and also, depending upon which specification of the oats and mixed corn acreage response function we choose, because of its dependence upon AB_t itself. Thus if we accept that $AOMC_t$ is generated by equation (5.31), which may be considered our 'best' result explaining the oats plus mixed cereal acreage, it is necessary to derive a reduced-form equation in order to permit the estimation of the short- and long-run barley acreage response elasticities to price. The results of forming the relevant reduced-form equation for results (5.31) and (5.36) is that the short-run barley response elasticity to the barley price is 0·49 and to the oats price is −0·29, while the adjustment coefficient turns out to be 0·33 indicating that the long-run elasticities are three times greater than those in the short-run. These results appear plausible, and are certainly worthy of further consideration; as (5.31) and (5.36) form what is strictly a simultaneous system of equations the results of estimating them by simultaneous procedures is considered below.

Alternative approach (b) for getting round the problems associated with (5.32) also appears to have potential: From the available census data it is not possible to identify the acreage devoted to dairying, which would be the obvious acreage variable to represent dairy competition in the barley acreage response equation. Some experimentation amongst available alternatives showed that the most promising results were obtained using as a variable the acreages of permanent and temporary grass plus fodder (APTGF); these results are presented as equations (5.37) and (5.38). The acceptable common features of these two results are that both the wheat acreage and relative barley-to-oats returns variables exhibit significant influences, and that the implied elasticities are reasonable. Equation (5.37) implies short-run barley acreage response elasticities of 0·62 to own price and −0·56 to the oats price, with comparable estimates from (5.38) of 0·77 and −0·69. These estimates for the elasticities with respect to the price of oats lie in the same range as those for the converse relationship obtained earlier. While such symmetry in the cross-price elasticities might seem appropriate, it would perhaps be more reasonable to look for cross-price symmetry in terms of the absolute magnitudes of the acreage responses. This being so, and given the much larger barley acreage than that for oats, it might be expected that the barley response elasticity to the oats price would be lower than for the converse relationship. This would favour the combined results (5.31) and (5.36) rather than either (5.37) or (5.38). Indeed the only distinct advantage of the latter results is the explicit inclusion of a variable to express the competition between barley growing and dairying, an advantage much diminished by the apparent nonsignificance of this variable. A further unsatisfactory feature of (5.37) and (5.38) is the very high coefficients of the lagged endogenous variable which implies much less adjustment flexibility than appears reasonable.

While little further discussion of equations (5.37) and (5.38) seems merited, the inclusion of the potato acreage in equation (5.38) does raise an opportunity to discuss a criticism which has arisen with respect to such results. The criticism is that equations which use other crop acreages as explanatory variables have a tautological quality. This might be thought to arise on the grounds that the inclusion of all major alternative crop acreages as explanatory variables is bound to explain the barley acreage by virtue of the sum of the acreages equalling the whole. While this cannot simply be rebutted, it is nevertheless true that not all alternative land use to cereals is accounted for by the explanatory variables. This combined with the independent entry of the explanatory acreage variables may mean that the identity problem is not real. It should also be recollected that in most instances these variables serve as proxies for unavailable price (returns) variables, and that their use is to some extent unavoidable.

In summary of the quality of the results in Table 12, it does not appear possible to select a best result. Equation (5.36) in combination with (5.31), and equations (5.37) and (5.38) all have features to commend them, and are all candidates for selection. In the absence of a clear cut 'winner' it will be especially interesting to consider the second acreage response model, in which explicit barley acreage response is omitted, and to go on to examine total cereal acreage response.

Before doing so, however, the results of re-estimating the system of equations (5.31) and (5.36) by means of two-stage least-squares (*2SLS*) will be presented. This is done to remove any simultaneous bias that may have been caused by estimating a simultaneous system by ordinary least-squares (*OLS*). The *2SLS* estimates are

(5.39)

$$AB_t = \underset{(2{\cdot}03)}{10{\cdot}99} - \underset{(0{\cdot}07)}{0{\cdot}32}AW_t + \underset{(0{\cdot}13)}{0{\cdot}14}RG_{t-1} + \underset{(0{\cdot}11)}{0{\cdot}38}AB_{t-1} - \underset{(0{\cdot}11)}{0{\cdot}53}AOMC_t$$

$$R^2 = 0{\cdot}99 \quad \bar{R}^2 = 0{\cdot}99 \quad D\text{-}W = 1{\cdot}78$$

(5.40)

$$AOMC_t = \underset{(3{\cdot}26)}{8{\cdot}12} - \underset{(0{\cdot}19)}{0{\cdot}52}(RB/RO)_{t-1} + \underset{(0{\cdot}20)}{0{\cdot}56}AOMC_{t-1} - \underset{(0{\cdot}22)}{0{\cdot}58}AB_t$$

$$R^2 = 0{\cdot}99 \quad \bar{R}^2 = 0{\cdot}99 \quad D\text{-}W = 2{\cdot}19$$

These results can be seen to be fairly similar to their *OLS* counterparts. Possibly the only seriously disappointing feature of the result is the non-significance of the cereal returns variable in the first equation. The economic implications of these estimates are nevertheless much the same as those obtained using (5.31) and (5.35). Response elasticities of the barley acreage to barley and oats prices are 0·56 and –0·37 (from the *OLS* equations we obtained 0·49 and –0·28), while the oats plus mixed corn acreage response elasticities to the same prices are –0·86 and 0·71 which compare reasonably with the *OLS* estimates from equation (5.27). Consistency between the two sets of estimates is not very surprising, but is encouraging.

Note that if the acreage of permanent and temporary grassland plus fodder were to be generated by an equation containing the current barley acreage as an explanatory variable, the results (5.37) and (5.38) would also give us a two-equation simultaneous model with AB_t and $APTGF_t$ as the endogenous variables. No further account will be taken of this at the current stage, but there will be some reference to it in the next section.

(d) *Total cereal acreage response.* Of the variables postulated to influence the total cereals acreage in the initial specification (5.11) only one, the spring aridity index, is not present in result (5.41) in Table 13; this omission reflects the failure of the variable to display any strong influence. One notable feature of result (5.41) is that all the included variables attain statistical significance. This is true for the relative returns of dairying to cereals variable, which conforms with the hypothesis that cereals and dairying are competitive enterprises, and also of the autumn aridity index which reflects the depressant effect on the final cereal acreage of a poor start to the year's planting operations. The most unsatisfactory feature of (5.41) is the appearance, yet again, of a coefficient exceeding one on the lagged endogenous variable, with all that this entails. Results (5.42) and (5.43) represent experiments to grapple with this problem by successively introducing as additional explanatory variables the current acreage of potatoes and the current acreage devoted to grazing livestock. The justification for considering the first of these variables is that competition between potatoes and cereals is of importance and should be considered, while justification for the second is on the grounds that there may be 'technical' competition between the grazing and cereal acreages as well as additional economic competition not reflected by the variable $(RM/RG)_{t-1}$. However neither experiment is successful in that neither variables achieves significance nor is the coefficient of the lagged endogenous variable greatly reduced. But it is worth noting that these experiments have only very slight effects upon the coefficients of the $(RM/RG)_{t-1}$ and W_{t-1} variables which possibly imbues them with greater confidence. Equation (5.44) reflects the impact of adding both the extra variables simultaneously, and this is that, while a positive adjustment coefficient is produced, four out of five variables exhibit a nonsignificant effect. In terms of the policy implications of the short-run elasticities implied by equations (5.41)-(5.44) there is little to choose between them. Result (5.41) implies total cereal acreage response elasticities of 0·12, 0·06 and 0·02 with respect to the prices (including subsidy) of barley, wheat and oats respectively, whilst equation (5.44) yields the comparable elasticities 0·09, 0·04 and 0·02. That these elasticities are so much lower than those for the individual cereal acreages is hardly surprising, and indicates that there is a relative inflexibility of the total acreage allotted to cereals but much greater flexibility in its composition.

An alternative approach to the problem is indicated by equations (5.45) and (5.46) in Table 13. The first of these results should be compared to

Table 13: Total grain acreage response

Equation	(5.41)	(5.42)	(5.43)	(5.44)	(5.45)	(5.46)
Intercept	−2·91	−1·25	5·71	12·38	0·32	10·92
	(1·39)	(2·33)	(11·13)	(12·19)	(0·64)	(7·87)
AG_{t-1}	1·34	1·24	1·03	0·73	0·86	0·54
	(0·16)	(0·20)	(0·43)	(0·49)	(0·09)	(0·24)
$(RM/RG)_{t-1}$	−0·18	−0·17	−0·15	−0·12		
	(0·08)	(0·08)	(0·09)	(0·09)		
W_{t-1}	−0·08	−0·09	−0·08	−0·08	−0·05	−0·05
	(0·03)	(0·03)	(0·03)	(0·03)	(0·02)	(0·02)
APO_t		−0·11		−0·16		
		(0·13)		(0·13)		
$APTGF_t$			−0·59	−0·89		−0·77
			(0·76)	(0·78)		(0·57)
RG_{t-1}					0·29	0·26
					(0·09)	(0·09)
R^2	0·94	0·94	0·94	0·95	0·95	0·96
$\overline{R}^2$	0·92	0·92	0·92	0·92	0·94	0·94
D-W	2·97	3·30	2·51	2·82	3·06	2·73

(5.41) in that the transition involves simply the substitution of the variable RG_{t-1} for $(RM/RG)_{t-1}$. That is the competitive element of dairying is removed. This procedure generates a positive adjustment coefficient, and tellingly the short-run acreage response elasticities to cereal prices are not markedly different; elasticities with respect to the barley, wheat and oats prices are 0·18, 0·08 and 0·03 respectively from (5.45), as opposed to 0·12, 0·06 and 0·02 from (5.41). Nevertheless result (5.45) is somewhat unsatisfactory in that no account is taken of competition from dairying and the negative autocorrelation problem of the residuals is made marginally worse. Both of these defects are overcome to some extent by introducing into specification (5.45) the proxy variable for competition with dairying, $APTGF_t$. From (5.46) it can be seen that this shift has little effect on the short-run acreage response elasticities to cereal prices, and it does generate a larger adjustment coefficient than the other results, which may well be considered an improvement. That these improvements are achieved at the expense of a nonsignificant coefficient on the $APTGF_t$ variable is insufficient to prevent (5.46) from qualifying as the 'best' result, although of the remaining results equation (5.41) still exerts appeal on account of its negative acreage response elasticity to milk returns. Acceptance of result (5.46) raises the possibility that the cereals acreage and the acreage of permanent and temporary grass plus fodder should be considered as being jointly determined by an interdependent set of equations. Simultaneous estimation of the determinants of these two acreages by means of two-stage least-squares has in fact generated the following results:

(5.47)

$$\underset{}{AG_t} = \underset{(16{\cdot}31)}{10{\cdot}21} + \underset{(0{\cdot}56)}{0{\cdot}72AG_{t-1}} - \underset{(0{\cdot}13)}{0{\cdot}17(RM/RG)_{t-1}} - \underset{(0{\cdot}03)}{0{\cdot}05W_{t-1}} - \underset{(1{\cdot}16)}{0{\cdot}75APTGF_t}$$

$$R^2 = 0{\cdot}96 \qquad \bar{R}^2 = 0{\cdot}95 \qquad D\text{-}W = 2{\cdot}77$$

(5.48)

$$APTGF_t = \underset{(2{\cdot}04)}{5{\cdot}87} + \underset{(0{\cdot}15)}{0{\cdot}60APTGF_{t-1}} + \underset{(0{\cdot}022)}{0{\cdot}038(RM/RG)_{t-1}} - \underset{(0{\cdot}06)}{0{\cdot}21AG_t}$$

$$R^2 = 0{\cdot}99 \qquad \bar{R}^2 = 0{\cdot}99 \qquad D\text{-}W = 2{\cdot}22$$

Considering the first half of the result first, it is notable that the magnitudes of all the coefficients (5.47) are very close to the most acceptable estimates achieved by ordinary least-squares and this is felt to outweigh the rather large standard errors associated with these coefficients. The short-run acreage response elasticities to cereal prices are well in line with those achieved using *OLS*, being 0·16, 0·07 and 0·03 to the prices of barley, wheat and oats respectively. The estimated adjustment coefficient of 0·28 implies long-run elasticities approximately 3·6 times greater than those in the short-run, which seems entirely plausible.

The levels of statistical significance of the coefficients in the second half of the result are superior to the first and the level of 'fit' is very high. This tends to corroborate the hypothesis that dairying and cereal growing are competitive, in spite of the crudity of the dependent variable as a measure of land devoted directly to milk production. That changes in the relative returns variable appear to exert only a small influence is perhaps not all that surprising when it is remembered that the average absolute magnitude of $APTGF_t$ has been about 2·5 times that of AG_t; the near significance of the relevant coefficient thus does imply that an improvement in cereal returns will induce a switch from grassland to cereals.

(2) *Cereal yields*

The results of the cereal yield analysis are presented in Table 14. The first four equations cover each of the four major cereals considered in

Table 14: Cereal yield response

Equation	(5.49)	(5.50)	(5.51)	(5.52)	(5.53)
Dependent variable	YB_t	YO_t	YMC_t	YW_t	YW_t
Intercept	1·69	0·33	0·87	1·73	2·00
	(0·29)	(0·33)	(0·21)	(0·45)	(0·47)
N_t	0·18	0·31	0·26	0·18	0·17
	(0·03)	(0·04)	(0·02)	(0·05)	(0·05)
Wr_{t-1}	–0·13	–0·10	–0·15	–0·16	–0·22
	(0·05)	(0·06)	(0·03)	(0·08)	(0·08)
$(AWW/AW)_t$					0·12
					(0·08)
R^2	0·77	0·87	0·93	0·61	0·68
$\bar{R}^2$	0·73	0·84	0·91	0·55	0·59
$D\text{-}W$	1·77	1·47	2·29	1·73	1·06

Equation	(5.54)	(5.55)	(5.56)	(5.57)	(5.58)
Dependent variable	YW_t	YW_t	YO_t	YMC_t	YB_t
Intercept	3·32	3·32	3·09	3·14	3·27
	(0·08)	(0·08)	(0·05)	(0·05)	(0·07)
Wr_{t-1}	–0·24	–0·13*	–0·07*	–0·11*	–0·10*
	(0·07)	(0·05)	(0·03)	(0·02)	(0·04)
$(AWW/AW)_t$	0·10				
	(0·07)				
T	0·10				
	(0·02)				
t		0·06	–0·006	0·02	0·03
		(0·02)	(0·009)	(0·01)	(0·01)
t^2		–0·002	0·002	0·0002	–0·001
		(0·001)	(0·001)	(0·0005)	(0·001)
R^2	0·75	0·78	0·95	0·94	0·79
$\bar{R}^2$	0·71	0·72	0·94	0·92	0·73
$D\text{-}W$	1·28	2·46	2·34	1·75	1·70

* In these instances Wr_{t-1}, enters in an untransformed manner.

YB, YW, YO, YMC = Yields of barley, wheat, oats and mixed cereals–cwt per acre

N = U.K. home deliveries of nitrogenous fertiliser–1,000 nutrient tons

Wr_{t-1} = De Martonne aridity index for June, July and August in England and Wales

t = linear trend (T is the logarithmic transform)

the supply analysis, and reflect the theoretical specification (5.12) minus the relevant explanatory cereal acreage variables, since these were found in general to add little to the explanatory power of the relationships.

In each case the index of rainfall and temperature for the months June, July and August, that is for the immediate preharvest and early harvest period, was found to exert a significant depressant influence on cereal yields. This variable was selected after experiments with alternative weather variables for different periods during the growing season. As was mentioned in Chapter 3, it must be expected that weather conditions outside this period will exert some influence on yields, but the cancelling-out effects of extreme conditions at critical periods in the construction of longer period indices makes it desirable to concentrate on the most critical (short) period, which in this case appears to be the three summer months. An interesting feature of the coefficients generated by the weather variable in equations (5.49) to (5.52) is their similarity in size, suggesting similar yield elasticities with respect to weather for all the cereals.

Also as anticipated is the significant positive relationship which emerges between the input of fertiliser and yields. The fertiliser variable employed, home deliveries of nitrogenous fertiliser, is however not the theoretically desired variable. Ideally a weighted index of fertiliser nutrients applied per acre to the individual cereals should be employed. Unfortunately no data is available on the basis of fertiliser applications to particular crops, either on an individual nutrient or total fertiliser basis. The only data available is on fertiliser deliveries, and it was thus decided to employ nitrogen deliveries on the assumption that these might reflect underlying changes in the intensity of fertiliser use on cereals. Certainly the results obtained exhibit some interesting features, chief amongst which is the differential yield responses to the fertiliser variable. It can be seen that wheat and barley exhibit almost identical elasticities of yield response, whilst those of oats and mixed cereals are higher. In view of the more commercial attitudes generally considered to be adopted in growing the former two crops, these differential responses seem likely to reflect the true technical situation; also note in this connection the smaller intercepts of the oats and mixed cereal equations.

Another difference between the barley and wheat yield equations and the others is the relatively low coefficients of determination achieved in the former cases. They are also low when compared to those obtained in the unrevised results for the period 1955-6 to 1966-7 (0·86 and 0·85 as opposed to 0·77 and 0·61 in equations (5.49) and (5.52) respectively). That this is so probably reflects fundamental changes which have taken place in wheat and barley production in the last few years—principally that the greater scale of cereal growing has created disease and soil fertility problems which seem to have severely curtailed the improvements in cereal yields which occurred fairly steadily until about 1967-8. It is partially to take account of this problem that experiments were conducted using various polynomials of time as explanatory variables, some of the results of which are recorded as equations (5.55) to (5.58). Because of the poor quality of the fertiliser variable it did not appear too unjust to consider that the variable had acted as a fairly simple trend variable, and that it could without much loss of meaning be replaced by a time trend. To take account of the possible nonlinearity in cereal yield growth rates the squared value of the time trend was introduced as an explanatory variable. By comparing the last four results of Table 14 with the first four it can be seen that this experiment succeeded in raising R^2 in each case, although only substantially in the case of wheat yields. It is also interesting that in the barley and wheat yield equations the squared trend collects a negative sign, indicating a downturn in yields over time. This is consistent with recent experience, and contrasts with the empirical results for the other two cereals which indicate continuously rising yields. Indeed these properties favour the selection of the last four equations as the representative yield equations for inclusion in the final model, since it is their forecasting abilities which are important.

The results (5.53) and (5.54) are also interesting in that they represent the sole cereal results in which changes in acreage level appear to directly affect yields. The positive but nonsignificant coefficients of the variable for the ratio of the acreage of winter wheat to the total wheat acreage, denotes what might be expected, which is that winter wheat yields exceed those of spring wheat, and that an increased proportion of winter to spring wheat therefore causes increased yields. In fact these coefficients can be used to estimate the differential yields of spring and winter wheat, and using equation (5.33) the relevant coefficient applied at the mean values of the other variables suggests spring wheat yields of 27·48 cwt per acre in comparison with 32·46 cwt for winter wheat. These are highly plausible results and invest equations (5.53) and (5.54) with considerable value, even though (5.55) is preferred for forecasting purposes.

6

Cereal demand—model specification and results

A. Specification of the model

Demand for cereals in this study is classified by three sources, (i) animal feed demand, (ii) human and industrial demand, and (iii) seed demand. The possibilities of further disaggregation, for example into feed demand for individual classes of livestock, were considered but had to be rejected for the lack of suitable data. All three of these outlets are of a derived demand type, and in each case cereals are complementary rather than competitive with the majority of other inputs into the production process.

Cereal seed and cereal feed inputs may be considered as technical complements to acreage and livestock inputs respectively; but whereas the cereal inputs may be readily adjusted in the short run land and livestock inputs can only be varied in the intermediate run. Annual producer intentions about livestock and cereal outputs are primarily embodied in decisions about the livestock inventories held and acreages planted. Seed demand is thus technically determined by the seed requirements per acre of crop. Over the annual period aggregate cereal feed demand will be principally determined by the numbers and types of livestock on hand, but the demand for individual cereals will be influenced by changes in the relative prices of competitive cereals and feedingstuffs. It therefore seems that only currently dated variables need appear in the seed and feed demand functions, as all long-run supply adjustment features are embodied in the decisions about acreage and livestock numbers.

Similarly only currently dated variables are required in the human and industrial demand functions. In most of their uses in this sphere, cereals are the only major raw material input and quantities may be readily altered in response to changes in economic factors—readily in the context of an annual analysis.

In addition to the three sources of cereal demand mentioned above, there is another outlet, which is the demand for cereal stocks. Unfortunately, however, the time series data on stock holdings of cereals are too short to permit stock demand functions to be estimated on an annual basis. (Data on stocks held by cereal processors are only available from the early 1960's, and there are some rough estimates of cereal stocks held on farms, which are available only from 1963 onwards.)

(1) *Feed demand*

Cereals for livestock feed are inputs into a productive process, and demand for them is of the derived type. Hence, according to the economic theory of production, feed demand functions should have the same general specification as supply functions. That is, feed demand should be considered as a function of output and input prices as well as of any institutional or exogenous factors which may influence demand.

However, as has already been argued, feed inputs are likely to be complementarily determined by the numbers of livestock on farms. For a particular cereal it is therefore argued that an index of total livestock numbers with appropriate cereal consumption weights should be employed as an explanatory variable; prices of protein feeds and competing cereals should also be included as changes in these may induce substitution between feeds; price changes in livestock and livestock products may induce changes in the intensity with which cereals are fed to livestock; and in the absence of a price series for grassland products it is proposed to use the quantity of forage fed to represent the competition to cereals of grassland production for which it is a proxy. On grounds already stated, that feed levels can be adjusted rapidly to the optimum given the numbers of livestock, the values of all variables in the demand relationships enter with the same dating. Thus, with *i* standing for the set wheat, barley, oats and maize, the general specification of the demand functions for cereal *i* is

$$iFe = f((+)L_w, (-)Pi, (+)Pj, (+)P'LP, (-)PP, (-)G, u_t) \quad (6.1)$$

iFe = Feed demand for cereal *i*
L_w = The number of livestock units on farms, weighted by consumption weights for cereal *i*
Pi = Market price of cereal *i*
Pj = Set of market prices for cereals other than the *ith*
$P'LP$ = Price of livestock and livestock products, including subsidy
PP = Price of protein feedingstuffs
G = The quantity of forage fed (as a proxy for total grassland output consumed).
u_t = Error term

Just a brief note on the anticipated signs on the variables on the right-hand side of (6.1). The negative sign attached to the protein-feed price variable reflects the assumption of complementarity between high-energy and protein feeds. By contrast it is assumed that grassland output (as primarily an energy source) is competitive with cereals, which explains the negative sign on the forage fed variable.

It has also been decided to estimate an aggregate demand function for feeding cereals. Because of the high degree of substitutability between feeding cereals, demand relations for individual cereals may prove unstable and difficult to estimate. It may well be that an estimated aggregate cereal feed demand function will yield coefficients which are more readily reconciled with economic expectations. The initial specification for such a function is a simple variant upon (6.1).

$$QCF = f((+)L, (-)PC, (-)PP, (+)P'LP, (-)G, u_t) \quad (6.2)$$

QCF = Quantity of cereal feed
PC = Price of feeding cereals
L = The number of livestock units on farms.

Cereals form the major part of the high-energy part of livestock rations, but there are nevertheless a number of feedingstuffs which also have a relatively high ratio of carbohydrate to protein and with which they are readily substitutable, e.g. molasses, and sugar-beet pulp. For the same reasons which have prompted estimation of an aggregate cereal feed demand function it is felt advisable to estimate an aggregate high-energy feed demand relation with the same basic rationale as (6.1) and (6.2):

$$QHF = f((+)L, (-)PE, (-)PP, (+)P'LP, (-)G, u_t) \tag{6.3}$$

QHF = Quantity of high-energy feed
PE = Price of high-energy feed

For the sake of completeness, and to gain additional insight into feed demand relations it has been decided to estimate a demand function for protein feeds of the form.

$$QP = f((+)L, (-)PP, (-)PE, (+)P'LP, (-)G, u_t) \tag{6.4}$$

QP = Quantity of protein feed

(2) *Human and industrial demand*

Cereals demand for human food and industrial use covers a multiplicity of different uses from barley for distilling, and wheat for flour to maize for starch and glucose production. For convenience, these will be discussed under the demand for a single item—food.

The essential characteristic of human demand for cereal foods is its stability and predictability. The price elasticity of demand is often low, especially for bread and flour, and the income elasticity of demand also tends to be extremely low, even negative for bread. It is fairly easy, therefore, to predict the level of human demand for cereals products given data on population, national disposable personal income and product prices. None of these three variables are likely to show dramatically rapid change, the first two because it is in their 'nature', and the third because product prices tend to be administered in the oligopolistic food-processing industries. Given this oligopolistic structure of industries processing cereals for human use, and the stable market shares of individual firms, it is probable that firms, and therefore the industries in aggregate, are able to accurately predict the demand for their products as functions of the prices they establish, population and personal disposable national income. We may therefore consider food demand to be determined by these variables rather than by the usual variables in a derived demand equation.

Again, as with feed, it should be possible to adjust cereals inputs to optimal levels in the short run, so that all variables in the demand equation may be specified in same period values. Thus a general specification of a demand function for cereals for human and industrial purposes is

(6.5) $$iFo = f((-)Phi, (-)Po, (+)H, (+)Y, (+)Pr, u_t)$$

iFo = Quantity of cereal i consumed in human and industrial uses
Phi = Price of cereal i–food grade
Po = Price of final output
H = Human population
Y = Personal disposable income
Pr = Prices of alternative products

(3) *Seed demand*

It has been argued that seed is such a minor item of cost in cereal production that its price will have virtually no impact upon the decision to produce cereals. Thus given the complementarity which exists between seed use and acreage, seed demand will be largely a function of acreage. However, technological developments have occurred to reduce the seed requirement per acre, and hence a time trend variable will be included in the specification as a proxy for technological change.

(6.6) $$iS = f((+)Ai, (-)t, u_t)$$

iS = Quantity of cereal i used for seed
Ai = Acreage of cereal i
t = Time

(4) *Import demand*

It is shown in Appendix 1 that there are good grounds for treating U.K. market prices for cereals as world prices. Assuming this to be the case the market prices in demand equations (6.1) to (6.5) are effectively world prices. Domestic supply is assumed to be determined by expected cereals prices which include an element of subsidy, but this output actually moves into the market at the lower, going market price. Thus net cereal imports (or exports) are simply the difference between U.K. demand for cereals, including stock demand, and the U.K. supply of cereals. This can be simply expressed as an identity

(6.7) $$iI = iFe + iFo + iS + \Delta T_i - QCi$$

iI = Net quantity of cereal i imported (exported)
ΔT_i = Change in stocks of cereal i
QCi = Domestic supply of cereal i

Unfortunately the inability to estimate cereal stock demand functions means that it is not possible to estimate a model which covers all the elements in equation (6.7). Only in the event that there are no changes in cereal stocks will the model estimated in this study be useful in predicting net cereal imports or exports. This is not a condition which seems likely to hold, for the little data which are available indicate that there are fluctuations in the cereal carryover from one year to the next, particularly in processors' stocks of barley.

It is however possible to check what the import predicting ability of the estimated model would be if it were assumed that a reliable stock demand predictor were available. This can be done for the period of stock data availability by adjusting predicted cereal demand for the actual stock changes and examining the relationship of the difference between predicted supply minus adjusted predicted demand and the volume of actual net imports (exports) for each cereal.

B. Cereal demand results

Unlike the cereal supply results the demand results have not been updated, and they were basically estimated for the period 1955-6 to 1966-7, although where data permitted the period of analysis covers the year 1954-5.

In many cases the coefficients and their standard errors in functions estimated using logarithmically transformed variables were less in accord with expectations than they were when no transformations were performed. Hence most of the results are presented for the untransformed variables.

The set of cereals for which demand functions are estimated excludes mixed cereals and includes maize. Mixed cereals are excluded because total output is assumed to be automatically used for animal feed on farms where it is produced, with none of its output being traded in the market; there is certainly no data recording either the volume of mixed cereal sales or mixed cereal prices. On the other hand maize is included, although not grown in any significant quantity in this country—there was an estimated 15,000 acres of maize grown in the U.K. in 1968[1]—because substantial quantities of imported supplies are used for both feed and food purposes, and are to some extent substitutes for domestically produced cereals. Sorghums, although imported in reasonable quantities over the period of analysis, have had to be omitted from consideration because of the lack of suitable price data.

(1) *Livestock feed demand for individual cereals*

An attempt has been made to estimate separate feed demand functions for the four cereals, wheat, barley, oats and maize. Because of the degree of substitutability of cereals for one another in high-energy feedingstuffs, a weighted price index of cereals other than that for which the demand function has been estimated has been employed as a measure of opportunity cost in most equations.

Cereal demand will depend largely upon the average number of livestock on farms during the harvest year $t/t + 1$. Crude averages of livestock unit numbers have therefore been constructed according to the formula: ((total livestock units at June census$_t$ + 2 (total livestock units at December census$_t$) + (total livestock at June census $t + 1$))/4. The double weighting for livestock at the December census means that the average calculated is

[1] *Farmers Weekly*, 28 June 1968.

effectively the average of two six-month averages. The variable produced by this procedure is designated by the symbol *l*, but a further weighting procedure has been adopted to produce consumption weighted livestock unit variables *lw*. These variables differ depending upon the cereal for which demand has been estimated; each component class of livestock has been weighted by the proportion of the relevant cereal in its concentrate ration in 1957-59, according to the principles established in Chapter 4.

For the purposes of comparing the impact of using the consumption weighted livestock variables, *lw*, in place of the unweighted variable, *l*, barley feed demand equations (6.8) and (6.9) are presented in Table 15. The difference in the size of the coefficients of these two variables is largely due to a difference in the units in which livestock numbers are expressed; this results from the weighting process. The use of *lw* in (6.9) can be seen to have led to a slight improvement in R^2, a relative reduction in the standard errors of the coefficients, and an increase in the value of the Durbin-Watson statistic from 1·03, which indicates positively auto-correlated residuals, to the nonsignificant value of 1·39. Thus the results of (6.9) seem to be marginally 'better' than those of (6.8), and, since similar encouragement has been obtained by using *lw* in some of the other functions, the unweighted livestock variable has been discarded for the purposes of further analysis of demand for individual cereals.

(a) *Barley*. Feed demand for barley rose rapidly over the period studied, and a high proportion of its variance appears to be explained by the two variables *pIB*/*pIOC* (the ratio of the feed barley price to the weighted price of other feeding cereals) and *lw*. In each of the equations (6.9)-(6.12) the coefficients of these variables have the appropriate sign and are statistically significant. As equation (6.9) shows these two variables explain 96 per cent of the variance of the dependent variable.

However, with the exception of the result in (6.12), the coefficients of the livestock variable are rather high from the technical point of view. The coefficient of 0·08 in equations (6.9) and (6.11) implies that an additional dairy cow causes barley feed demand to increase by 1·08 tons. This seems a very high estimate in view of the fact that the technical concentrate requirements of a dairy cow are about 1·25 tons per annum, and by no means all of this will be supplied by barley. (It must be admitted that actual concentrate usage per cow may well exceed the experimentally determined requirement). Much more reasonable is the result in equation (6.12) which implies that one dairy cow requires 0·52 tons of barley. This estimate still seems a little high however, and this may be the result of failing to reduce the livestock unit weights of cattle to allow for the proportion of cattle feed provided by grassland. Any reduction in these weightings would reduce the estimate of barley feed requirements for a given number of cattle.

Such a modification would however reduce the size of the aggregate live-stock unit variable, and might well increase the size of its coefficient, which

Table 15. Demand for feed barley, 1954-5 to 1966-7

Equation	(6.8)	(6.9)	(6.10)	(6.11)	(6.12)
Dependent variable	*bFe*	*bFe*	*bFe*	*bFe*	*bFe*
Intercept	–11,174·17	–4,766·12	–5,573·173	1,518·49	–1,754·30
	(5,570·36)	(4,344·23)	(3,983·138)	(4,264·68)	(3,516·34)
l	1·85				
	(0·21)				
lw		0·08	0·07	0·08	0·04
		(0·01)	(0·01)	(0·01)	(0·02)
pIB/pIOC	–81·70	–113·00	–100·36	–107·93	–58·36
	(35·79)	(29·75)	(28·04)	(23·95)	(30·06)
g			0·27		
			(0·16)		
pLP′				–66·27	
				(25·92)	
aB					0·56
					(0·20)
Own-price elasticity	–2·01	–2·78	–2·47	–2·66	–1·44
R^2	0·94	0·96	0·97	0·97	0·98
$\bar{R}^2$	0·93	0·95	0·96	0·97	0·97
D-W	1·03	1·39	2·33	2·43	1·21

N.B. (1) All variables are in natural units.
(2) The ratio variable (*pIB/pIOC*) has been multiplied by 100.

bFe = Quantity of barley consumed by livestock in the U.K. (1,000 tons)
pIB = Price index of feeding barley
pIOC = Weighted price index of other cereals, i.e. other than barley
g = Quantity of hay preserved in the U.K. (1,000 tons)
pLP′ = Price index of livestock and livestock products
aB = U.K. acreage of barley (1,000 acres)
l = Average number of livestock units on U.K. farms, with shifting coefficients to reflect changes in feed conversion efficiency and yield per animal for several livestock classes[2]
lw = As *l*, but with a further weighting procedure according to the importance of the relevant cereal (dependent variable) in the rations of each livestock class[3]

[2] Since livestock unit coefficients are designed to express livestock numbers in terms of the feed they require, it seems important that changes in livestock feed requirements should be reflected by these coefficients, and that to represent successive years a vector of coefficients should be used for each livestock class in place of the usual static coefficients.

[3] It is acknowledged that the appropriate consumption weightings will have changed, but the only reliable source for such weightings is the M.A.F.F. Livestock Feeding Practices Survey of 1957-1959.

would result in a larger increase in barley demand being attributed to increases in pig and poultry numbers. This would be highly undesirable for the implication of (6.12) is that an additional sow causes an increased feed demand for barley of 0·94 tons, which would appear a very high estimate. Judged solely upon the criterion of the properties of the coefficient of *lw*, it would appear that (6.12) is the least unsatisfactory result, for the coefficients are even larger in the other equations.

The prices of feeding barley and of other cereals also appear to exert considerable influence on the demand for barley; the coefficients of *pIB*/*pIOC* being significant in each case. In fact it turns out that the estimates of the elasticity of demand with respect to the barley price exceed two in all of the equations presented, except (6.12). This is perhaps not overly surprising in view of the relative ease of substitution of cereals for one another in animal feed uses over a certain range. With respect to the effect of prices of feeding barley and other cereals none of the results in Table 15 appears preferable to any other.

In order to be consistent with the theoretical demand function, equation (6.1), an output price variable for the price index of livestock and livestock products, *pLP*, has been included in equation (6.11). Its effect turns out to be statistically significant, but to be not of the expected sign. As there is no obvious explanation for a negative effect of the product price upon feed demand, the result would appear to add little value to the empirical results in the other equations.

It was also anticipated that an increase in forage supply would reduce the demand for barley, and (6.10) was estimated in an attempt to test this hypothesis. Unfortunately, the estimated effect turned out to be positive and nonsignificant, as it also did in the demand functions for the other cereals. It may well be that this unsatisfactory outcome is due to the inadequacy of the forage supply series, for it must be admitted that the hay preservation variable is very roughly estimated and is not a particularly good proxy for total forage supply.

Thus it appears that, for reasons concerned with the technical properties of the coefficient of the livestock variable, (6.12) is the most satisfactory barley feed demand result. It has however only been achieved by including as an explanatory variable, the acreage of barley. As acreage is a supply variable it may well be considered an inappropriate variable to explain demand. Acreage is however not the same as production, and there is no identity between barley feed demand and the U.K. barley acreage. Inclusion of this variable can be justified on the following grounds. These are that much barley is grown for feed utilisation on the farm where it is produced, hence an expansion of the barley acreage may well increase barley demand by inducing livestock producers to substitute their own home-grown barley for feedingstuffs purchased off the farm. In the circumstances of the time period of this study however, there can be no doubt that the barley acreage variable operates to some degree as a trend variable, and that it captures some of the trend influence otherwise attributed to livestock numbers.

(b) *Maize.* Feed demand for maize stayed fairly steady from 1954-5 to 1956-7, rose sharply until 1962-3 and has exhibited a subsequent decline. It is generally accepted that the recent reduction in feed maize utilisation has resulted from the much increased U.K. barley output, and therefore exhibits the influence of domestic cereal supply conditions on maize demand.

As equations (6.13) and (6.14) (Table 16), show about 80 per cent of the variance in maize demand is explicable by variables *lw* and either the relative price of maize to other cereals (*pIM*/*pIOC*) or the relative price of barley to maize (*pIB*/*pIM*). The coefficients in both these equations have the expected sign, are of similar magnitude, and are highly significant, while R^2 is also similar in both cases. The estimated own-price elasticities of demand for maize are also similar, and of roughly the same magnitude as those estimated for barley. The coefficients of *lw* are again very high–a coefficient of 0·13 implying that an extra dairy cow will require 1·17 tons of maize. Obviously this is technically unreasonable, and the arguments used concerning the livestock variable coefficients in the barley feed

Table 16: Feed demand for maize, wheat and oats, 1954-5 to 1966-7

Equation	(6.13)	(6.14)	(6.15)	(6.16)
Dependent variable	*mFe*	*mFe*	*mFe*	*wFe*
Intercept	−2,889·11	−14,525·02	−94·37	3,383·53
	(1,915·88)	(2,644·07)	(4,925·09)	(1,271·78)
lw	0·12	0·13	0·09	0·03
	(0·02)	(0·02)	(0·02)	(0·01)
pIM/*pIOC*	−54·04			
	(16·91)			
pIB/*pIM*		53·06	33·91	
		(15·30)	(12·60)	
pIW/*pIOC*				−50·61
				(15·48)
pLP′			−89·62	
			(28·19)	
Own price elasticity	−2·20	−2·18	−1·39	−2·51
R^2	0·82	0·84	0·92	0·57
$\overline{R}^2$	0·79	0·81	0·90	0·48
D-W	1·43	1·27	2·22	0·91

Equation	(6.17)	(6.18)	(6.19)	(6.20)
Dependent variable	*wFe*	*wFe*	*oFe*	*oFe*
Intercept	–841·88	–5,389·64	6,547·52	612·69
	(1,481·37)	(1,678·68)	(2,555·21)	(355·69)
lw	0·02	0·04	–0·02	
	(0·01)	(0·01)	(0·004)	
pIW/pIOC	–15·17	–47·25		
	(14·60)	(7·69)		
aW	1·00			
	(0·28)			
aO				0·75
				(0·05)
pLP′		72·36	0·27	
		(12·83)	(0·29)	
pIO/pIOC			20·73	
			(13·93)	
pIO				–3·65
				(4·39)
Own-price elasticity	–0·75	–2·34	1·29	–0·20
R^2	0·82	0·91	0·84	0·97
$\bar{R}^2$	0·76	0·87	0·79	0·96
D-W	1·70	2·60	1·47	2·44

N.B. (1) All variables are in natural units.
(2) Ratios of variables are multiplied by 100.
mFe, wFe, oFe = Quantities of maize, wheat and oats consumed by livestock in the U.K. (1,000 tons)
pIM, pIW, pIO = Price indices of maize meal, feeding wheat and feeding oats
pIOC = Weighted price index of feeding cereals other than the one whose price index comprises the numerator of the ratio variable in which *PIOC* is the denominator
aW, aO = Acreages of wheat and oats harvested in the U.K. (1,000 acres)

demand analysis are equally applicable here. Somewhat more reasonable is the prediction (using a coefficient of 0·13) that 1,000 laying hens would require 21·37 tons of maize per annum or 0·43 cwt per bird, but this estimate is still high. This would seem to imply that more work is required to obtain the correct livestock unit coefficients and consumption weights for the various classes of livestock.

Equation (6.15), which contains the livestock and livestock product price variable improves upon (6.13) and (6.14) in respect of decreasing the coefficient of *lw* and increasing R^2. As a predictive equation it is likely to do better than the others, but this gain is obtained at the expense of having a coefficient of the wrong sign on the *pLP* variable. Thus these results each have their positive points, and there is no adequate criterion to select a 'best' result.

(c) *Wheat.* As equation (6.16) indicates the coefficients of variables *lw* and *pIW/pIOC* both have statistical significance, but in contrast to the barley and maize feed demand functions the R^2 is only 0·57. In addition the value of the Durbin-Watson statistic (0·91) indicates the presence of positively autocorrelated residuals, and examination of the residuals reveals that with the exception of 1958-9 they are negative for all the years 1957-8 to 1963-4. These years constitute a period when the U.K. wheat acreage was less than in both the preceding and subsequent periods, suggesting that the demand pattern might (again) be directly influenced by domestic supply considerations. Since the relative price of wheat to other cereals did not rise, and since evidently imports of feeding wheat did not increase in the fashion one might expect in an open market, it is clear that no excess demand for feed wheat developed in the U.K. and that demand must have been satisfied by some substitute. This being so it seems entirely justifiable to include the supply variable *aW* in the demand equation as has been done in (6.17). The consequences of this move are to significantly improve R^2, to increase the Durbin-Watson statistic, to reduce the magnitude of the other coefficients so that the coefficient of *pIW/pIOC* becomes nonsignificant, and to generate a significant coefficient for *aW* itself. The coefficient of *lw* in (6.17) predicts that 1,000 dairy cows would require 61 tons of wheat which is approximately 1·2 cwt per cow—a not unreasonable estimate.

However, result (6.18) in which *pLP′* (the price of the product) substitutes for *aW*, is also a highly satisfactory one from an *a priori* point of view. It is the sole cereal demand function in which the price of livestock and livestock products has been estimated to have a significant positive influence upon feed demand. The other coefficients are also significant and of the anticipated sign, and although the estimated amount of wheat consumed per dairy cow increases to 3·6 cwt, this still does not seem unreasonable.

Thus there are two wheat demand functions (6.17) and (6.18) both of whose structures are justifiable, and both of which yield acceptable results. However, because of doubts about the validity of introducing an explanatory supply variable into a demand equation (6.18) would appear to be the marginally preferable result.

(d) *Oats.* Oats feed consumption has declined steadily throughout the period, and since oats prices have declined relative to other cereal prices while livestock numbers have increased, no permutation of these variables produces a logically sound explanation of feed oats demand. This is revealed by equation (6.19) (Table 16) in which the signs of the coefficients of *lw* and *pIO/pIOC* are both contrary to expectations, as is that of *pLP* also. Once again inclusion of the supply variable *aO* offers an apparent solution to the problem (see 6.20), a solution which can be justified if there is a high degree of substitutability between cereal feeds. The simple correlation between *aO* and *oFe* is 0·98, and in consequence the inclusion of *aO* in (6.20) leads to a very high R^2. Other variables do little to detract from the size of the coefficient of *aO*, and no coefficients of other variables are significant in the presence of the oats acreage variable.

(e) *Conclusions.* It appears that there is a close relationship between the U.K. acreages of wheat, barley and oats and the quantities of these cereals consumed for feed; although it is possible for the feed demand for wheat and barley to be satisfactorily explained without resort to the use of an acreage or supply variable. One feasible interpretation of the fact that shortages of oats (and wheat) supplies have not caused either relative prices or imports to rise is that cereals are such close substitutes in livestock feeds that short supplies of one can be offset by plentiful supplies of another. Further evidence of interdependence of this type appears to be provided by the decline in maize utilisation in recent years. The high estimates of own-price elasticities of demand also imply ready substitutability between cereals.

These cumulative arguments suggest that it may be more appropriate to estimate an aggregate high-energy feed demand function rather than functions for individual cereals–given that the bulk of high-energy feed is supplied by cereals. This will also overcome any identification problem which is posed by the inclusion of cereals acreage variables in cereals demand functions.

However in order that the model of the cereal economy should be able to predict import requirements for cereals it is desirable that a cereal feed demand function should be estimated in preference to one for total high-energy feed which also includes wheat offals, dried sugar-beet pulp and molasses. Even so, employing a model which considers aggregate cereal feed demand only will not permit any estimate of individual cereal import requirements to be made, but merely the aggregate requirement. For this reason it will be as well to discover how much predictive 'mileage' can be obtained from the individual feed demand equations before rejecting them completely. The results of prediction tests will be reported in Chapter 8.

(2) *Aggregate demand for cereal, high-energy and protein feeds*

This section presents the results of estimating aggregate demand functions for feeding cereals, high-energy feed, and also for protein feed. This latter is added for the sake of completeness and in order to assist evaluation of the relationship between protein and high-energy feeds–whether they are substitutes or complements.

It has not proved possible to demonstrate a positive relationship between livestock plus livestock product prices and the demand for these aggregate classes of feed. As equation (6.22) (Table 17) indicates inclusion of this variable in the total cereal feed demand equation explained little additional variance in the dependent variable and generated a nonsignificant negative coefficient. This was also the case in demand equations for the other two feed aggregates.

Table 17. Demand for cereal, high energy, and protein feeds, 1954-5 to 1965-6

Equation	(6.21)	(6.22)	(6.23)	(6.24)	(6.25)
Dependent variable	*QCF*	*QCF*	*QCF*	*QHF*	*QPF*
Intercept	–14·51	–13·14	–9·80	–9·84	–13·98
	(4·50)	(8·09)	(5·04)	(3·63)	(4·04)
L	2·52	2·45	1·72	2·07	2·38
	(0·41)	(0·55)	(0·62)	(0·33)	(0·37)
PE	–0·29	–0·29	–0·50	–0·22	0·52
	(0·38)	(0·40)	(0·37)	(0·31)	(0·34)
PP	0·28	0·34	0·45	0·17	–0·65
	(0·28)	(0·41)	(0·28)	(0·22)	(0·25)
PLP'		–0·21			
		(0·99)			
G			0·33		
			(0·21)		
R^2	0·94	0·94	0·96	0·95	0·93
$\bar{R}^2$	0·92	0·91	0·94	0·93	0·90
D-W	2·42	2·45	2·53	2·42	1·95

N.B. All variables logarithmically transformed.

QCF, QHF, QPF = Quantities of total cereals, high-energy feed, and protein feed consumed by livestock (1,000 tons)

PE, PP, PLP' = Price indices of high-energy feed, protein feed and livestock plus livestock products

L = Average number of livestock units on U.K. farms centred on December

G = Quantity of hay preserved (1,000 tons)

The other two price variables considered, the prices of high-energy and protein feeds, are common to all the equations presented in Table 17, and in each case their coefficients have the expected sign. However with the exception of the protein feed price variable in equation (6.25) (the demand equation for protein feed) the coefficients of these two variables are nonsignificant in each case, and are less than their standard errors in equations (6.21), (6.22), and (6.24). However the low price elasticities of demand obtained with respect to *PE* and *PP*—these are much lower than the price elasticites estimated in the individual cereal demand equations in the last section—imply that there is some marginal substitution between high-energy and protein feeds. Although this conflicts with the *a priori* hypothesis of complementarity between the two feeds, the result is plausible in view of the arbitrary division of feeds into these classes—a feed is defined as a protein feed if its digestible crude protein content exceeds 13 per cent.[4] Such a classification may cause close substitutes to be consigned to different feed aggregates.

It appears that the nonsignificance of the price variable coefficients is due to the very high correlation between livestock unit numbers and feed demand. This is to be expected in view of the principles underlying the construction of the livestock unit index; in fact the simple correlation between the two variables exceeds 0·92 in each case. Because of this high correlation the effects of other variables are small and are overshadowed. For example, inclusion of the preserved forage variable, which is itself highly correlated with feed demand (0·85), collects an unanticipated negative sign when introduced into (6.23). The introduction of this variable does cause an increase in the negative size and significance of the coefficients of the feed price variables. However, since this improvement is achieved at the cost of an unjustifiable sign on the preserved forage variable equation (6.21) is preferred for the ensuing analysis in Chapter 8.

As might have been expected the coefficient of the livestock variable is significant in all equations in Table 17. It is also noteworthy that the livestock coefficients are similar in size for all the feed aggregates, so that a 1 per cent increase in livestock numbers appears to cause both high-energy (or cereal) and protein feed use to increase by just over 2 per cent. This would appear to imply a broad complementarity in demand for the two basic feeds, a result which is not nullified by the weak substitution between the two feed aggregates at the margin. A further feature of the livestock coefficients is the higher response of cereal feed demand to livestock numbers than of high-energy feed aggregate as a whole, which may be considered to reflect that cereals have been the most rapidly increasing fraction of the aggregate.

The technical properties of the livestock variable coefficients are again such that they imply a rather high response of feed demand to increased livestock numbers. Using the 1967-8 values of all the relevant variables, the livestock variable coefficients of equations (6.21), (6.24) and (6.25) respectively imply that an extra livestock unit would require 2·13 tons of cereals or 2·14 tons of high energy feed and 0·48 tons of protein feed per year. Given that a livestock unit is defined as a cow yielding 600 gallons of milk and requiring 1·87 tons of starch equivalent or 2·67 tons of concentrate feed at 70 per cent starch equivalent per ton,[5] it is evident that the predicted feed concentrate requirement (2·14 + 0·48 tons) is slightly high on a purely technical basis. This is so because it must be assumed that grassland is going to make some contribution to feeding any additional grazing livestock on U.K. farms.

[4] The figures are taken from McDonald, P., R. A. Edwards, and J. F. D. Greenhalgh, *'Animal Nutrition'*, Oliver and Boyd, 1966; and are figures for digestible crude protein in ruminant rations.

[5] If it were to be assumed that all feed requirements were provided by concentrates.

The coefficients are, however, only slightly out of line and refinement of the livestock coefficients used might well lead to the construction of a livestock variable which could generate entirely acceptable coefficients. In any case some of the 'overestimation' may result from the failure of the specified demand functions to take account of changes in feeding practices, which, insofar as they have been secular, would be reflected in the livestock variable coefficients. Also it may well be that the physiological feed requirement of 1·87 tons is exceeded in the actual feeding practices of producers. Furthermore some doubts must be expressed about the quality of the data on home-grown cereals fed to livestock, for these are calculated as residuals and may well be subject to secular error due to improvement in methods of data collection.

In view of all the above factors the results seem quite satisfactory. The close relationship between the cereal and high-energy feed demand results suggest that no great error will be committed by using the cereal feed demand function (thus ignoring the other high-energy feed components) in a model of the cereal economy. In that the coefficients on the livestock variables are somewhat too high as a result of secular features which may be expected to persist, there appears to be no cause for alarm. Satisfaction can also be gained from the fact that the complementary 4 : 1 relationship between high-energy and protein feed demand is consistent with technical expectations.

(3) *Cereal demand for human consumption*

Analysis of cereal demand for human consumption has been rendered difficult by the trends in the dependent variables; barley and maize consumption have risen steadily, while demand for wheat and oats has exhibited a steady decline—although wheat demand has exhibited more variability about trend than the other cereals. Because most of the theoretical explanatory variables have also moved in secular fashion problems of multicollinearity rapidly emerge as additional variables are admitted, as manifested by instability in the coefficients. For this reason only two explanatory variables are presented in the cereal food demand equations (6.26) to (6.29) (Table 18).

In all cases the income variable has proved highly significant, but with the possible exception of wheat demand the income elasticities implied are suspiciously high; the suspicion being that the coefficients reflect the effects of omitted variables in addition to the effects of income. The signs of all the income variable coefficients are however in accord with expectations. Both wheat and oats appear to be inferior goods which is generally accepted,[6] while the demand for maize and barley, which are largely used in brewing and malting, appear to respond positively to income increases.

[6] See for example National Food Survey, *Domestic Food Consumption and Expenditure: 1963*, Table 10, H.M.S.O., 1965.

Table 18: Cereal demand for human consumption, 1954-5 to 1966-7

Equation	(6.26)	(6.27)	(6.28)	(6.29)
Dependent variable	*wFo*	*mFo*	*bFo*	*oFo*
Intercept	7,976·37	–1,518·20	–96·93	389·29
	(972·21)	(294·12)	(281·13)	(49·60)
y	–5·90	7·87	4·68	–0·70
	(1·04)	(0·67)	(0·48)	(0·08)
pBr	–4·88			
	(6·70)			
pM'		–10·24		
		(4·43)		
pBM/PM			–219·02	
			(174·51)	
pO				–2·02
				(2·51)
Own-price elasticity	–0·10	–0·31	–0·18	–0·17
Income elasticity	–0·33	3·42	1·28	–1·51
R^2	0·81	0·98	0·93	0·91
$\bar{R}^2$	0·77	0·98	0·92	0·90
D-W	2·71	1·60	1·34	2·29

N.B. All variables in natural units.
wFo, mFo, bFo, oFo = Quantities of wheat (including flour at wheat equivalent) maize, barley and oats for human consumption in the U.K. (1,000 tons)
y = Personal disposable income per capita, deflated by the retail price index of all items (R.P.I.)
pBr = Average retail price of bread, deflated by R.P.I.
pM = Average price of imported maize
pM' = Average price of imported maize, deflated by R.P.I.
pBM = Average price of malting barley
pO = Price of oatmeal and oats products, deflated by R.P.I.

Similarly the coefficients of the price and relative price variables all bear the expected negative sign, although only the maize price variable in (6.27) has a coefficient significantly different from zero. All of the cereals appear to exhibit inelastic price demand, with maize and then barley showing the highest price responsiveness. In view of the greater possibilities for substitution of other cereals for barley and maize than for oats and wheat this result appears highly plausible.

(4) *Cereal seed demand*

There is a well-defined technical complementarity between seed and land inputs in cereal production. Hence it is not surprising to find that most of the variance in seed demand is explained by variations in the acreages of the different cereals.[7]

In each of the equations (6.30)-(6.35) (Table 19) the coefficient of the acreage variable is highly significant, and the implied rates of seed application are well in line with quoted technical coefficients. A coefficient of 0·05 would indicate a rate of 1 cwt of seed per acre. Hence the acreage variable coefficients of (6.30, (6.32) and (6.34) respectively indicate seed

Table 19: Cereal demand for seed 1955-6 to 1966-7*

Equation	(6.30)	(6.31)	(6.32)	(6.33)	(6.34)	(6.35)
Dependent variable	wS_t	wS_t	bS_t	bS_t	oS_t	oS_t
Intercept	18·81	22·91	4·52	–7·66	33·44	87·51
	(11·64)	(8·63)	(2·43)	(6·06)	(7·30)	(68·10)
aW_{t+1}	0·07	0·06				
	(0·01)	(0·00)				
AB_{t+1}			0·06	0·07		
			(0·00)	(0·00)		
aO_{t+1}					0·06	0·04
					(0·00)	(0·03)
T		0·70		–2·72		–3·26
		(0·22)		(1·27)		(4·08)
R^2	0·94	0·97	0·999	0·999	0·95	0·95
$\bar{R}^2$	0·94	0·97	0·999	0·999	0·95	0·94
D-W	1·28	2·28	1·21	2·05	1·30	1·39

N.B. All variables in natural units.

* The use of $t + 1$ subscripts on the explanatory acreage variables results from the fact that the acreage sown in year t (and measured at the June census in year t) is harvested in year $t + 1$. This dating procedure is consistent with that used throughout the study.

wS, bS, oS = The quantities of wheat, barley and oats utilised as seed in the U.K. (1,000 tons)

T = A time trend increasing by annual increments of one from a base of one in 1955-6

applications per acre of 1·4 cwt for wheat, 1·2 cwt for barley and 1·2 cwt for oats. These compare well to the input coefficients quoted in the N.A.A.S. Farm Management Handbook, 1967, which are 1·0-1·25 cwt for winter wheat, 1·5-1·75 cwt for spring wheat, 1·25 cwt for barley and 1·5 cwt for oats.

Various technological improvements in the breeding, testing and sowing of seed have occurred in recent years, and might reasonably be expected to have caused a continuous decline in the seed requirement per acre. In

[7] It is even less surprising if one acknowledges that the data are generated (as opposed to measured) by multiplying cereals acreages by a seed input coefficient.

order to allow for this a time (technological proxy) variable was introduced into the analysis. Only in the case of barley is the time variable coefficient significantly negative (6.33), and in the case of wheat (6.31) the time variable has quite inexplicably generated a significant positive coefficient. For all three cereals the addition of time has caused the Durbin-Watson statistic to assume a value nearer to two, and has slightly improved R^2. Only in the case of barley, however, does there appear to be a basis for selecting the specification which includes time as the preferable one. For the other two cereals the specifications involving acreage as the sole explanatory variable seem preferable.

7

Livestock inventories–model specification and results

In setting up the cereal feed demand equations it was inferred that livestock numbers would not immediately respond to changes in feed or other prices, but that the response would be of the distributed lag type. Thus increases in feed prices would not be expected to depress feed demand as a result of causing an immediate decline in livestock numbers, but would have a delayed impact in later periods. In order to test the strength of these lagged responses it has been decided to estimate livestock inventory functions with feed prices as explanatory variables. The livestock considered are cattle, pigs and poultry. Sheep are omitted because they consume very little concentrate feed, and therefore can be left out of account in the context of the present study. The three types of livestock which are considered are divided as far as possible into separate breeding and fattening aggregates, as it is anticipated that these aggregates will respond differently to change in cereal and other prices.

Both annual and quarterly data are employed in estimating the functions in this chapter. Annual equations are estimated to conform to those in the previous two chapters. However with livestock production there are certain well-defined technical lags, such as the gestation and fattening periods. Typically, the duration of these is not in multiples of one year, but can more readily be approximated by multiples of quarterly periods. Thus in an attempt to more accurately identify the effects of cereal price changes upon the livestock economy quarterly inventory functions are estimated.

Sections A and B respectively are devoted to developing specifications of the annual and quarterly functions to be estimated. The results of estimating the annual results are then presented in Section C and a set of summary remarks on these results is presented in the next section. Section E presents the quarterly inventory results and this is followed by some conclusions concerning the results presented throughout the chapter.

A. Annual model

Since livestock are inputs into a productive process, livestock numbers can be assumed to be determined in accordance with general derived demand functions of the type used in estimating feed demand, and cereal acreage response. More particularly livestock inventories may be assumed to be determined by returns to the livestock, returns to other types of livestock and the price of inputs, particularly feed. Because of the production lags, the inventory functions will be specified to incorporate a Nerlove-type partial adjustment model, and with expected prices assumed equal to prices in the preceding period. Consequently the one-period lagged inventory of livestock of type i will enter as an explanatory variable of inventories of livestock i, and all other explanatory variables will enter with a one-period lag in the following way

$$(7.1) \qquad iL_t = f((+)iL_{t-1}, (-)PE_{t-1}, (-)PP_{t-1}, (+)R'_{it-1}, (-)R'_{jt-1}, u_t)$$

i = Cattle or pigs or poultry
j = The set of two livestock classes excluding the ith
L = Livestock numbers
PE = Price of high-energy feed
PP = Price of protein feed
R' = Returns (including subsidy) to a particular class of livestock
u = Error term

An additional variable for the stock of capital available to the relevant livestock enterprise should also be included in (7.1), but since there exists no prospect of obtaining such data it has been omitted.

Functions of the general form (7.1) are considered to be appropriate for estimating the coefficients of the determinants of inventories of both total livestock and breeding livestock aggregates. For fattening livestock a different formulation is required in which the numbers are dependent upon the number of breeding stock in previous periods as well as upon previous feed and livestock prices. Such a specification is based on the assumption that decisions about the number of young stock produced will largely determine the number of fattening animals in later periods. Hence the general proposed form of the fattening livestock inventory function is

$$(7.2) \quad iLF_t = f((+)iLB_{t-1}, (-)PE_{t-1}, (-)PP_{t-1}, (+)Ri'_{t-1}, Rj'_{t-1}, u_t)$$

LF = Fattening livestock
LB = Breeding livestock

It is important to note with respect to these livestock inventory functions that the guaranteed prices of livestock are adjusted according to a formula which takes account of changes in feed prices, as well as being altered for reasons of policy. Thus the inclusion of both the feed price and livestock returns adjusted for subsidy payment variables might appear superfluous. However, because guaranteed prices are announced in advance there may be a divergence between the anticipated feed price on which the livestock guarantee is based and the feed prices which actually prevail in any given period. Also because changes in guaranteed prices may reflect factors other than feed price changes, it is unlikely that producers necessarily equate the two. For both of these reasons, the inclusion of both sets of variables appears justified.

B. Quarterly livestock inventory functions

Changes in the numbers of pigs and poultry can be effected relatively rapidly, and the use of annual time series analysis is likely to mask much of the short-run economic response of pig and poultry producers. It is for this reason that some quarterly analyses have been performed. In the case of cattle the production cycle is a long one, and the benefits of quarterly as opposed to annual analysis may not be great. Nevertheless quarterly cattle inventory functions have also been estimated.

It has been felt desirable to disaggregate the inventory functions into two relationships for each type of livestock. The first of these functions is for the inventory of breeding livestock, which in the case of poultry is defined to include laying hens, and the second is for the inventory of livestock destined solely for slaughter. The inventory of breeding animals is assumed to reflect producers' intentions concerning the supply of livestock and livestock products, and the inventory of fattening livestock is assumed to be largely explicable as a technical function of the number of breeding animals in earlier periods.

(1) *Pig inventories*

The equations specified for pig inventories are taken directly from the model developed by McClements in his recent study of pig production in Northern Ireland.[1] The rationale for the structures which he developed from technical data seem equally applicable to the U.K. as a whole. Although McClements' model comprises a total of four equations the three equations used here form the prediction model which he selects as best representing the industry.

Feed prices are assumed to have their main impact upon pig numbers through the first function, which is for the determination of the size of the breeding herd. The number of fattening pigs is then assumed to be technically determined as a function of the number of breeding pigs, with only minor additional influences of the price of feed. The number of sows not in pig is also assumed to be largely a function of the size of the breeding herd in previous periods.

(a) *Size of the breeding herd.* The size of the breeding herd (number of sows and gilts in pig) is assumed to depend upon the conventional price variables determining the returns to, and costs of, production; upon the number of breeding sows not pregnant in the previous quarter; the opportunity cost of sows as represented by their sale value for meat; and upon the returns to the other major supplementary enterprise, poultry, which may be expected to compete for resources with pig production.

$$(7.3) \quad HB_t = f((+)HB_{t-1},(+)HOS_{t-1},(-)PFS'_{t-1},(+)RFH'_{t-1} \\ (-)PE_{t-1},(-)PP_{t-1},(-)RF_{t-1}, Dr, u_t)$$

HB = Number of sows and gilts in pig
HOS = Number of other sows
PFS = Price of fat sows
PFH' = Returns to fat pigs other than baconers, including subsidy
RF = Returns to poultry
Dr = Quarterly seasonal dummy variables

[1] McClements, L. D., *'A Quarterly Model of Pig Supply'*, Manchester Univ. Dept. Agric. Econ., Bul. No. 123, Oct. 1968.

The returns to fat pigs other than baconers is used instead of the returns to baconers in regard of the fact that only about one-third of U.K. pig output is of bacon pigs.

(b) *Fattening-pig numbers.* The rather unusual lag structure of this equation is justified by McClements in terms of the gestation period of the sow and other technical features of the pig production cycle. Feed price variables are included in the formulation to test the hypothesis that increases in feed prices cause producers to sell fat pigs, at a lower weight, an outcome which would be reflected in a reduction of fattening-pig numbers.

(7.4) $$HF = f((+)HBS_{t-3},(+)HBG_{t-3},(-)PE_{t-1},(-)PP_{t-1},Dr,\ u_t)$$

HF = Number of fat pigs
HBS = Number of sows in pig
HBG = Number of gilts in pig

(c) *Sows not in pig.* In order that all pigs should be accounted for an additional function has been fitted to explain the number of sows not in pig. Because farmers attempt to minimise the barren period for sows it may reasonably be assumed that numbers are largely dependent upon the number of sows and gilts farrowing in the recent past, and the proxy which appears most appropriate for this is the number of sows and gilts in pig in the previous quarter. Other variables which are likely to influence barren pig numbers are (a) the price of fat sows, which should be inversely related, (b) feed prices which should also have a negative sign, and (c) fat-pig prices, an increase in which should encourage the retention of sows. In view of the possibilities for short-term response to these variables it is not clear whether these price variables should be specified with current datings or with one quarter lags. Hence the specification is as follows:

(7.5) $$HBO_t = f((+)HB_{t-1},(-)PS_t \text{ or } (-)PS_{t-1},(+)RFH'_t \text{ or } (+)RFH'_{t-1},(-)PE_t \text{ or } (-)PE_{t-1},Dr,\ u_t)$$

HBO_t = Number of barren sows
PS = Price of fat sows

(2) *Poultry inventories*[2]

Two poultry inventory functions are to be estimated, (a) to determine the numbers of breeding and laying fowls, and (b) to determine the number of broiler and table fowls. The reasons for aggregating poultry classes on this basis are due to limitations in the available data, but it should be borne in mind that the number of breeding fowls is small relative to the number of laying fowls and hence the first function could be interpreted as being for laying fowls. Because of the enforced level of aggregation it is not possible to estimate the numbers of laying and table

[2] Turkeys are omitted from consideration in this analysis.

birds as a function of the number of breeding fowls, or to estimate the effects of increased feed prices upon breeding-fowl numbers.

In consequence of the rapid adjustments which can be made in the numbers of all classes of poultry only one-period lags are considered, and both relationships are treated as conventional supply functions. In both relationships an independent variable for the 'price of fat pigs other than baconers' is included as a measure of the opportunity cost of poultry production.

(a) *Laying and breeding-fowl inventories.*

$$(7.6) \quad FL_t = f((+)FL_{t-1},(+)RX'_{t-1},(+)PC_{t-1},(-)PE_{t-1},(-)PP_{t-1},(-)RFH'_{t-1},Dr, u_t)$$

FL = Number of laying and breeding fowls
RX' = Returns per laying fowl, including subsidy
RFH' = Returns to fat pigs other than baconers, including subsidy
PC = Price received for table and broiler fowls

(b) *Table and broiler-fowl inventories.*

$$(7.7) \quad FF_t = f((+)FL_{t-1},(+)PC_{t-1},(-)PE_{t-1},(-)PP_{t-1},(-)RFH'_{t-1}, Dr, u_t)$$

FF = Number of table and broiler fowls

The number of laying and breeding fowls is included in (7.7) as a proxy for the number of breeding fowls, data on which are not available over the period studied.

(3) *Cattle inventories*

Here again two major functions are to be estimated; the first is for dairy and breeding cows and heifers; the second is for other cattle (excluding bulls for service) which it is assumed is equivalent to a fattening-cattle inventory function. In addition a third function is to be estimated for the determinants of the number of calves slaughtered. This is expected to illuminate the way in which fat-cattle numbers are determined, and will influence the specification of the fattening-cattle inventory function.

The production cycle for cattle is a long one, and there is typically a lag of two-and-a-half years or more from conception to production. This makes the problem of choice of the appropriate variables and lag structures in a quarterly model extremely difficult, for there are a number of ways in which initial plans to produce so many dairy heifers or so many fat cattle may be modified before they come to fruition.

At conception producers will have intentions of producing either a beef-type calf or a dairy-type calf. Nearly all male calves will go for fattening, but dairy heifer calves may be diverted either into dairying or into fattening for slaughter.

Examination of calf slaughter data indicates large year-to-year fluctuations in the number of calves slaughtered in the first few months after birth. For example 666,000 calves were slaughtered in 1959, and this was increased to 898,000 in 1960. The lowest slaughter figure recorded during the study period was 407,000 in 1965. It may fairly be assumed that these large variations in calf slaughterings are mainly of calves which might be diverted to beef production, rather than representing changes in the numbers of dairy heifers retained. This being so, it is evident that the scale of calf slaughterings represents a major decision about the future size of the fattening herd. Such a decision might be expected to be made on the conventional basis of the expected prices of fat cattle, feed, and other agricultural outputs and inputs, and to be influenced by the number of calves born in any quarter. If it is assumed that the average age of fat cattle is one year, then changes in calf slaughterings will have their maximum impact upon fat-cattle inventories with a four quarter lag. Hence in specifying the fattening-cattle inventory function those variables which are expected to affect calf slaughterings should be included with an additional four quarter lag. Since this calf slaughtering decision appears likely to prove the major one influencing fat-cattle numbers, the fattening-cattle inventory function will be specified accordingly. It is of course also true that dairy replacement heifers may be transferred to a fattening regime even after the age of one year, but the scale of such changes seems likely to be dominated by the calf slaughter decision.

(a) *Calf slaughter function.*

$$(7.8) \quad CV_t = f((+)CB_{t-1},(-)PIC'_{t-1},(+)PE_{t-1},(+)PP_{t-1},(-)RFH'_{t-1},Dr,\, u_t)$$

CV = Number of calves slaughtered
CB = Number of breeding and dairy cows and heifers
PIC' = Price of fat cattle (including subsidy)

(b) *Fattening-cattle inventory.*

$$(7.9) \quad CF_t = f((+)CB_{t-5},(+)PIC'_{t-5},(-)PE_{t-5},(-)PP_{t-5},(-)RFH'_{t-5},Dr,\, u_t)$$

CF_t = Number of fattening cattle

The reason for expecting a positive coefficient on the breeding-cattle variable in both equations is that an increase in calf births may be expected to cause an increase in both calf slaughter and retention, whereas the other variables expected to increase calf slaughter should have the eventual effect of reducing fat-cattle numbers.

As has already been mentioned replacement heifers can be diverted from dairy or beef breeding to slaughter at any point up to mating. Hence replacement of the dairy and breeding herd can be reduced in quite quick time. Similarly older cows can either be slaughtered prematurely or retained for longer than usually expected, to respectively either deplete or expand the breeding herd. In view of these relatively short-period possibilities for modifying the size of the breeding herd only one quarter lags are proposed for the dairy and breeding-herd inventory.

(c) *Dairy and breeding-herd inventory*

$$(7.10)\quad CB_t = f((+)CB_{t-1},(+)RM_{t-1},(-)PBC_{t-1},(?)PIC_{t-1},(-)PE_{t-1},(-)PP_{t-1},(-)RG_{t-1}\text{ preceding crop year}, Dr, u_t)$$

RM = Milk return per cow
PBC = Price of breeding cows
PIC' = Price of fat cattle (the reason for the indeterminate expected sign is that increases in the price of fat cattle may either cause (a) an expansion in the breeding herd, or (b) a reduction by encouraging immediate slaughter of heifers. There is no way of knowing which should be dominant)
RG = Return to cereals production (this variable is introduced to represent the opportunity cost of cattle, particularly dairy, production).

C. Annual inventory results, U.K.

(1) *Cattle*

Functions have been estimated for the inventories of all cattle in the U.K. at the December census and also for the subaggregates of breeding (including dairy) cattle and fattening cattle. Some of the results of this estimation are presented in Table 20.

(a) *All cattle.* The relatively small coefficients on the lagged endogenous variable in equations (7.11) and (7.12) suggest that, in comparison with the acreage response results, the rate at which cattle numbers can be adjusted to the optimum is a high one. From a methodological point of view this contrast is of particular interest in view of the presence of strong trends in the cereal acreage variables and their absence in cattle inventories. (Trends are also weak in pig inventories but strongly upward in poultry numbers.) Discussion of this point will be reopened later.

In both equations the weighted returns index for cattle and milk generates a significant positive coefficient, with implied short-run returns elasticities of 0·31 (7.11) and 0·32 (7.12), and long-run elasticities of 0·62 and 0·84 respectively. The quality of these estimates is difficult to assess, but there are no grounds for rejecting them as infeasible.

The results of estimating cattle inventory responsiveness to changes in feed prices are disappointing. For while the coefficients of the price of all feedgrains variable in equations (7.11) and (7.12) are both negative as expected, they are nonsignificant, and alternative feed price variables failed to generate even a negative coefficient. Nevertheless acceptance of these coefficients at their face value indicates a short-run feed price elasticity of response of 0·14 or 0·13 respectively. These are extremely low values and do little to support the notion that cereals policies have a major impact on the livestock economy.

The feature which differentiates equations (7.11) and (7.12) is the inclusion of a returns to cereals variable in the latter. This variable has produced a negative, albeit nonsignificant coefficient which suggests a certain amount of competitiveness between the cereal and cattle enterprises.

Table 20: Cattle inventories in December, 1955-6 to 1966-7

Equation	(7.11)	(7.12)	(7.13)	(7.14)	(7.15)
Dependent variable	c_t	c_t	cB_t	cF_t	cF_t
Intercept	3,695·92	2,862·59	1,220·16	1,857·91	1,423·99
	(2,285·90)	(2,617·57)	(1,078·69)	(1,730·24)	(1,764·79)
c_{t-1}	0·50	0·62			
	(0·21)	(0·27)			
cB_{t-1}			0·67		
			(0·20)		
cF_{t-1}				0·43	0·56
				(0·24)	(0·27)
$rICM'_{t-1}$	33·97	35·50			
	(14·37)	(14·95)			
rM_{t-1}			9·90		
			(7·32)		
PIC'_{t-1}				22·88	28·48
				(9·95)	(11·19)
pF_{t-1}	–16·98	–16·16	–6·15	–6·36	–6·47
	(13·98)	(14·45)	(6·85)	(11·46)	(11·37)
rG_{t-1}		–22·48			–29·45
		(30·78)			(27·75)
Own returns elasticity	0·31	0·32	0·21	0·38	0·48
Feed price elasticity	–0·14	–0·13	–0·12	–0·09	–0·09
R^2	0·92	0·92	0·81	0·85	0·87
$\overline{R}^2$	0·89	0·88	0·74	0·79	0·79
D-W	1·90	1·91	1·89	1·46	1·55

N.B. All variables in natural units.
c, cB, cF = The numbers of total, breeding, and fattening cattle at the U.K. December census (1,000)
rICM' = An index of cattle and milk returns, including subsidy
rM = An index of milk returns per cow
pIC' = A price index of clean cattle, including subsidy
pF = The price index of all feedingstuffs
rG = Return per acre of grain (£'s)

(b) *Breeding cattle.* Estimation, using annual data, of the coefficients of variables influencing breeding-cattle numbers has proved unrewarding, and equation (7.13) bears witness to this. It should be remembered, however, that breeding cattle include beasts of all ages from dairy heifers to elderly cows, and there are many points of decision as to the disposal of a cow over a life of 10 years or more. It is quite possible that the complex of decisions which can be made with respect to the numbers of cows and heifers for breeding cannot be adequately treated in a naïve annual aggregate model.

As it is, only the lagged endogenous variable bears a significant coefficient, and while both the returns to milk and price of feed variables possess coefficients of the anticipated sign they are not significantly different from zero.

(c) *Fattening cattle.* Insofar as inclusion of the returns to cereals variable causes the coefficient of the lagged endogenous variable to become significant without materially affecting the coefficients of the PIC_{t-1} and pF_{t-1} variables, result (7.15) seems preferable to (7.14).

The coefficient of the price of cattle variable in (7.15) represents a short-run returns elasticity in fattening cattle inventories of 0·48, and the equation yields a long-run elasticity of 2·26. That both of these estimated elasticities are higher than those for total cattle inventory response is entirely reasonable in view of the fact that the other component of total cattle, breeding cattle, has a higher average age and will therefore be slower to adjust than fattening-cattle numbers.

Again the estimate of feed price responsiveness is disheartening, the coefficient of the feed price variable being nonsignificant and its small size implying a very low elasticity of response, although a fairly low elasticity was to be expected in view of the fact that a fair proportion of the diet of cattle is provided by grassland.

As in equation (7.11) the cereals return variable has generated a negative coefficient. The fact that this result was not duplicated in the breeding-cattle inventory function suggests that if cereals acreage is expanded it is the number of fattening cattle, which graze off land surplus to immediate arable requirements, which is reduced in preference to the less easily adjustable numbers of breeding stock.

In specifying annual livestock inventory functions it was hypothesised that the number of fattening animals will depend upon the number of breeding cattle in earlier periods. Unfortunately it has not proved possible to uncover this relationship between fattening and breeding cattle with the annual model.

(2) *Pigs*

(a) *All pigs.* The results in equation (7.16) and (7.17) (see Table 21) seem very satisfactory on the whole. The coefficients of the lagged endogenous variable are significant, and of a size which implies an acceptably fast rate of adjustment. The estimated short-run elasticity of inventory response to pig returns is either 1·25 (7.16) or 1·45 (7.17). These may appear to be rather large, but it should be borne in mind that a full year is a fairly long time in terms of the pig breeding and fattening cycle, and the elasticity of response for pig numbers over one year should be expected to be considerably larger than that for cattle. For similar reasons it is not surprising to note the relatively high elasticities of response to feed prices.

Also encouraging is the fact that the coefficient of the feed price variable is highly significant in both equations, thus indicating a fairly strong relationship running from the cereal to the livestock sector such as has been persistently hypothesised. Alternative feed price variables have also been tested, and while these also generated negative coefficients their statistical significance was less than that of the variable selected.

Inclusion of a returns to fowls variable (rF_{t-1}) in (7.17) appears to have marginally improved the coefficients on the three variables which are common with (7.16); this improvement is adjudged on the basis of the increased response elasticities in (7.17) as compared to (7.16). At the same time the rF_{t-1} variable has collected a negative, although nonsignificant coefficient. This suggests the possibility that pig and poultry production are in some measure competitive, as might be expected from the fact that they are both supplementary enterprises which are not in general directly land using.

With consideration to all of the above factors equation (7.17) is selected as the basis of any further discussion of total pig inventory 'supply'.

(b) *Breeding pigs.* As was the case for total pigs, the results on the inventories of breeding pigs, which are presented in equations (7.18) and (7.19) yield the anticipated signs on the coefficients of all variables, although the results are somewhat less consistent.

In both equations the coefficient of the lagged endogenous variable is small, which implies a very rapid, but not infeasible, rate of adjustment. In neither case is the coefficient significant.

Result (7.18) has the advantage of producing significant coefficients on the pig returns and feed price variables, with high and acceptable response elasticities for both. On the other hand equation (7.19), which includes the variable for the current price of sows (pSt) explains a considerably larger proportion of the dependent variable, 85 as opposed to 68 per cent. In addition the coefficient of pSt turns out to be significantly negative, implying, quite reasonably, that a high sow price induces producers to sell relatively more breeding sows for slaughter. In view of the probable predictive superiority of (7.19), and in the absence of any clear evidence about the 'true' response elasticities of breeding pigs, the second equation, (7.19), seems preferable.

(c) *Fattening pigs.* Equation (7.20) presents the result of a specification similar to (7.16) and (7.18). The outcome is also similar; the implied rate of adjustment is suitably high, the feed price variable coefficient is negative and highly significant, and the pig returns variable coefficient, while not quite significant, implies a high positive response of fattening-pig inventories to increases in pig returns.

It is, however, equation (7.21) which is of most interest. The mean number of breeding pigs (hB) at $t-1$ is 841,000. Of these about 220,000 are sows which are not pregnant, and 45,000 are boars, leaving 576,000 pregnant sows and gilts. If the coefficient of hB_{t-1} is adjusted so that it represents the relationship of fattening-pig numbers to pregnant sow and gilt numbers only, its value becomes 7·62, (5·22 x 841/576). In view of the Northern Ireland Survey result reported by McClements,[3] that the average number of pigs weaned per litter was 9·1, the coefficient of hB_{t-1} is somewhat low, but is fairly acceptable from a technical standpoint, especially when it is borne in mind that a three quarter lag is more appropriate than an annual one. For this reason alone equation (7.21) seems superior to (7.20), but in addition R^2 is improved from 0·76 to 0·85. It is also interesting to find in (7·21) that, in spite of the stringent technical constraint on fattening pig numbers, both pig returns and feed prices have the expected influence, although the coefficient of the latter variable fails to achieve significance.

(3) *Fowls*

The data has not permitted examination of separate inventory response functions for laying, breeding or fattening fowls on an annual basis, and

Table 21: Pig inventories in December 1955-6 to 1966-7

Equation	(7.16)	(7.17)	(7.18)
Dependent variable	h_t	h_t	hB_t
Intercept	59·56	4,355·30	–132·51
	(419·27)	(5,836·26)	(601·36)
h_{t-1}	0·55	0·52	
	(0·19)	(0·19)	
hB_{t-1}			0·33
			(0·23)
rH_{t-1}	85·86	99·41	14·61
	(48·74)	(50·11)	(6·88)
pE_{t-1}	–61·06	–81·20	–8·46
	(22·82)	(29·69)	(3·52)
rF_{t-1}		–33·04	
		(31·44)	
Own returns elasticity	1·25	1·45	1·73
Feed price elasticity	–0·80	–1·07	–0·91
R^2	0·76	0·79	0·68
$\bar{R}^2$	0·67	0·67	0·57
D-W	1·91	1·66	2·15

[3] McClements, L. D., op. cit. p. 19.

Equation	(7.19)	(7.20)	(7.21)
Dependent variable	hB_t	hF_t	hF_t
Intercept	457·13	289·36	–970·90
	(484·26)	(3,714·68)	(2,760·83)
hB_{t-1}	0·32		5·22
	(0·17)		(1·14)
hF_{t-1}		0·57	
		(0·19)	
rH_{t-1}	9·19	71·61	54·30
	(5·36)	(43·20)	(30·11)
pE_{t-1}	–4·92	–53·52	–31·15
	(2·85)	(20·04)	(17·04)
pS_t	–3·75		
	(1·32)		
Own returns elasticity	1·09	1·19	0·90
Feed price elasticity	–0·53	–0·80	–0·47
R^2	0·85	0·76	0·85
$\bar{R}^2$	0·77	0·67	0·80
D-W	2·12	2·08	1·95

N.B. All variables in natural units.
h, hB, hF = The number of total, breeding and fattening pigs at the U.K. December census (1,000)
rH, rF = Indices of returns to pigs and fowls
pE = Price of high-energy feed
pS = Price index of sows

hence a result is presented for total fowl numbers only. This is done for the years 1955-6 to 1966-7.

As in the acreage response results, the problems of using the distributed lag estimation procedures with a dependent variable exhibiting a strong trend cause some difficulty. This is reflected in the high coefficient of the lagged dependent variable in (7.22), with its implied low rate of adjustment of fowl numbers. This is not the result which should be expected from an animal with such a short life cycle. It would reasonably be expected that the rate of adjustment would be at least as high as those which have been estimated for cattle and pig inventories.

In (7.22) only the coefficient of the lagged endogenous variable attains statistical significance, although the coefficients of both other variables bear the anticipated sign and are greater than their standard errors. The short-run elasticity of response of fowl numbers to fowl returns

$$(7.22)\quad f_t = \underset{(3{,}171{\cdot}46)}{875{\cdot}88} + \underset{(0{\cdot}06)}{0{\cdot}90}\,f_{t-1} + \underset{(166{\cdot}89)}{272{\cdot}98}\,rF_{t-1} - \underset{(166{\cdot}50)}{195{\cdot}59}\,pE_{t-1}$$

$$R^2 = 0{\cdot}99 \quad \bar{R}^2 = 0{\cdot}98 \quad D\text{-}W = 2{\cdot}26$$

f = Number of fowls at the December census (1,000)
rF = Index of returns to fowls

appears to be relatively inelastic at 0·34 while that to feed prices is even lower at 0·20. These are considerably lower than the estimated elasticities of pig numbers; whereas they might reasonably have been expected to be higher—unless the relative value of the fixed plant in poultry production is so much higher than that in pig production that the costs of underutilisation of capacity are also relatively higher. There is no particular reason to believe that this is so—as Table 3 showed specialist pig and poultry producers are grouped together in terms of the capital intensity of production. In view of this it does not appear that the result presented adequately reflects the economic determinism of fowl numbers.

D. Remarks on the annual results

In view of the many arguments concerning the use of distributed lag models it seems particularly relevant to compare the annual cattle and pig inventory results with those for fowls. Neither cattle nor pig numbers have moved in any steady fashion; over the twelve annual observations used both types of livestock have exhibited a number of upward and downward movements. In contrast fowl numbers have increased rapidly and uninterruptedly, total fowls having almost doubled in number over the twelve years. It is therefore telling that the coefficient of lagged poultry numbers is much greater than those estimated for lagged cattle and pig numbers. This does not accord with expectations formed on the basis that the livestock with the longest life cycle should be the most difficult, and therefore slowest, to adjust—fowls have the shortest life cycle of the three classes of livestock. The clear implication is that the presence of a strong trend in fowl numbers impedes estimation of the true economic relationship when a distributed lag specification is employed.

Further criticism may be directed at the use of annual data in analysing the determinants of livestock inventories. The first criticism concerns the appropriateness of using difference equations with annual lags to estimate the response of variables subject to continuous change—shorter period analysis would appear to be more suitable. This is possibly not too serious where the time which elapses between initiating a production process and realising its output is stable, and where this production period is longer than the observation period. In the case of cattle the period from conception, or birth, to either slaughter or the commencement of milk production is almost invariably greater than one year, and hence the problem is not one of the life cycle being shorter than the observation period. The problem with cattle arises from the fact that there are a relatively large number of alternative methods of producing beef, and cattle can be switched rapidly from one production process to another should economic circumstances require it. Cattle can be moved quickly from one plane of nutrition to another, with the consequence that the production period is either lengthened or shortened and the inventories of cattle increased or reduced respectively. Alternatively slaughter weights may be adjusted with similar effect, and dairy cows can be slaughtered before the end of their natural milking lives. Thus with cattle the fact that average age exceeds one year does not preclude significant changes in cattle inventories over shorter periods. Failure to account for this may be responsible for the relatively weak relationship which has been isolated between feed prices and cattle numbers, something which might well be overcome by the use of quarterly data.

Paradoxically perhaps, using annual data to analyse changes in pig numbers may have been perfectly satisfactory, despite the fact that the life cycle of pigs is shorter than that for cattle. This is due to the relative fixity in the length of the production process; fewer opportunities exist for modifying the period from birth to slaughter, and since the time which elapses from conception to slaughter averages more than one year annual data may be quite adequate in analysing the response mechanism. Nevertheless, since there is some flexibility, and because numbers of breeding stock can always be modified over periods shorter than one year, use of quarterly data with appropriate lags should enable an even more satisfactory analysis to be performed.

Because of the presence of a 'trend' problem it is not possible, in a way similar to the above, to attribute the success or failure of the fowl inventory analysis to the choice of observation period. However, it is probable that quarterly data will prove more suitable in view of the typically short life of table birds and broilers. Also, quarterly data should give more leverage in identifying the underlying economic and technical relationships as a result of the presence in the data of marked seasonal variations about the increasing trend of fowl numbers.

E. Quarterly livestock inventory results, England and Wales

Because of the high degree of seasonality in many of the dependent livestock variables it was decided to employ quarterly dummy variables–March has been used as the base period in all cases. As a result of this decision, in order to avoid correlation between seasonal movements in the various explanatory variables used and the seasonal dummies it was also decided to deseasonalise all price and return variables. The method of deseasonalisation involved taking four quarter moving averages of the basic data, and then taking a further two quarter moving average of the resultant series in order to centre the moving average on the quarterly census dates. In the following section all variables subjected to this procedure will be denoted by an asterisk.

In virtually no case has logarithmic transformation of the variables enhanced the quarterly livestock inventory results. Therefore because coefficients denoting the relationship between breeding and fattening stock are easier to read for untransformed data, all variables in the ensuing results are expressed in original units.

Because of the more detailed breakdown of the census data for England and Wales the quarterly cattle and pig results are for these two countries only. It is assumed that little difference will exist between the appropriate structures, or the relevant parameters, for England and Wales and those for the U.K. as a whole.

(1) *Cattle (England and Wales)*

(a) *Breeding Cattle, Jan. 1960-Dec. 1966.* Four equations for breeding-cattle inventories are presented in Table 22, the difference between them being the outcome of permuting two explanatory variables (pC_{t-1} and rG_{t-1}). This scheme of permutations can be seen to have no effects upon the signs of the coefficients of the six variables common to these equations; the signs of all these coefficients accord with expectations.

Returns to milk generates a positive coefficient in each of the equations, and statistical significance is attained in all except (7.25). Also according to expectations is the estimated negative response to the price of compound feedingstuffs for cattle, and it too is statistically significant in all equations save (7.25). On the face of things it is surprising that the estimated short-run elasticity of inventory response to milk returns does not appear to be higher than that to feed prices. This may however be due to the stability of legislated liquid milk prices, and the higher degree of uncertainty associated with prices of feedingstuffs.

What is nevertheless surprising about the estimates of the short-run response elasticity to feed is that they are higher than the values derived from the annual data. These estimated elasticities might reasonably have been expected to be below those of the annual model and to have been accompanied by lower estimated adjustment coefficients than those estimated and presented in equations (7.23) and (7.25). Such a combination of results would have produced similar long-run elasticities to those of the annual model, plus a similar period of time to full adjustment, whereas the results obtained indicate a similar long-run effect but a much shorter time in achieving it. That such estimates have been obtained may be due to the fact that purely seasonal fluctuations in the data series (as opposed to the underlying movements) have not been fully countered by the use of dummy variables and deseasonalised explanatory variables. Certainly the quarterly rates of adjustment in breeding cattle inventories seem rather high by the standards of rates previously estimated in this study.

In both equations which incorporate the price of cows variable the coefficient of this variable carries the expected negative sign. It turns out to be significant in both of them, and its effect is only slightly reduced on introducing a return to cereals variable. This cereals return variable is an odd one insofar as it is the annual one developed for the total cereals acreage response analysis. It therefore assumes the identical value in four consecutive quarters. The negative coefficient generated by this variable

Table 22: Breeding-cattle inventory results

Equation	(7.23)	(7.24)	(7.25)	(7.26)
Dependent variable	cB_t	cB_t	cB_t	cB_t
Intercept	1,334·17	2,633·01	1,277·56	2,522·02
	(493·45)	(558·86)	(481·89)	(595·75)
cB_{t-1}	0·76	0·35	0·79	0·39
	(0·11)	(0·15)	(0·11)	(0·17)
rM^*_{t-1}	3·49	8·81	2·84	8·20
	(1·68)	(2·10)	(1·69)	(2·36)
$pCOM^*_{t-1}$	−7·45	−6·77	−5·40	−6·02
	(2·99)	(2·45)	(3·24)	(2·76)
pC^*_{t-1}		−3·15		−2·93
		(0·94)		(1·02)
rG_{t-1}			−4·71	−1·82
			(3·24)	(2·93)
D_1	−84·04	−48·47	−88·49	−52·63
	(18·25)	(18·27)	(18·03)	(19·76)
D_2	−74·27	−48·53	−78·29	−51·85
	(17·55)	(16·23)	(17·30)	(17·34)
D_3	−129·79	−107·82	−133·77	−110·86
	(17·53)	(15·71)	(17·28)	(16·71)
Milk-return elasticity	0·09	0·24	0·07	0·22
Feed-price elasticity	−0·19	−0·17	−0·14	−0·15
R^2	0·83	0·89	0·85	0·89
$\bar{R}^2$	0·78	0·85	0·79	0·85
D-W	2·24	2·29	2·38	2·38

N.B. All variables in natural units. The asterisk denotes that the variable is a four quarter centred moving acreage.

$pCOM$ = Price index of compound feedingstuffs for cattle
pC = Index of the price of cows
D_1, D_2, D_3 = Quarterly dummy variables for June, Sept., and Dec. respectively
rM = Milk return per cow

exceeds its standard error in equation (7.25) but is somewhat less than it in equation (7.26). However these results do lend tentative support to the hypothesis of competition between cereal growing and the cattle economy.

Differences between the four equations are slight and hence no unequivocal choice of a best result can be made. However, as already stated, the estimated adjustment coefficients in equations (7.24) and (7.26) are unexpectedly high, and therefore the choice has been narrowed down to (7.23) and (7.25). Of these (7.25) gets the vote by virtue of its slightly higher R^2, which results from inclusion of the returns to cereals variable.

(b) *Calves slaughtered, March 1959-March 1967.* The dominant variables determining the number of calves slaughtered appear to be clean cattle prices and the number of breeding cattle, both lagged one quarter. On the other hand, although result (7.27) suggests that increased feed prices may cause an increase in calf slaughter, as expected, this variable is nonsignificant and does not appear to exert a major influence. Thus when the feeding barley price variable is dropped from (7.27) and the function is re-estimated it causes only very minor changes in the coefficients of the remaining variables and in R^2 (see equation (7.28)).

$$(7.27)\quad \underset{}{cVt} = \underset{(218{\cdot}99)}{583{\cdot}96} \; \underset{(0{\cdot}66)}{-7{\cdot}84plC^*_{t-1}} \; \underset{(3{\cdot}85)}{+1{\cdot}00pFB^*_{t-1}} \; \underset{(0{\cdot}06)}{+0{\cdot}44cB^*_{t-1}}$$

$$\underset{(9{\cdot}58)}{-88{\cdot}64D_1} \; \underset{(9{\cdot}57)}{+2{\cdot}24D_2} \; \underset{(9{\cdot}57)}{-12{\cdot}37D_3}$$

$$R^2 = 0{\cdot}90 \qquad \bar{R}^2 = 0{\cdot}88 \qquad D\text{-}W = 0{\cdot}88$$

$$(7.28)\quad cVt = \underset{(167{\cdot}82)}{-548{\cdot}24} \; \underset{(0{\cdot}63)}{-7{\cdot}80plC^*_{t-1}} \; \underset{(0{\cdot}05)}{+0{\cdot}43cB^*_{t-1}} \; \underset{(9{\cdot}43)}{-88{\cdot}68D_1}$$

$$\underset{(9{\cdot}42)}{+2{\cdot}20D_2} \; \underset{(9{\cdot}42)}{-12{\cdot}34D_3}$$

$$R^2 = 0{\cdot}90 \qquad \bar{R}^2 = 0{\cdot}88 \qquad D\text{-}W = 0{\cdot}88$$

cV = Number of calves slaughtered during the quarter (1,000)
plC = Price index of clean cattle
pFB = Price of feeding barley (£'s per ton)

From these results it appears that an increase in clean cattle prices has a highly significant effect in reducing calf slaughterings, and therefore in increasing retentions of calves. Increased breeding-cattle numbers, which stand as a proxy for increased calf births, also appear to exhibit a highly significant influence in increasing the numbers slaughtered.

It is true that the Durbin-Watson statistic has a low value, indicating the presence of positive serial correlation. Examination of the residuals shows that this is due to underestimating the peaks and troughs of slaughter, and is not attributable to any trend. Thus far no feasible variable has been found to improve 'the fit' in this respect.

In view of the large year-to-year variation in calf slaughter and the effect which this must have upon fattening cattle numbers at a later date, the above result is of considerable importance. It appears that a fundamental decision concerning the future numbers of fattening cattle is made in the first few months after the birth of calves, and that this decision is strongly influenced by the formation of clean cattle price expectations.

The role of the feed prices in this decision process appears to be more indirect than direct, and to operate through their effects on breeding-cattle numbers.

(c) *Fattening cattle, March 1959-Sept. 1967.* In setting up the quarterly fattening-cattle inventory equation (7.9), the variables hypothesised as affecting calf slaughterings were specified as entering into the relationship with additional lags of four quarters. However, testing this specification produced coefficients of unexpected sign on most of the variables, and the level of explained variance was considerably lower than when calf slaughterings four quarters previously were explicitly included in the function. Hence the results presented below include calf slaughter as an explanatory variable in preference to the determinants of the variable.

Despite this the results are far from satisfactory and they are unsatisfactory in a most fundamental way. This is that the coefficient of the calf slaughter variable is negative and frequently exceeds one, while the coefficient of the number of breeding animals is not significantly different from zero and in many of the estimated functions (not presented) actually bore a negative sign. The significance of this will become most clearly apparent when the effects of feed price increases upon livestock numbers are calculated (See Table 34 in the next chapter), but in essence it is that, given the breeding-cattle inventory and calf slaughter functions estimated above, the quarterly model predicts that an increase in feed prices will cause an increase in fat-cattle numbers as opposed to an expected decrease. This happens because the predicted reduction in calf slaughter resulting from reduced inventories of breeding cattle causes a predicted increase in fat-cattle numbers which outweighs the partial decrease in fat-cattle numbers directly caused by the reduction in numbers of breeding stock. Given this unfortunate overall picture the most satisfactory result is the one with the smallest negative coefficient on the calf slaughter variable and the largest positive coefficient on the breeding-cattle variable. This is presented in the following equation.

$$(7.29)\quad \underset{(1{,}051\cdot97)}{cF_t = 1{,}099\cdot31} \; + \underset{(0\cdot13)}{0\cdot74cF_{t-1}} - \underset{(0\cdot23)}{1\cdot03cV_{t-4}} - \underset{(3\cdot48)}{2\cdot18PIC_{t-1}} + \underset{(0\cdot22)}{0\cdot15cB_{t-5}}$$

$$R^2 = 0\cdot83 \quad \bar{R}^2 = 0\cdot80 \quad D\text{-}W = 2\cdot12$$

It required the inclusion of the lagged endogenous variable in order to obtain a positive coefficient on cB_{t-5} and this perhaps provides the key to the failure to uncover a satisfactory set of results. During the period studied there has been an underlying reduction in calf slaughter, and an underlying increase in fat-cattle numbers, but no basic change in breeding-cattle stocks. What has happened is that there has been a progressive increase of the crossing of dairy cows and heifers with beef bulls, so that more of the progeny of the dairy herd have been suitable for fattening and fewer have required slaughter. Thus, for the same size of breeding herd, fat-cattle numbers have been increased while calf slaughter (wastage) has decreased. In the regression analysis performed this has resulted in an exaggeratedly high inverse correlation between calf slaughter and fat cattle and a weak relationship between breeding stock and fat cattle numbers. Only when the lagged endogenous variable is introduced to take up some of the underlying increase in fat-cattle inventories does the negative coefficient of cV_{t-4} fall absolutely to around one, its expected value, and does the coefficient of cB_{t-5} become positive—other lags were tried with these variables without any success. However as (7.29) shows the coefficient of cB_{t-5} is nonsignificantly different from zero, and is small. Removal of the price of clean cattle variable from (7.29) causes the size of the coefficient of the cB_{t-5} variable to diminish even further, which only serves to emphasise its fragility.

If the demands of the overall model are disregarded, the best short-term predictive equations for fat-cattle numbers are obtained by deseasonalising the explanatory variables and introducing dummy variables. This serves to considerably increase R^2 and the coefficient of cV_{t-4} but causes the coefficient of cV^*_{t-5} to become negative, and this variable is omitted in presenting the following results.

$$(7.30)\quad \underset{}{cF_t} = \underset{(3{,}670{\cdot}37)}{1{,}845{\cdot}09} + \underset{(0{\cdot}07)}{0{\cdot}64cF_{t-1}} - \underset{(0{\cdot}22)}{1{\cdot}19cV^*_{t-4}} + \underset{(20{\cdot}33)}{140{\cdot}15D_1} + \underset{(18{\cdot}99)}{101{\cdot}97D_2} + \underset{(19{\cdot}56)}{148{\cdot}53D_3}$$

$$R^2 = 0{\cdot}94 \quad \bar{R}^2 = 0{\cdot}93 \quad D\text{-}W = 1{\cdot}95$$

What emerges from the two presented results is the apparent dominance in the determination of fat-cattle numbers of the calf slaughter decision, although for reasons already explained its strength appears to be overestimated.

(2) *Pigs (England and Wales)*

(a) *Breeding pigs, March 1958-Sept. 1966*. In order to illustrate a methodological point concerning the coefficient of the lagged endogenous variable two results are presented:

$$(7.31)\quad hBSG_t = \underset{(129{\cdot}97)}{-240{\cdot}69} + \underset{(0{\cdot}05)}{1{\cdot}05hBSG_{t-1}} - \underset{(2{\cdot}09)}{7{\cdot}69pFB^*_{t-1}} + \underset{(1{\cdot}36)}{4{\cdot}08pH^*_{t-1}} + \underset{(5{\cdot}58)}{37{\cdot}10D_1} - \underset{(5{\cdot}58)}{8{\cdot}24D_2} + \underset{(5{\cdot}74)}{20{\cdot}36D_3}$$

$$R^2 = 0{\cdot}95 \quad \bar{R}^2 = 0{\cdot}94 \quad D\text{-}W = 1{\cdot}77$$

$$(7.32)\quad hBSG_t = \underset{(79\cdot39)}{-41\cdot22} + \underset{(0\cdot05)}{0\cdot91}hBSG_{t-1} - \underset{(2\cdot10)}{5\cdot78}pFB^*_{t-1} + \underset{(0\cdot71)}{1\cdot86}rH^*_{t-1} + \underset{(5\cdot76)}{35\cdot88}D_1 - \underset{(5\cdot76)}{7\cdot71}D_2 + \underset{(5\cdot92)}{18\cdot30}D_3$$

$$R^2 = 0\cdot94 \quad \bar{R}^2 = 0\cdot93 \quad D\text{-}W = 1\cdot55$$

$hBSG$ = The number of sows and gilts in pig (1,000s)

The only difference between the specification of these two equations involves a substitution of a returns to pigs variable in (7.32) for the price of pigs (7.31). The returns variable is merely the price variable transformed by a feed efficiency index which exhibits an upward trend. This definition of returns is a somewhat crude one, but given that price variables are usually expected to reflect changes in profitability, on the understanding that costs and technology are constant, it is clear that they fail to do this if *ceteris paribus* conditions do not obtain. In the case of pig fattening important changes in feed efficiency have occurred which will have increased profitability for any given set of product and input prices. Thus it appeared that some better indicator of profitability than price was called for, and price multiplied by the change in feed efficiency was the measure opted for.

The principal effect of switching from the price to returns variable has been a reduction in the coefficient of the lagged endogenous variable from 1·05 to 0·91. If it is assumed that equation (7.31) was misspecified as a consequence of failing to take account of a change in an important technical coefficient (feed input per pig) then the implication is that the effects of this misspecification are lodged in the coefficient of hB_{t-1}. If this interpretation is accepted equation (7.32) would appear to be preferable to (7.31). There is, of course, no guarantee that other mis-specification effects are not carried in the coefficient of the lagged endogenous variable in (7.32), which would render its estimates of the adjustment coefficient and the long-run elasticities unreliable. Nevertheless on *a priori* grounds the results of (7.32) are quite plausible. All coefficients, except that of D_2, are statistically significant. The estimated short-run elasticity of breeding-pig inventories with respect to pig returns is 0·41, while that for feed barley prices is 0·26–lower as would be expected. In addition the estimated coefficient of adjustment is markedly lower than that estimated from annual data, and this too is as expected.

(b) *Fattening pigs, March 1959-March 1967.* From the findings of the 1954-5 Disease Survey cited by McClements[4] a clear basis exists for evaluating the coefficients of the sows and gilts in pig variables. The Survey discovered that sows in Northern Ireland produced an average of

[4] McClements, L. D., op. cit., p. 20.

9·4 weaned pigs per litter, and gilts produced 7·3. If allowance is made for improved breeding performance since the Survey date of 1954-5 and for differences between England plus Wales and Northern Ireland, it appears, according to the technical criterion, that equation (7.33) is a satisfactory result. Certainly the implied ratio of pig output per sow to that of gilts, which is 1·1, does not differ greatly from that of the survey data.

The explanatory power of the estimated function is however improved when quarterly dummy variables are added, but a reaction between the dummys and the pig returns variable produces results which, infeasibly, imply that gilts produce litters of 12·6 or 13·2 pigs ((7.36) and (7.37)). Nevertheless, it appears ((7.33), (7.36), (7.37)) that returns to pigs are a highly significant determinant of fattening-pig numbers in the following period and hence cannot reasonably be ignored. Unfortunately the simultaneous inclusion of the feed barley price variable with that for pig

Table 23: Fattening-pig inventories

Equation	(7.33)	(7.34)	(7.35)
Dependent variable	hF_t	hF_t	hF_t
Intercept	–1,735·65	–599·28	414·67
	(1,468·10)	(352·47)	(659·25)
hBS_{t-3}	10·46	11·50	11·78
	(1·23)	(0·87)	(0·86)
hBG_{t-3}	9·57	9·76	10·50
	(2·67)	(1·96)	(1·95)
pFB^*_{t-1}	–40·72		–59·65
	(45·07)		(33·21)
rh^*_{t-1}	26·24		
	(12·09)		
D_1		261·94	270·94
		(90·36)	(87·43)
D_2		423·76	430·55
		(92·23)	(89·17)
D_3		475·59	486·34
		(89·43)	(86·59)
Feed barley price elasticity	–0·17	–	–0·26
Pig returns elasticity	0·56	–	–
R^2	0·81	0·89	0·90
$\overline{R}^2$	0·78	0·87	0·88
$D\text{-}W$	2·16	1·26	1·47

Equation	(7.36)	(7.37)	(7.38)
Dependent variable	hF_t	hF_t	hF_t
Intercept	−3,679·09	−2,697·28	2,155·41
	(763·81)	(870·96)	(815·54)
hBS_{t-3}	10·03	10·32	
	(0·77)	(0·75)	
hBG_{t-3}	12·60	13·20	
	(1·71)	(1·65)	
$hBSG_{t-3}$			10·55
			(0·58)
pFB_{t-1}		−53·32	−32·63
		(26·10)	(25·89)
rh_{t-1}	32·67	31·87	24·56
	(7·54)	(7·18)	(6·39)
D_1	295·35	302·58	163·41
	(72·43)	(68·97)	(67·81)
D_2	486·76	491·27	450·69
	(74·93)	(71·79)	(67·05)
D_3	471·86	481·57	458·32
	(71·28)	(67·95)	(68·02)
Feed Barley price elasticity	–	−0·23	−0·14
Pig returns elasticity	0·69	0·68	0·52
R^2	0·93	0·94	0·94
$\bar{R}^2$	0·92	0·93	0·93
$D\text{-}W$	1·96	2·27	0·81

hBS = Number of sows in pig (1,000)
hBG = Number of gilts in pig (1,000)

returns compounds the effect of the latter upon the coefficient of the gilts in pig variable (compare (7.36) and (7.37)). At the same time result (7.37) is the only one which indicates a significant response of fattening pigs to feed prices.

Ample justification has been demonstrated for treating the breeding herd in its components of sows and gilts. However, because of the absence of a separate treatment of sows and gilts in determining the breeding pig numbers, in tracing through the effects of changes in feed prices from breeding to fattening pigs it will be necessary to employ a function which has an aggregate breeding-pig variable. Equation (7.38) is such an equation, and is a simple modification of (7.37) resulting from the aggregation of the sows and gilts in pig variables. The outcome of this is to generate a plausible, but slightly high, 10·55, coefficient on the sows plus gilts in pig variable. It also causes a reduction in the Durbin-Watson statistic to a level indicating positively autocorrelated residuals and reduces the influence attributed to the feeding barley price and pig returns variables below the levels indicated by preceding equations. These changes may indicate a slightly diminished sensitivity by this form of the fattening-pig inventory relationship, but it is nevertheless reasonably satisfactory, and is the one which will be employed in the final application and evaluation of the results.

(c) *Sows not in pig.* The caution displayed in specifying equation (7.5) with respect to the appropriate lags on the price variables, seems to have been entirely justified. In the event there appears to be nothing to choose between the result produced with current dated variables and that with prices lagged one quarter.

$$(7.39)\quad \underset{}{hBO_t} = \underset{(25{\cdot}41)}{58{\cdot}01} + \underset{(0{\cdot}02)}{0{\cdot}40hB_{t-1}} - \underset{(0{\cdot}11)}{0{\cdot}48pS_t^*} - \underset{(0{\cdot}71)}{2{\cdot}79pFB_t^*} + \underset{(0{\cdot}17)}{0{\cdot}63rH_t^*} - \underset{(1{\cdot}86)}{10{\cdot}65D_1} + \underset{(1{\cdot}85)}{8{\cdot}11D_2} - \underset{(1{\cdot}84)}{3{\cdot}53D_3}$$

$$R^2 = 0{\cdot}98 \quad \bar{R}^2 = 0{\cdot}97 \quad D\text{-}W = 1{\cdot}95$$

hBO = Number of other sows, i.e. sows not in pig (1,000)
pS = Price index of sows.

$$(7.40)\quad hBO_t = \underset{(30{\cdot}33)}{31{\cdot}62} + \underset{(0{\cdot}03)}{0{\cdot}39hB_{t-1}} - \underset{(0{\cdot}13)}{0{\cdot}44pS_{t-1}^*} - \underset{(0{\cdot}80)}{2{\cdot}39pFB_{t-1}^*} + \underset{(0{\cdot}21)}{0{\cdot}81rH_{t-1}^*} - \underset{(2{\cdot}04)}{10{\cdot}05D_1} + \underset{(2{\cdot}03)}{8{\cdot}30D_2} - \underset{(2{\cdot}01)}{3{\cdot}40D_3}$$

$$R^2 = 0{\cdot}97 \quad \bar{R}^2 = 0{\cdot}97 \quad D\text{-}W = 1{\cdot}69$$

As can be seen the differences between these two results are negligible. Each on its own is excellent, all of the coefficients are highly significant, and of the expected sign. It is worth mentioning, without presenting the results, that permuting the price variables does not cause any of the coefficients to become statistically nonsignificant, nor does it cause major changes in the size of the coefficients.

The sizes of the various coefficients also appear entirely acceptable. The sow price and pig return variables both have means of about 100 while the mean feed barley price is about £20 per ton. Hence, multiplying the coefficients of the sow price and pig returns variable by five permits a comparison of the price and return coefficients as if they were elasticities. On doing this it can be seen that the elasticity of sow numbers with respect to pig returns is greater in both equations than that to feed barley prices. This should be expected, because as feed costs represent about 70 per cent of pig production costs one would expect that the elasticity with respect to pig returns would be greater than that to feed prices, *ceteris paribus.*

The responsiveness to sow prices appears to be slightly less than that to feed prices, and there are no good reasons to suppose that this is not so.

(3) *Fowls, March 1960-March 1967 (U.K.)*

It appears to have been unduly optimistic to expect that the fowl inventory functions specified in Section B2 would prove adequate for the job. It will be remembered that these specifications resulted from the lack of suitable data on breeding-fowl numbers. Ideally fowl inventory structures should be estimated for (1) breeders for laying fowls, (2) breeders for broilers and table fowls, (3) laying fowls as a function of, amongst other things, breeders for layers at $t-1$, and (4) broiler and table fowls as a function of breeding fowls for broilers and table fowls at $t-1$. The absence of breeding fowl data, which has been remedied in the statistics published since 1966, has apparently proved critical. Results for the breeding-laying fowl aggregate defied rational interpretation and hence have been omitted. This is not surprising as the three major components of the aggregate respond to very different factors.

For broilers and table fowls an acceptable result has been obtained. However, the breeding-laying fowl aggregate did not prove a satisfactory proxy for the appropriate breeding-fowl variable, and the endogenous variable with a one-period lag is substituted in its place.

$$(7.41) \quad \underset{}{FF_t} = \underset{(1{\cdot}67)}{-2{\cdot}13} + \underset{(0{\cdot}07)}{0{\cdot}98FF_{t-1}} + \underset{(0{\cdot}26)}{0{\cdot}65RF^*_{t-1}} - \underset{(0{\cdot}25)}{0{\cdot}23PFW^*_{t-1}}$$

$$+ \underset{(0{\cdot}03)}{0{\cdot}18D_1} + \underset{(0{\cdot}03)}{0{\cdot}06D_2} + \underset{(0{\cdot}25)}{0{\cdot}23D_3}$$

$$R^2 = 0{\cdot}93 \qquad \bar{R}^2 = 0{\cdot}91 \qquad D\text{-}W = 2{\cdot}74$$

FF = Number of broiler and table fowls (1,000)
RF = Returns to fowls
PFW = Price of feeding wheat

Equation (7.41) is presented for logarithmically transformed variables since untransformed variables yield a coefficient on the lagged endogenous variable greater than one. This very low estimate of the rate of adjustment is once again due to the fact that the endogenous variable has exhibited an extremely rapid upward trend.

The result implies that a significant direct relationship exists between lagged fowl returns and broiler plus table fowl numbers. The price of feed on the other hand appears to have a weak influence; this is especially so in view of the fact that other feed price variables generated even less-significant coefficients than that presented for the feeding wheat price.

F. Conclusion

The annual livestock inventory results, particularly for pigs go some way to supporting the hypothesis that feed (cereal) prices influence livestock inventories with a one year lag. This confirms the suspicion that the effects of policies such as a minimum import price policy, which operate upon user prices for cereals, cannot be fully evaluated without consideration of their direct effects upon the livestock economy and the implications of this for cereal demand.

The quarterly livestock inventory results provide even stronger evidence of an inverse relationship between cereal prices and livestock numbers. At the same time they shed some doubt upon the appropriateness of assuming annual lags between price movements and changes in livestock numbers as was done in the annual analysis. In the cases of breeding cattle and pigs, feed prices seem capable of influencing numbers with only a one quarter lag. This is also probably true for fowls, in spite of the lack of empirical confirmation. For fattening cattle and pigs it appears that feed prices lagged five and four quarters respectively exercise more influence on numbers than do more recent prices; they do this through the important technical link between breeding and fattening stock. Thus the majority of quarterly results imply that the true lags are either shorter or longer than one year, which might appear to render the annual results inappropriate. Some theoretical evidence about the unsuitability of the annual results can be derived from work by Strotz[5] and Telser.[5] Both authors examined the problem of using annual time series data where one quarter lags exist in the true economic relationship, but each primarily considered flow data as opposed to stock data of a livestock inventory type. Strotz basically examined biases resulting from suppressing the lag and using currently dated annual data, while Telser examined estimation biases where one year lags are assumed. A recent study of Chandler[6] set out to examine the magnitudes of the estimation biases under the Strotz and Telser misspecifications for a particular two-equation system. Amongst his conclusions were that estimating the Telser misspecified model for a non-oscillatory system using ordinary least-squares does not result in large errors. This case would seem to parallel the estimation of the annual breeding-pig and cattle inventory functions in this study, and it may thus be implied from Chandler's results that these results do not suffer from large biases as a result of misspecifying the lag period. There, therefore, appears to be no reason why some of the annual livestock inventory results should not be employed to examine the impact of changes in cereal prices upon livestock numbers in the analysis in the following chapter.

[5] Strotz, R. H., 'Interdependence as a Specification Error', *Econometrica*, Vol. 28, 1960, pp. 428-442. Telser, L. 'Discrete samples and Moving Sums in a Stationary Stochastic Process', *J. Am. Statist. Ass.*, Vol. 62, 1967, pp. 484-498.

[6] Chandler, A. I., 'An Analysis of the Econometric Problems Involved in Misspecifying the Unit Time Period of an Economic Model', Unpublished M.A. dissertation, Manchester University, 1969.

8

Evaluation of empirical results

In this chapter the results presented in the three preceding chapters will be evaluated. This will be done in three parts:

(a) The predictive accuracy of the chosen best estimates of the cereal supply and demand relationships will be considered, and their usefulness in predicting imports will be assessed. Similar treatment will not be accorded to the livestock inventory results, since these are not central to the main argument of the study and do not enter directly into the system for estimating cereal imports.

(b) Various estimated relationships will be used to numerically forecast the outcomes of certain policy changes with a view to assessing the effectiveness of these policies. Changes will be assumed in the guaranteed prices and minimum import prices of cereals for some stated year and the predictions based on actual and hypothetical policies will be compared.

(c) The general policy implications of the results will be discussed with particular reference to the lags in response to changes of policy, and the size of the responses.

A. The predictive ability of the estimates

In the ensuing analysis the term 'prediction' is used with a certain amount of licence, in that what is basically examined for the estimated relationships is their goodness of fit during the latter part of the estimation period plus an extra year beyond it. In other words the fit of each chosen acreage and yield equation is examined for the period 1963-4 to 1970-1, while the performance of the demand equations is examined for the years 1963-4 to 1967-8. Use of the word 'prediction', therefore, may perhaps only be considered strictly apposite for the last year's figures in each exercise performed in this section, although its employment throughout is in line with common usage.

Errors of prediction are calculated by subtracting the actual from predicted values of the variables, thus indicating directly whether the predictions are too high (positive errors) or too low.

(1) *Cereal acreage predictions*

For some cereals more than one set of predictions are given in Table 24 and, in order to permit discrimination between different sets of estimates in the text, a prediction number is assigned to each set of estimates in the Table. This convention will also be employed in calculating the cereal production estimates in Section 3, and in the graphic presentation of the acreage prediction errors in Figure 5.

Insofar as the prediction test is an illustration of goodness of fit during the estimation period, the magnitudes of the prediction errors in Table 24 simply reflect the multiple correlation coefficients of the equations which generate them. Thus the errors for the wheat results are fairly high, a number of them exceeding 10 per cent, while the errors associated with acreage response equations for the other cereals are in nearly all years less than 5 per cent. With respect to these latter results in particular, it is conceivable that the generating equations provide the basis of an acreage prediction system which is at least as satisfactory as anything at present available. Certainly, as will be noted more fully later, these equations perform in a generally superior way to the most naïve one-year forecast procedure, which is that next year's acreage will be the same as this years's. In this connection two further general points are noteworthy. The first is that the prediction errors for 1970-1 are not essentially better or worse than those in previous years, so that this slight extrapolation of the results does not erode any confidence there may be in the usefulness of the results. Secondly, an important turning point occurred towards the end of the estimational period, *c.* 1967-1968, with a downturn in barley acreage and upswing in the acreages of oats and mixed cereals. From Figure 5 it can be seen that these features are captured by the results presented, which gives a further degree of confidence in the basic structural properties of the equations.

The errors associated with the winter wheat acreage predictor (1) are certainly considerable and exceed 10 per cent in three out of the eight years examined. Nevertheless these predictions based on equation (5.13) are seen from Table 24 to be superior to the naïve one-year forecast assumption that acreage will equal that in the previous year. But, for winter wheat, with its high sensitivity to weather conditions, the naïve forecast procedure would probably not be entertained seriously. A more realistic alternative forecast procedure for the winter wheat acreage might be to assume current acreage equal to the average of the previous three years' acreage, although, with errors of over 500,000 acres in two of the eight years, this too proves inferior to prediction (1).

It is of course difficult to see any genuine forecasting role for winter wheat equation (5.13), in that predictions of acreage one or more years in advance based on assumptions of normal weather conditions are of little interest when the largest source of acreage variation is weather conditions in September, October and November, and when the December sample census gives an early indication of the true acreage. However, given a December estimate (1) of winter wheat acreage, equation (5.15) can be used to generate a useful forecast of spring wheat acreage and hence of the final total wheat acreage of the following year. In particular, as shown by prediction (3) in Table 24, a fairly reliable estimate of the final wheat acreage could be generated some nine months before the official statistics on it become generally available. It should however be admitted that

Table 24: Cereal acreage predictions, 1963-4 to 1970-1* (thousand acres)

	(1) *Winter wheat acreage*			(2) *Spring wheat acreage*		
	Predicted by (5.13)	Error	Naïve forecast error	Predicted by (5.15) given (1)	Error	Naïve forecast error
1963-4	1,533	282	275	647	–30	53
1964-5	1,390	–8	–147	781	–27	–131
1965-6	1,880	–89	–571	586	20	242
1966-7	1,420	–79	470	691	–38	–163
1967-8	1,548	203	154	751	–209	–231
1968-9	1,314	–363	–332	922	183	–220
1969-70	1,487	120	310	693	1	48
1970-1	1,887	–80	–609	534	–26	141

	(3) *Total wheat acreage*		(4) *Oats acreage*		
	(1) + (2)	Error	Predicted by (5.19)	Error	Naïve forecast error
1963-4	2,180	252	1,347	52	224
1964-5	2,171	–35	1,162	37	170
1965-6	2,466	–69	1,021	7	111
1966-7	2,111	–117	952	–15	107
1967-8	2,299	–6	881	–131	–105
1968-9	2,236	–181	967	22	67
1969-70	2,180	120	984	38	–1
1970-1	2,421	–106	1,141	99	4

	(5) *Oats acreage*		(6) *Mixed cereal acreage*		
	Predicted by (5.20)	Error	Predicted by (5.25)	Error	Naïve forecast error
1963-4	1,299	4	96	–3	26
1964-5	1,162	37	85	5	19
1965-6	1,047	33	75	2	7
1966-7	936	–31	74	1	0
1967-8	912	–100	89	1	–15
1968-9	968	23	97	–15	–24
1969-70	972	26	164	8	–44
1970-1	1,004	56	182	–5	–31

* A selection of these predictions are presented in a graphic form in Figure 5.

	(7) *Mixed cereal acreage* Predicted by (5.21)	Error	(8) *Oats & mixed cereals acreage* Predicted by (5.40)	Error	Naïve forecast error
1963-4	104	5	1,400	6	250
1964-5	86	6	1,234	29	189
1965-6	72	–1	1,114	27	118
1966-7	74	1	1,013	33	107
1967-8	83	–5	998	–102	–120
1968-9	99	–13	1,070	13	43
1969-70	168	12	1,134	32	–45
1970-1	214	27	1,179	50	–27

	(9) *Oats & mixed cereals acreage* Predicted by (5.39) and (5.40)	Error	(10) *Barley & acreage* Predicted by (5.39)	Error
1963-4	1,392	–2	4,751	38
1964-5	1,228	23	5,190	158
1965-6	1,122	35	5,418	23
1966-7	1,035	55	6,065	–65
1967-8	972	–128	5,901	–126
1968-9	1,069	12	5,966	33
1969-70	1,139	37	6,041	45
1970-1	1,175	47	5,604	44

	(11) *Barley acreage* Predicted by (5.39) and (5.40)	Error	Naïve forecast error	(12) *Total cereal acreage* Predicted by (5.41)	Error
1963-4	4,745	32	–726	8,347	312
1964-5	5,128	96	–319	8,229	–214
1965-6	5,078	–317	–363	9,085	68
1966-7	5,880	–250	–735	9,145	–203
1967-8	6,287	260	103	9,430	–2
1968-9	5,918	–15	94	9,338	–69
1969-70	5,925	–71	–63	9,212	55
1970-1	5,568	8	436	9,317	102

	(13) Barley acreage		(14) Barley acreage	
	(12) - (3) - (9)	Error	(12) - (3) - (4) - (7)	Error
1963-4	4,775	62	4,716	3
1964-5	4,830	–202	4,810	–222
1965-6	5,497	102	5,526	131
1966-7	5,999	–131	6,008	–122
1967-8	6,159	132	6,167	140
1968-9	6,033	100	6,036	103
1969-70	5,893	–103	5,880	–116
1970-1	5,717	157	5,730	170

* A selection of these predictions are presented in a graphic form in Figure 5.

predictions (2) and (3) (even for 1970-1) benefit from having employed data on actual spring weather conditions, whereas a true forecasting exercise would presumably operate under the assumption of average weather conditions, and this works to the advantage of the published figures.

A surprising feature of the spring wheat acreage prediction (2), which is dependent upon the predicted winter wheat acreage, is that its errors are smaller than when actual *aWW* is employed as an explanatory variable. The errors are also markedly less than for the naïve predictor. In fact large errors are registered only in 1967-8 and 1968-9, and the interesting feature of these is that they do much to cancel out the large winter wheat prediction errors in the same years; this results from the compensation feature of equation (5.15). Indeed it is largely as a result of this compensation feature that the resulting total wheat acreage predictions err by more than 10 per cent in only one year. This outcome is markedly superior to any results obtained (but not presented in the book) by attempting to treat the wheat acreage as a single acreage.

The reason for presenting two oats acreage predictions in Table 24 is to permit comparison of the performance of two equations of differing potential as forecasting tools. Equation (5.19) which gives rise to prediction (4) contains as explanatory variables AO_{t-1}, $(RB/RO)_{t-1}$, and T; given that producers receive prices close to an established guaranteed level, as is the case, the values of all these variables can be determined by, say, November and used to predict the harvested oats acreage in the following year. In contrast equation (5.20), which generates prediction (5), uses the current barley acreage to explain the current oats acreage and would therefore be a rather inconvenient forecasting tool. Surprisingly the additional information available in the latter equation does not give it much predictive advantage over (5.19) as will be readily appreciated from the Table. There is in fact very little to choose between the two results, both of which perform as well as might have been expected from their high

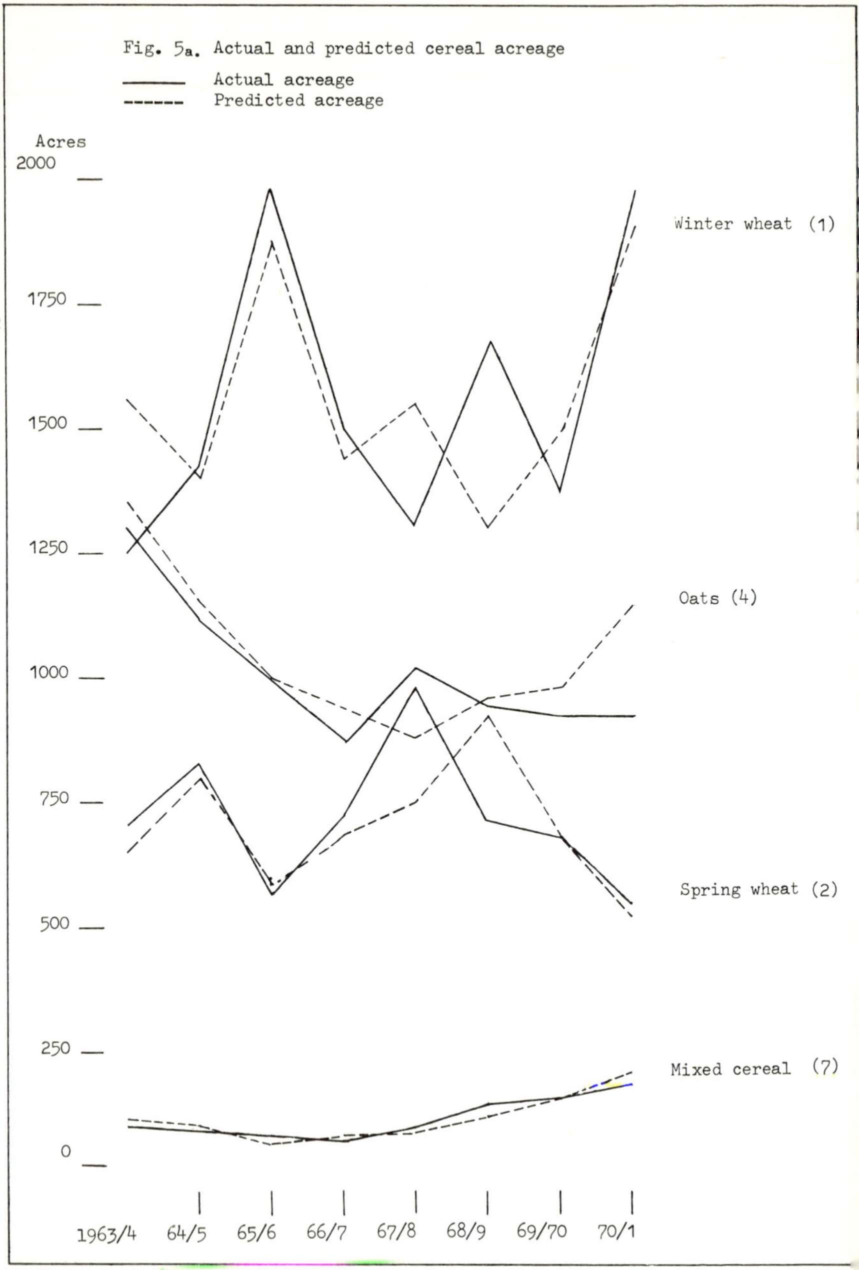

N.B. Acreage figures in thousands.

Fig. 5b. Actual and predicted cereal acreage

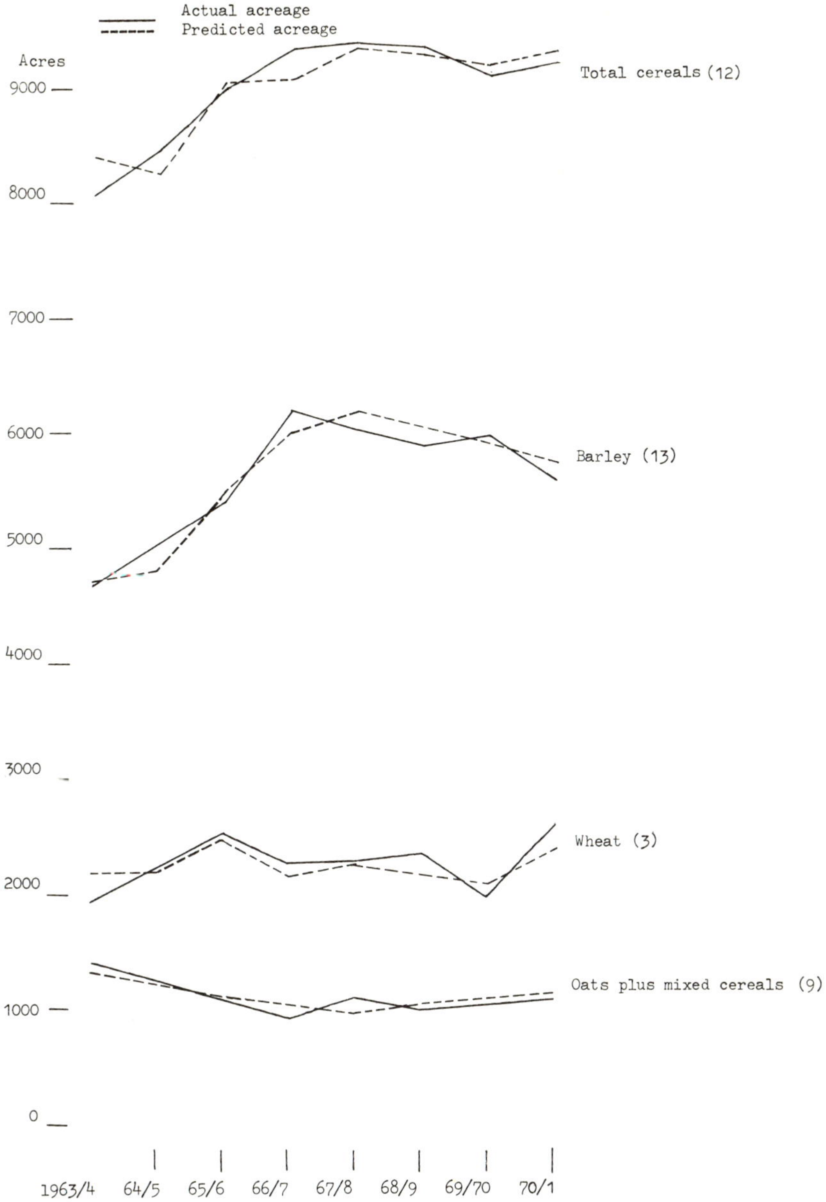

N.B. Acreage figures in thousands.

R^2's, and both of which are superior to the naïve forecaster. In view of the possibility of using equation (5.19) as a one-year forecasting tool, prediction (4) will be employed later to generate the estimate of oats production.

A very good explanation of the mixed cereals acreage is achieved when equation (5.25) is used to produce prediction (6). Unfortunately this accurate descriptive model, with its clear superiority over the naïve predictor, employs the current barley acreage (aB_t) as explanatory data thus diminishing its usefulness as a purely predictive tool. An alternative not suffering from this problem is equation (5.21); but, as prediction (7) shows, its performance is, as might be expected, less accurate than (5.25). However, since in subsequent exercises we wish to employ a mixed cereal acreage prediction to generate an estimate of the barley acreage in the same period, it is important that we have an non-interdependent system such as exists if we employ (7).

Two alternative predictions are also presented for the combined oats plus mixed cereal acreage; prediction (8) which uses information about the current barley acreage, and prediction (9) which is produced by the appropriate reduced-form of equations (5.39) and (5.40) using only lagged explanatory variables plus the current wheat acreage which can be estimated in advance. Prediction (8) seems to have derived little benefit from contemporaneous information about aB, and there is very little to choose between the two results on grounds of accuracy. Thus in view of the reduced-form equation's capability as a one-year forecast tool, prediction (9) is preferred as the basis for subsequent exercises requiring an estimate of the oats plus mixed cereal acreage. There is a further alternative way of achieving such an estimate, which is by summation of the separate estimates of the acreages of the two cereals. Comparing the errors in prediction (9) to the combined errors of predictions (4) and (7), which are also the products of equations with a one-year forecast role, indicates that prediction (9) is the more accurate. This provides a further vindication for going to the length of estimating the oats and mixed cereals acreage jointly as well as separately. Nor is this evaluation debased by the fact that the combined errors of the separate predictions (5) and (6) are marginally less than those of (9), for these results depend upon contemporaneous information about aB and could not readily fulfil a forecasting role.

It will be recollected that two different versions of the acreage response model were examined, one in which the barley acreage was estimated directly, and another in which it was approached indirectly as the difference between the total cereals acreage and the combined acreage of cereals other than barley. To illustrate the possibilities associated with these two approaches four alternative predictions of the barley acreage are shown in Table 21.

Turning to the direct estimational approach first: Paralleling the already established practice there is a prediction (11), based on the relevant reduced-form of equations (5.39) and (5.40), and prediction (10) which requires knowledge of the contemporaneous acreages of oats and mixed cereals. Again there is very little to choose between these alternatives, although there are fewer large errors in prediction (10) than in (11). Indeed, the largest error in the former set is one of 3 per cent in 1964-5, while in the latter set there are three errors in excess of 4 per cent. But, by most standards these errors are not large, and both results can be considered satisfactory from the viewpoint of accuracy.

The indirect approach to predicting the barley acreage also performs satisfactorily, and an important basis of this success is rooted in the very accurate way in which equation (5.41) predicts the total cereals acreage. As prediction (12) indicates this equation generates errors of less than 1 per cent in four out of the eight years, and errs by more than 3 per cent in only one year, 1963-4. Furthermore, equation (5.41) can perform a one-year forecast role by virtue of containing only lagged explanatory variables and a time trend, so that in several respects this is a useful result.

Total cereal acreage prediction (12) is used to provide two alternative predictions of the barley acreage, both of which could in principle be published about 9-12 months in advance of the true acreage value becoming known. In both of these estimates wheat acreage estimate (3) is subtracted from (12), but whereas prediction (13) employs the 'reduced-form' estimate of the combined oats plus mixed cereal acreage, prediction (14) uses separate estimates of the acreages of these two cereals as derived in predictions (4) and (7). On the basis of their errors there is very little to choose between these two estimates of the barley acreage. Possibly result (13) is marginally superior, but this might have been expected in view of the superiority of the combined oats and mixed cereals acreage estimate over their separate estimates. What is perhaps most important about these two indirect estimates of the barley acreage, is that they compare very favourably with the direct approach. This means that the rather unconventional second acreage response model in which the barley acreage is determined as a 'residual' may not have been misconceived. It also means that there are a number of satisfactory alternative acreage estimates on which to base predictions of barley production.

Before passing on to examine the usefulness of the cereal yield equations it is worth explaining the repeated use of the term 'one-year forecaster' in the current section. It will be recognised that all the equations whose performance has been scrutinised in this section are structural economic relationships. That is, they explain acreages in terms of the values of prices, cereal yields and other economic variables. Where these variables enter with a one-year lag their values might be known with a fair degree of certainty at a time which permits us to produce a forecast of the dependent variable about one year in advance of its true value becoming known. However, if we wish to forecast cereal acreages in the more distant future, we would also need to forecast values for the explanatory economic variables, which itself presents considerable difficulties. Of course we could adopt some simple extrapolative scheme for generating future values of these variables, but in view of the recent history of cereal growing in this country—there has been a downturn in the barley acreage and an upturn in other cereal acreages—it seems unlikely that such crude methods will have success. By the same token it does not seem probable that equations expressing acreages as functions of time (such equations having no structural pretensions but being envisaged in a purely forecasting role) would produce more reliable forecasts of the longer term than do the structural equations here examined. In other words, there seems to be no simple pattern in recent cereal acreage changes to suggest that long-term forecasting can be undertaken by either structural or extrapolative equations with any degree of confidence.

(2) *Cereal yield predictions*

The most striking feature of the results presented in Table 25 is the large size of the prediction errors generated for 1970-1, the only year outside the sample period. For this year the yields of oats, mixed cereals and barley have all been overestimated by more than 10 per cent. These results can be attributed to rather unusual weather conditions which arose in 1970. More particularly, wet and cold weather in April delayed sowing of spring cereals, and subsequent dry weather in May and June retarded the development of the crops, causing especially low yields. These circumstances lead to a number of criticisms which can be made about the cereal yield equations.

Firstly, only weather conditions in June, July and August are taken into account in the yield equations, but it is clear from the 1970 evidence that weather conditions in April and May might influence yields—although on the evidence of the other years this omission does not seem too serious. Possibly, therefore, a number of explanatory weather variables for different periods should have been used. This was done to effect in Guise's[1] study of wheat yields in New Zealand, although he had more statistical latitude through using long time-series from 1918 to 1967. However, as was pointed out in Chapter 3, there are many difficulties associated with choosing the time periods for constructing weather indices, and for this reason it was decided to concentrate on identifying the single most critical period; a strategy which seems to have been reasonably successful in the years prior to 1970-1.

Another interesting feature of the May-June weather in 1970 is that it was lack of rainfall which caused a reduction of cereal yields. This illustrates a further problem in constructing weather indices; that different

[1] Guise, J. W. B., 'Factors associated with variations in the aggregate yield of New Zealand wheat (1918-1967)', *Am. J. Agric. Econ.*, Nov. 1969.

Table 25: Cereal yield predictions, 1963-4 to 1970-1 (Hundredweights per acre)

	(1) *Wheat yield* Predicted by (5.55)	Error	(2) *Oats yield* Predicted by (5.56)	Error
1963-4	30·7	–0·4	22·3	0
1964-5	32·7	–1·1	23·7	0·1
1965-6	31·6	–0·8	24·2	0·2
1966-7	30·7	0·1	24·9	0·5
1967-8	32·7	–0·6	27·1	0·6
1968-9	30·3	2·3	27·5	–1·1
1969-70	31·4	–0·7	29·9	0·2
1970-1	31·1	–1·8	31·9	5·8

	(3) *Mixed cereals yield* Predicted by (5.57)	Error	(4) *Barley yield* Predicted by (5.58)	Error
1963-4	23·5	–0·3	27·3	–0·7
1964-5	25·1	–0·2	28·8	–0·6
1965-6	25·0	0·2	28·3	–1·6
1966-7	24·9	–0·8	28·0	0
1967-8	27·1	0·6	29·8	–0·9
1968-9	26·2	0·7	28·4	1·2
1969-70	28·2	–0·3	29·7	0·8
1970-1	29·1	3·3	29·9	3·3

influences may be exerted by weather variations in different ranges of the index. Stated more fully, there may be an optimum set of weather conditions such that upward or downward changes in the weather index from this level may cause diminution of yields. It is not obvious that this problem can be handled by any simple index of weather conditions.

A further noteworthy point is that winter wheat did not suffer any depression of yield in 1970, due to the fact that it was already well established by April and May. Because winter wheat makes up the bulk of the wheat crop, the overall wheat yield was similarly not greatly depressed, and indeed it was actually underestimated for 1970-1 by the relevant equation. This suggests that in a more sophisticated analysis where several explanatory weather variables were used it might be appropriate to use different sets of weather variables to explain the yields of different cereals.

The comparatively poor results for 1970-1 must not be allowed to obscure the fact that all four equations established fairly good fits in the more normal years of the sample period. (The wheat yield equations performs slightly less accurately than the other equations, but this is hardly surprising in view of its smaller multiple correlation coefficient.) Similarly there is no strong reason to suppose that the four simple yield response equations will not provide reasonable explanations of the data for future years which would not be expected to exhibit the unusual weather characteristics of 1970.

(3) *Cereal production predictions*

The predictions of cereal output in Table 26 and represented in Figure 6 are obtained by multiplying acreage predictions from Table 24 by the appropriate yield predictions. All of the results presented use acreage response equations which can produce genuine one-year forecasts. The yield response equations can only be used in a similar fashion under some arbitrary assumption about prevailing weather conditions, which is obviously unsatisfactory in view of the fact that the main cause of cereal yield fluctuations is random fluctuations in weather conditions. Consequently the yield predictions in Table 25 were produced using knowledge of the actual weather conditions, so that the production predictions discussed in this section are likewise dependent upon these factors and do not therefore amount to one-year forecasts.

It is apparent from the results that in some cases there is no cancelling out of the yield and acreage forecasting errors but rather a cumulation of them. This has led to large errors in predicting the output of each of the cereals in one year or another. Not surprisingly in view of the large yield prediction errors in 1970-1, the production prediction errors are also especially large in this year—only in the case of wheat is the error not the largest recorded in any of the eight years examined. But further discussion of 1970-1 forecasting errors will be set aside.

The least satisfactory output prediction results are achieved for wheat output with errors in three years exceeding 10 per cent, and being close to this level in three of the remaining five years. This was, however, to be anticipated, given the relatively low multiple correlation coefficients associated with the wheat acreage and yield response equations. For the remaining cereals the prediction performance in years other than 1970-1 is not at all bad. This is especially true for mixed cereals, for which the prediction only errs by much over 5 per cent in one of the seven years.

In the case of barley two alternative results are presented, one, prediction (4), employing a directly estimated acreage response equation, and the other based upon the indirect method. Comparison of these two alternatives reveals little in terms of error size on which to select between them. Each prediction errs by large absolute amounts in years when the other performs more accurately, and is accurate to within 2 per cent in a number of years. Thus despite glaringly large errors in 1970-1, and in 1965-6 from prediction (4) both barley production estimates provide a

Table 26: Cereal production predictions, 1963-4 to 1970-1 (thousand tons)

	(1) *Wheat production*		(2) *Oats production*	
	Acreage (3) x yield (1)	Error[a]	Acreage (4) x yield (2)	Error[a]
1963-4	3,587	589	1,542	98
1964-5	3,542	–186	1,379	51
1965-6	3,818	–289	1,236	19
1966-7	3,174	–250	1,185	78
1967-8	3,948	110	1,195	–146
1968-9	3,076	–308	1,330	–21
1969-70	3,580	275	1,473	68
1970-1	3,650	–508	1,519	288

	(3) *Mixed cereal production*		(4) *Barley production*	
	Acreage (7) x yield (3)	Error[a]	Acreage (11) x yield (4)	Error[a]
1963-4	122	4	6,477	–121
1964-5	108	7	7,384	–13
1965-6	90	1	7,185	–881
1966-7	92	–2	8,232	–350
1967-8	112	–5	9,368	117
1968-9	130	–13	8,404	335
1969-70	237	15	8,799	135
1970-1	311	71	8,324	929

	(5) *Barley production*	
	Acreage (13) x yield (4)	Error[a]
1963-4	6,518	–80
1964-5	6,926	–471
1965-6	7,758	–208
1966-7	8,399	–183
1967-8	9,177	–74
1968-9	8,567	498
1969-70	8,751	87
1970-1	8,533	1,138

[a] The true values of production used for the purposes of calculating these errors equal the acreage times yield values employed as true values in the preceding sections. The resultant figures vary slightly from official published production data.

Fig. 6. Actual and predicted cereal production

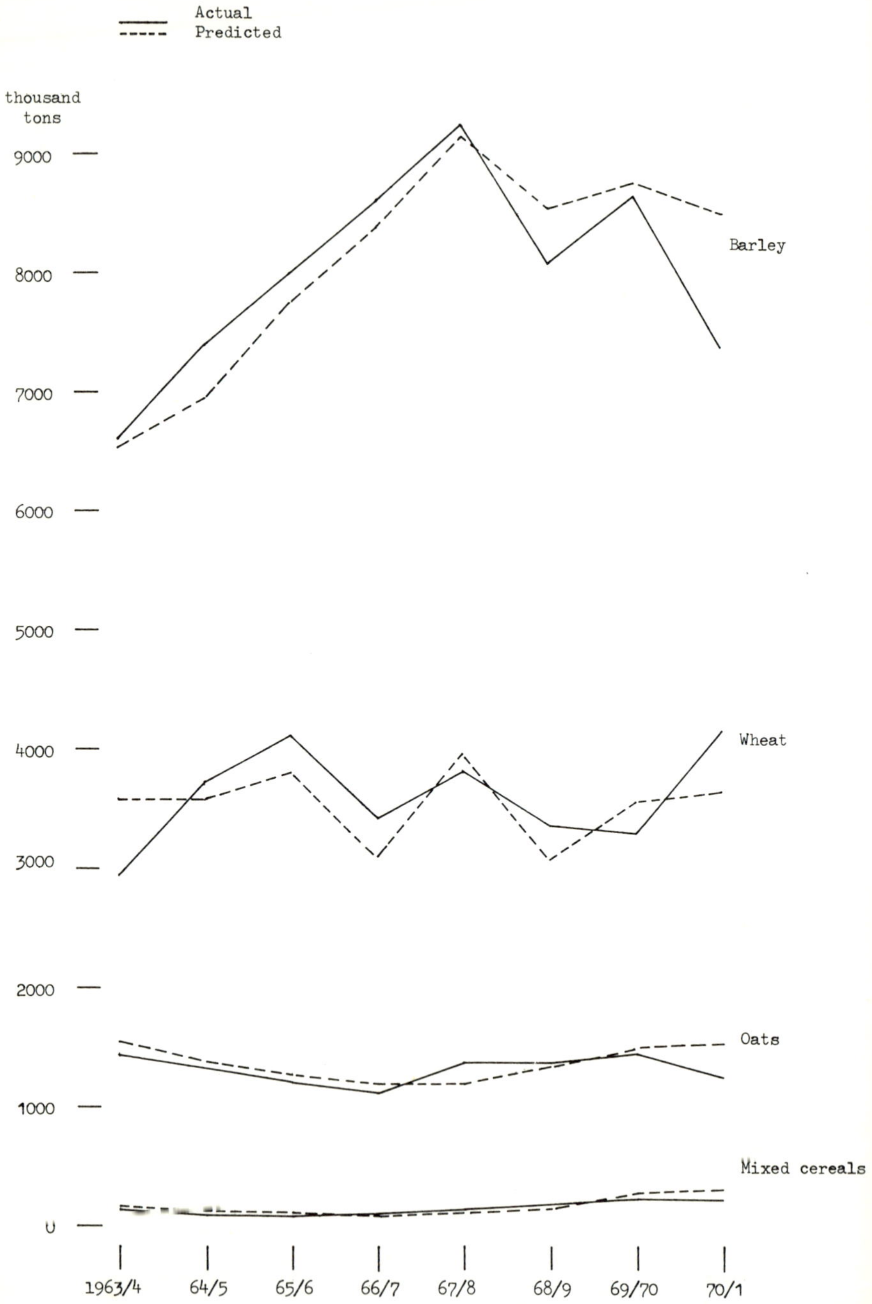

relatively accurate explanation of the data in the majority of years. Hence it appears that either approach (direct or indirect) to estimating the barley acreage lays a reasonably successful foundation for a barley supply model. Similarly, for oats and mixed cereals it can be argued that developing supply models in which acreage and yield are estimated separately shows considerable promise. For wheat this approach has been less successful, although there is no reason to suppose that a more direct approach, in which output was the dependent variable of an estimated equation, would prove superior.

(4) *Cereal demand predictions*

Less difficulty was encountered in estimating demand functions for cereals in the U.K. than supply functions, and this is reflected in the results presented in Table 27. On the whole predictive error[2] is appreciably less than that encountered on the supply side and is in many instances less than 1 per cent. Furthermore there appears to have been slightly less problem of using the individual demand equations to forecast for an extra year (1967-8) beyond the sample period than with the supply model. Only maize food demand, and the rather minor wheat and barley seed demand equations produce higher prediction errors in 1967-8 than in preceding years. This is certainly an encouraging feature of these results.

It should cause no surprise that the seed demand predictions are as accurate as they are; for the data series on seed usage, which provided the dependent variables, are not directly measured, but are estimated by a procedure which uses the planted acreage and some technical coefficient. It could thus be argued, that if this coefficient were published no estimation would be required to explain the series.

The predictive performance of the food demand equations is also gratifying. But what is surprising is that equation (6.26) with an $\bar{R}^2 = 0{\cdot}77$ should perform relatively more accurately over the five-year period examined than the maize food demand equation which has $\bar{R}^2 = 0{\cdot}98$. This could not have been anticipated, but somewhat similar results have been obtained with the feed demand equations. The barley feed equation with an $\bar{R}^2 = 0{\cdot}97$ produces some quite sizeable errors over the five years, while the wheat and maize equations with $\bar{R}^2$'s of 0·87 and 0·81 respectively do not seem to perform in a much more inaccurate manner. Nevertheless the prediction errors associated with the feed demand equations only exceed 10 per cent in one instance (maize in 1966-7) and this appears to be an acceptable level of performance, although it is less good than for the food and seed equations.

Summing the predicted components of demand for each of the cereals produces the predicted total demand column of Table 27. The errors in

[2] Errors are calculated as predicted values minus the data series on cereal utilisation which provided the endogenous variables in the statistical analysis. There have been subsequent minor revisions of these series, but these revisions have not been taken into account in calculating prediction errors.

Table 27: Cereal demand predictions, 1963-4 to 1967-8 (thousand tons)

(1) *Wheat demand*

	Food demand pred. by (6.26)	Error	Feed demand pred. by (6.18)	Error
1963-4	5,456	–22	1,808	–28
1964-5	5,412	45	2,342	–52
1965-6	5,393	–97	2,552	167
1966-7	5,371	81	2,067	90
1967-8	5,339	0	2,505	136

	Seed demand pred. by (6.30)	Error	Predicted total demand	Error
1963-4	170	0	7,434	–50
1964-5	192	–2	7,946	–9
1965-6	172	–1	8,117	69
1966-7	176	–5	7,614	–14
1967-8	176	–11	8,020	125

(2) *Barley demand*

	Food demand pred. by (6.28)	Error	Feed demand pred. by (6.12)	Error
1963-4	1,260	42	5,150	–320
1964-5	1,309	–33	5,692	–83
1965-6	1,316	–26	5,656	–103
1966-7	1,337	–55	6,417	462
1967-8	1,372	20	6,059	–419

	Seed demand pred. by (6.33)	Error	Predicted total demand	Error
1963-4	328	–2	6,738	–280
1964-5	352	1	7,353	–115
1965-6	401	1	7,373	–128
1966-7	391	–2	8,145	405
1967-8	381	–9	7,782	–408

(3) *Oats demand*

	Food demand pred. by (6.29)	Error	Feed demand pred. by (6.20)	Error
1963-4	128	2	1,287	26
1964-5	124	1	1,135	–4
1965-6	123	–6	1,023	20
1966-7	122	4	996	73
1967-8	117	2	1,084	13

	Seed demand pred. by (6·34)	Error	Predicted total demand	Error
1963-4	99	0	1,514	28
1964-5	93	3	1,352	0
1965-6	86	5	1,232	19
1966-7	93	4	1,211	81
1967-8	89	1	1,290	16

(4) *Maize demand*

	Food demand pred. by (6.27)	Error	Feed demand pred. by (6.14)	Error
1963-4	928	–35	2,230	–182
1964-5	994	14	2,251	–14
1965-6	1,036	–45	2,542	205
1966-7	1,054	–2	2,631	379
1967-8	1,103	95	2,612	–36

	Predicted total demand	Error
1963-4	3,158	–217
1964-5	3,245	0
1965-6	3,578	160
1966-7	3,685	377
1967-8	3,715	59

predicting total demand for wheat and oats are especially small. Despite the fact that for wheat the 1967-8 prediction error is the largest of all the five years, it still only amounts to a 1·5 per cent error, which only serves to underline the overall predictive qualities of the demand equations for wheat. In comparison the overall predictive accuracy of the barley demand equations looks poor. However, only one total barley demand forecast is in error by more than 5 per cent, and even this error, unfortunately recorded for 1967-8, amounts only to a 5·7 per cent error. The least successful predictive performance is associated with maize demand, and this is highlighted by the substantial overestimate of demand in 1966-7. This error, due to an overestimate of feed demand, coincides with sizeable overestimates of feed demand for barley and oats in the same year. Some unusual event seems to be signified here, which has not been accounted for by the explanatory variables used.

Despite this latter result, it does appear in general from the evidence of Table 27 that a fairly satisfactory cereal demand model has been developed.

(5) *Cereal import and export predictions*

One purpose of the study was to develop a model which could explain the effects of cereal price policies upon U.K. trade in cereals. Insofar as it has not proved possible to develop equations to explain producers' and processors' demand for cereal stocks it is not possible to use our model to obtain a direct prediction of net cereal exports and imports (reasons for this were fully examined in Chapter 6). It is however a simple matter to examine the trade prediction (description) errors which result from applying the supply and demand equations which have been developed. If it is assumed that stock demand has been exactly explained, then the trade prediction errors would equal the sum of the supply and demand errors generated by our model. An overestimate of domestic cereal demand will lead to an identical overestimate of imports or underestimate of exports, while an overestimate of domestic supply will cause under-estimation of imports or overestimation of exports. Using these rules and applying them to the production and demand prediction errors in Tables 26 and 27 produces the trade prediction errors presented in Table 28. (*N.B.* the barley trade prediction has been derived using production estimate (5)). In the case of maize there is no domestic supply equation and hence the import prediction errors are identical to the demand forecast errors in Table 27.

It will be immediately obvious that unless the demand and supply errors cancel out the trade prediction errors will be large. Furthermore, small relative errors in predicting supply and demand may cause large relative errors when set against net import or export totals if trade is a small fraction of domestic consumption and production. This is made evident on examining the oats trade prediction errors; relatively small errors can be seen to exceed the true values by over 200 per cent in three of the five years. Clearly in this situation it is unrealistic to expect accurate trade volume estimates from the model which has been developed. A somewhat similar position arises in the case of trade in barley. Here again trade is a fairly small proportion of domestic production and demand so that the cumulated supply and demand errors produce large percentage errors in the trade prediction. These errors are in fact so large, although they exceed 100 per cent only in the year of lowest net trade, that the model cannot even be adjudged to operate better than the assumption that trade will be

Table 28: Net cereal imports* and import prediction errors (thousand tons)

	Wheat		*Barley*	
	Net imports	Prediction errors	Net imports	Prediction[a] errors
1963-4	4,524	–639	344	–200
1964-5	4,112	177	165	356[c]
1965-6	4,581	358	–477[b]	80[c]
1966-7	4,101	236	–905[b]	588[c]
1967-8	3,993	15	–676[b]	–334[d]
	Oats		*Maize*	
	Net imports	Prediction errors	Net imports	Prediction errors
1963-4	17	–70	3,431	–217
1964-5	22	–51	3,140	0
1965-6	33	0	3,490	160
1966-7	25	3	3,334	377
1967-8	–67[b]	160[c]	3,722	59

[a] Derived using barley production prediction (5)
[b] Net exports of cereals
[c] Underestimate of exports (corresponds to overestimate of imports)
[d] Overestimate of exports (corresponds to underestimate of imports)

**Source:* Home Grown Cereals Authority, Annual Reports

at last years' level–the errors under this assumption equal the differences between adjacent net import figures.

In terms of percentage errors, it is the wheat model which performs best. This is however due to the large volume of wheat trade, which outweighs the large absolute size of the errors, with the consequence that the largest prediction error is only about 15 per cent off course. In addition the prediction errors of this model are less than those generated by the naïve forecast assumption. This is also true of the maize trade predictions, which is a slight source of encouragement. Despite these two results, it cannot be claimed that the supply and demand models developed in this study have sufficient accuracy in predicting trade to warrant their use in this way. Nevertheless, the objective with respect to cereal trade was more limited than this; it was to be able to identify the effects of domestic policy upon cereal trade. The model can still be used to achieve this goal; that is it can be employed in comparative static analysis to predict how much different the cereal trade volume would be after some hypothetical change in policy.

B. An appraisal of the guaranteed price policy for cereals

A major objective of the study was to construct and estimate a model capable of evaluating the guaranteed price policy for cereals.[3] The current section aims to accomplish this objective by using the estimated acreage response model to forecast the effects of changes in cereal price guarantees. Because of the nonlinear (logarithmic) form of the majority of the equations, the outcome of policy is dependent upon the levels of the relevant explanatory variables. For this reason it was decided to use the cereal acreage and market prices which prevailed in 1969-70 as the basic data for testing the effects of policy. Thus, as a consequence of the one-year lags in the cereal acreage response model, the predicted outcomes of price policy changes are in terms of the acreages in 1970-1.

In the procedure adopted it is assumed that the deficiency payment system makes up the average cereal price received by producers to the guaranteed price. Thus employing 1968-9 guaranteed prices and 1969-70 values of the relevant yield, acreage and weather variables enables us to use the acreage response equations to predict what the 1970-1 acreages of cereals would have been if the 1968-9 policy had prevailed in 1969-70. This gives us the first line in Table 29. It is now possible to rework the predictions assuming alternative guaranteed price policies in 1969-70, and assessing their effects by comparison with the first prediction. For example, if we employ actual 1969-70 guaranteed prices to generate predictions about the 1970-1 acreages, we can attribute the difference between these predictions and those under the assumption of 1968-9 guaranteed prices to the change of policy between the two years. In the same manner it is possible to estimate the partial effects of the different components of the changed policy package (see lines three and four of Table 29).

Before proceeding further it is important to stress that what the ensuing evaluation reveals is the effects of cereal price changes under the assumption that the estimated price coefficients in the acreage response equations are the true values. In fact, a number of the critical coefficients involved in the prediction process, such as the returns coefficient in the spring wheat acreage equation, are not statistically significant, and there is a low probability that such coefficients are the true values. Hence some of the results presented are subject to large margins of error, but these margins

[3] In the historical context guaranteed producer prices have been achieved by the deficiency payment system, and this section will assume this to be the relevant policy. However the probability is that producer prices will in future be guaranteed or supported through a minimum import price policy. The findings of this section should also be relevant to such a policy.

will not be presented as they would be difficult to calculate. It is important to bear these facts in mind while reading the ensuing section.

All the policy effect calculations shown in Table 29 have been worked out through equations with the one-year forecasting property. For barley, oats and mixed cereals alternative sets of results are presented in order to reflect the different equational systems which could be used to explain these acreages. Hence the effects of price policy changes upon the acreages of oats and mixed cereals are worked through for the two acreages treated separately and in combination. Only one major difference arises from these alternative treatments; this is that wheat price changes have no effects upon the oats and mixed cereals acreages when handled separately, but do produce an impact when the two acreages are examined in combination using a reduced-form of equations (5.39) and (5.40). It is the second outcome which would appear to be the most realistic. Also, since the effects of changes in the oats and barley prices upon acreages of oats and mixed cereals are similar whether the two acreages are treated separately or in combination, it is the results of the latter treatment to which remarks are addressed in the rest of this section. In the case of barley two sets of calculations have been performed, one for the direct, the other for the indirect acreage model. The direct estimator employed is the appropriate reduced-form of equations (5.39) and (5.40) and this can be seen to generate larger acreage changes in response to price policy changes than does the indirect method which produces the set of results in the last column of Table 29. The direct estimate involves fewer equations than the indirect method, and so requires the accumulation of fewer errors. For this reason, and because of the relationship of the direct estimator to the equation selected to analyse policy effects upon the oats plus mixed cereal acreages, remarks about price policy effects upon the barley acreage are largely confined to those generated by the direct estimate.

Comparison of the first two rows of Table 29 enables the predicted effects of the change in cereal guarantees from 1968-9 to 1969-70 upon 1970-1 cereal acreages to be identified. This policy change was in fact to increase the guaranteed price of wheat by 1*s.* 7*d.* and the barley guarantee by 10*d.* The estimated effects of these separate components of the policy package are shown by comparing rows three and four of the Table to the first row. The overall effect is estimated to have been a large increase in the barley acreage, a small increase in the wheat acreage, and a relatively large reduction of the oats plus mixed cereal acreage. One of the objectives of the policy package was to promote additional output of both wheat and barley. Whilst the model suggests that this would in fact have been accomplished, it also suggests that with respect to the encouragement of additional wheat the two elements of the policy operated in opposition to one another. For, according to the spring wheat equation (5.15), the extra wheat output induced by the increased wheat guarantee was offset to the extent of about 50 per cent by the effect of the increased barley guarantee. As the increased guarantee for barley was about half of that for wheat, the result suggests that equal increases in both guarantees would succeed in stimulating additional barley sowings but would have virtually no effect upon the wheat acreage. A clear implication of this is that where the primary policy objective is to increase wheat output, care should be taken not to simultaneously increase the barley guarantee along with that for wheat, but preferably to reduce it. A further complication for this policy arises by virtue of the fact that an increased wheat guarantee is predicted to increase the barley acreage by more than it increases the wheat acreage. This outcome depends upon two characteristics of the model used. The first of these is that the barley acreage is made directly dependent upon the weighted average return per acre of grain which will, of course, increase if the wheat guarantee is increased. However the barley acreage is also inversely related to the wheat acreage, and this is where the second characteristic of these results enters. For if the wheat acreage were sufficiently own-price elastic it would cause changes in the wheat acreage which would operate through the barley acreage equation to produce an opposing change in the barley acreage. But this is not the case, and the own price elasticity of wheat is found to be small. This principally results from the non-price responsiveness of the winter wheat acreage

Table 29: Predicted effects of different producer prices in 1969-70 upon 1970-1 cereal acreages (in thousand acres)*

	Spring[a] wheat acreage (5.15)	Oats acreage (5.19)	Mixed cereals acreage (5.21)	Oats plus mixed cereals acreage (5.40) & (5.39)
1968-9 guaranteed prices	447·7	985·2	239·8	1,239
1969-70 guaranteed prices	456·3 (8·6)	968·4 (–16·8)	226·5 (–13·3)	1,213 (–26)
1968-9 g.p. plus 1/7*d.* on wheat	464·0 (16·3)	985·2 (0)	239·8 (0)	1,236 (–3)
1968-9 g.p. plus 10*d.* on barley	440·0 (–7·7)	968·4 (–16·8)	226·5 (–13·3)	1,205 (–34)
1968-9 g.p. plus 1/- on wheat	457·9 (10·2)	985·2 (0)	239·8 (0)	1,237 (–2)
1968-9 g.p. plus 1/- on oats	447·7 (0)	1,004 (18·8)	254·8 (15)	1,271 (32)
1968-9 g.p. plus 1/- on barley	438·4 (–9·3)	965·1 (–20·1)	224·0 (–15·8)	1,199 (–40)

	Barley acreage (5.39) & (5.40)	Total cereals acreage (5.41)	Barley acreage $aG_t - aWW_t{}^b - aSW_t - aO_t - aMC_t$
1968-9 guaranteed prices	5,399	9,280	5,640·3
1969-70 guaranteed prices	5,510 (111)	9,339 (59)	5,720·8 (80·5)
1968-9 g.p. plus 1/7*d.* on wheat	5,416 (17)	9,306 (26)	5,650·0 (9·7)
1968-9 g.p. plus 10*d* on barley	5,494 (95)	9,315 (35)	5,713·1 (72·8)
1968-9 g.p. plus 1/- on wheat	5,410 (11)	9,296 (16)	5,646·1 (5·8)
1968-9 g.p. plus 1/- on oats	5,328 (−71)	9,287 (7)	5,613·5 (−26·8)
1968-9 g.p. plus 1/- on barley	5,511 (112)	9,321 (41)	5,726·5 (86·2)

[a] Estimate depends upon the actual winter acreage in 1970-1
[b] Actual acreage of winter wheat in 1970-1

* Figures in parentheses indicate the change in acreage from the base level shown in the first row of the table.

which makes up the bulk of the wheat crop. A great deal of experimenting with alternative functions failed to reveal any evidence that winter wheat is responsive to prices. Thus the low (and nonsignificant) short-run own-price elasticity of spring wheat of 0·29 becomes 0·11 when spread over the total wheat acreage. Evidently this has serious implications for the guaranteed price policy, in that it suggests that expansion of the wheat acreage can only be achieved at high cost to the taxpayer, especially in view of the earlier result that wheat expansion may be accompanied by unwanted extra output of barley.

A further striking feature of the results in Table 29 is the way in which they illustrate the high degree of competitiveness between oats and barley. Not only are the oats and mixed cereal acreages highly responsive to the price of barley, but the barley acreage is also influenced by the price of oats. Using the two reduced-forms of equations (5.39) and (5.40), the results in the Table imply a short-run response elasticity of the oats plus mixed cereal acreage to the barley price of −0·86, and a converse relationship of −0·37. These are by no means the highest cross elasticity estimates obtained for these cereals in the current study, a number of higher estimates having been presented in Chapter 5. In policy terms the implication of these results is that the guaranteed price policy might be used quite effectively to alter the balance of cereal output as between barley and oats, a view reinforced by the relatively high short-run own-price elasticities of these two crops.

One further point about the estimates in Table 29 which is worth drawing attention to concerns the magnitudes of the responses of the total cereal acreage to changes in producer prices. These responses are seen to be less elastic than those of the individual cereal acreages. This is no more than might have been expected, for on technical grounds one would suppose that farmer's would have greater flexibility to shift production from one cereal to another than to switch from cereals to some completely different type of crop. Furthermore it does serve to underline one point, which is that raising the guaranteed price of a cereal to encourage extra output may be successful, but is as likely to succeed at the expense of some other cereal as of a non-cereal crop.

The calculations in Table 29 have basically served to illustrate with numbers the acreage response elasticities estimated from a number of chosen equations. However there were a large number of equations estimated in the study which could provide alternative estimates of these elasticities. It is therefore thought to be useful to present in Table 30 a summary of the directly estimated elasticities underlying the calculations in Table 29, the chosen elasticities as it were, and to supplement this information by presenting, in parentheses, the full range of alternative estimates obtained. It will be noted that where the range of estimates is wide the chosen estimate lies towards the centre of the range. This was of course not necessarily the basis upon which the selection was made (rather this was upon grounds already fully explored in Chapter 5), but it may nevertheless support the credence of the chosen estimates.

One elasticity not presented in Table 30 is that for the total cereals acreage with respect to the price of milk. The principal reason for selecting total cereal acreage response equation (5.41) for the tests performed in this chapter was that it provides a statistically significant estimate of this elasticity, which reflects a relationship which was considered to be important on *a priori* grounds. In fact the short-run elasticity of all cereals to the price of milk implied by this result is –0·18, an estimate which is in close accord with that of –0·24 derived from the reduced form of the simultaneously estimated equations (5.47) and (5.48). It is encouraging that these two estimates should lie so close to each other. But more importantly, the fact that the size of these elasticities is not trivial when compared to the elasticities presented in Table 30 lends strong support to the notion that cereals and dairying are competitive. The elasticity of –0·18, is as should be expected, close to the response elasticity of total cereals to a general change in all cereal prices. This is obtained by summing the elements of the last column of Table 30 and equals 0·20. From a policy point of view this result is most significant, in that it emphasises the interrelated character of major agricultural enterprises.

Until now mention has only been made of the short-run responsiveness of cereal supply to price policy, and, insofar as the short-run acreage response elasticities are less than one (with the exception of mixed cereals), the suggestion has been that proportional changes in public expenditure on deficiency payments will exceed proportional changes in cereal supply.

Table 30: Summary of short-run acreage response elasticities, 1970-1*

Cereal acreage

	Spring wheat	Total wheat	Oats	Mixed cereals	Oats plus mixed cereals	Barley	Total cereals
Wheat price or subsidy	0·29 (0·29 to 0·32)	0·11 (0·11 to 0·12)			−0·04	0·06 (0·03 to 0·06)	0·06 (0·04 to 0·08)
Oats price or subsidy			0·51 (0·24 to 0·97)	1·57 (0·91 to 4·93)	0·71 (0·21 to 3·33)	−0·37 (−0·17 to −0·69	0·02 (0·02 to 0·03)
Barley price or subsidy	−0·25 (−0·25 to −0·32)	−0·10 (−0·10 to −0·12)	−0·57 (−0·27 to −0·80)	−1·91 (−0·91 to −4·93)	−0·86 (−0·34 to −1·68)	0·56 (0·14 to 0·77)	0·12 (0·07 to 0·18)

*The figures in parentheses indicate the range of elasticity estimates obtained in the study. The principal figure in each cell is the elasticity estimate relevant to the calculated policy change effects which are presented in Table 29.

However, a basic hypothesis of the study is that it takes time to adjust to optimum supply levels, and that policy changes exercise their influence over a number of years. To cope with this, distributed lag models were estimated for all cereals except wheat; this latter for reasons already explained. Thus the results obtained do provide for the calculation of the long-run supply elasticities. These estimates are equal to the short-run elasticity multiplied by $1/(1-\gamma)$ where γ is the relevant coefficient of the lagged dependent variable. However, as has already been pointed out, problems of trends in the data make it probable that the γ's may have been overestimated in many cases, and this would lead to overestimation of the long-run elasticities. Nevertheless a number of seemingly reasonable estimates of the adjustment coefficients, $(1-\gamma)$, have been obtained from simultaneously estimated sets of equations.

The reduced-forms of equations (5.39) and (5.40) yield adjustment coefficients of 0·45 for the barley acreage and 0·19 for oats plus mixed cereals, implying that the respective long-run elasticities exceed those in the short-run by approximately twice and five times. The estimate of the adjustment coefficient for barley certainly seems reasonable, because it may be supposed that there is a fair degree of flexibility to adjust the acreage of a particular cereal from year-to-year. An implication of this result is that the own-price elasticity of barley supply is elastic in the long-run, which is acceptable and indicates that price policy might be used successfully to manipulate the barley acreage.

If the reasoning applied to the barley acreage is accepted then the relatively low adjustment coefficient estimated for oats and mixed cereals appears too low. It would certainly be surprising if oats were that much more difficult to adjust than barley, and in any case the high short-run own-price elasticity for oats and mixed cereals suggests a fair degree of flexibility. It may well be, therefore, that the adjustment coefficient for these cereals is also around 0·5, a view which could be supported by some ordinary least-squares estimates of the acreage response of oats and mixed cereals—see for example equations (5.20), (5.25) and (5.31). Even if we accept an adjustment coefficient as high as 0·5, it still indicates a highly elastic long-run responsiveness of oats and mixed cereals to price changes.

Turning to the total cereal acreage, one would of course expect a lower adjustment coefficient than for individual cereals, because it is more difficult to change. In fact all the available estimates of the parameter suggest that it is less than 0·28. This highest estimate is obtained from the simultaneous equations (5.47) and (5.48), whilst slightly lower estimates are obtained from the ordinary least-squares results (5.44) and (5.45). Acceptance of this highest estimate would imply long-run total cereal supply elasticities which exceed those in the short-run by approximately three-and-a-half times. Thus, given that the short-run elasticity of total cereal supply to a general cereal price change is estimated at 0·20, the long-run elasticity would be 0·70. Even acceptance of the lower adjustment coefficient of 0·2 would only imply a unitary long-run supply elasticity. Either estimate suggests that a policy of controlling the level of overall cereal output by means of guaranteed prices may prove costly.

The major implications of the estimated cereal supply model for the operation of a guaranteed price policy may be summarised as follows:

(a) The ability of the policy to stimulate an expansion in wheat production appears to be severely limited.

(b) Increases in the guaranteed price of wheat are as likely to bring about expanded barley output as to encourage wheat production.

(c) The policy could be used effectively to encourage substitution between oats and barley.

(d) It is easier to promote substitution between different cereals than between cereals and other crops.

(e) Because of the interrelationship between dairying and cereal production, expansion of one of these enterprises is likely to cause contraction of the other.

(f) The evidence suggests that in the long-run the barley and oats (including mixed cereals) acreages respond elastically to their own and each other's prices.

C. Assessment of the minimum import price policy

The minimum import price policy operates by imposing levies on imported cereals other than oats and rye, and on some cereal products in order to raise the price which importers have to pay to some minimum level. One of the basic assumptions of this study has been that domestic cereal prices are largely determined by prices on the international market. (See Appendix 1 for an investigation of this assumption.) It may therefore be assumed that raising minimum import prices by a given amount, and making them effective by the imposition of levies, will increase domestic cereal prices by a comparable amount.

It is with certain reservations that this assumption is adopted in this part of the analysis, and one of these concerns its applicability to barley prices at the current time. U.K. barley production has been in surplus for several years and considerable quantities of barley have been exported. Hence no real possibility exists at the current time of making minimum imports' prices for barley effective, that is of imposing the minimum import price by imposing levies on barley imports. Another reservation results from the fact that imported grains are not necessarily of the same quality as those domestically produced. Wheat is the major case in point here; most imported wheat is of milling quality while much domestic production of wheat goes for animal feed. Thus it is possible to make the minimum import price (m.i.p.) effective for milling wheat, but not for feeding wheat, of which little is imported, and, because of the market conditions of substitution between feeding and milling wheat, raising the market price of the latter by operating the m.i.p. policy may not have an equal effect upon the price of the former. Nevertheless, despite these reservations, it will be assumed that the policy can be used to raise the market prices of wheat, barley and maize of all qualities by predetermined amounts, and the current analysis will proceed as if this had been done in 1967-8.

The analysis of the effects of hypothetical cereal price increases in 1967-8 (induced by the m.i.p. policy) will be pursued in three stages, (1) the direct effects upon cereal demand, (2) the effects upon the livestock economy as predicted by the annual livestock inventory equations, and (3) the effects upon the livestock economy as predicted by the quarterly livestock inventory equations.

(1) *The direct effects of cereal price increases on cereal demand*

The equations used to predict demand in Table 27 have been used in Table 31 to estimate the effects on cereal demand of increasing cereal prices by 1 per cent (as a result of implementing the m.i.p. policy). Oats demand is also considered, despite the fact that it is not currently covered by the m.i.p. policy, because the results are of interest.

Table 31: Effect of a 1 per cent increase in cereal prices upon cereal demand in 1967-8[a,b]

	Wheat demand	Barley demand	Oats demand	Maize demand
				(Changes, in tons)
Feed demand	–51,499	–54,857	–2,907	–48,812
Human use demand	–3,334[c]	–1,960	–116[d]	–1,863
		(Change as a percentage of 1967-8 demand)		
Feed demand	2·17	0·90	0·27	1·84
Human use demand	0·07	0·14	0·10	0·18

[a] It is assumed that only the price of the cereal in question has increased. In the feed demand equations for wheat, maize and barley, prices enter as ratios to other cereal prices. If all prices were to rise by 1 per cent simultaneously there would be no predicted change in feed demand.

[b] The same equations were used to obtain these results as were used in predicting cereal demand in Table 31.

[c] A 0·25 per cent increase in the price of bread is assumed.

[d] A 0·5 per cent increase in the price of oats and oatmeal is assumed.

In estimating the effects upon wheat and oats demand for human and industrial use, arbitrary assumptions have had to be made about the impact of cereal price changes upon the final product prices used in the relevant equations ((6.26) and (6.29)). Thus it has been assumed that 1 per cent increases in the wheat and oat prices would increase the prices of bread and of oats and oatmeal by 0·25 and 0·5 per cent respectively.[4]

The size of the predicted demand effects, presented in Table 31, are in line with the price elasticities of demand in the equations used to make the forecasts. Thus the effects of price increases upon feed demand are

[4] This assumes a farm-retail margin, of 75 per cent for processed wheat products, and 50 per cent for processed oats products. These margins are arbitrarily established, below margins known for cereals in the U.S.A., on the assumption that processing and transport costs are less in the U.K. than in the U.S.A. It also assumes that more processing goes into the preparation of wheat products than into oats products. A figure of 85 per cent for farm-retail margins for cereal products in the U.S.A. was obtained from data in, *The Farm Food Marketing Bill and Its Components*, Ag. Econ. Report No. 105, E.R.S., U.S.D.A., Jan. 1967.

relatively and absolutely much greater than the influence upon cereal demand for human and industrial use. This is largely because the substitution between cereals which is possible in animal feeds exceeds that between cereals in their various food and industrial uses. It is the relative price variables in the feed demand equations which reflect this substitutability, the only exception being the feed demand equation for oats which contains simply an oats price variable. It is thus noteworthy that the responsiveness of feed demand for oats to its own price is small relative to that of other cereals.

The relative feed price variables in the feed demand equations for wheat, barley and maize (equations (6.18), (6.12) and (6.14) respectively) have other important implications for the applicability of the model. Consider the predictions by the model of the effects of equiproportional increases in the prices of all feeding cereals induced by the m.i.p. policy. If oats were excluded from the general price increase as it is under the current m.i.p. legislation, then there would be no forecast change in maize demand because *pIB/pIM*, the ratio of the prices of feeding barley and maize, would be unchanged, but there would be a predicted decrease in the demand for wheat and barley. This would occur because of slight increases in the ratios *pIW/pIOC* and *pIB/pIOC* which would result from the fact that a minor component in the denominator of the ratios is the price of feed oats, and this would not increase along with the other components and the numerator. Were the price of oats to rise along with the others, all components of the ratios would rise equiproportionately and there would be no forecast change even in the demand for wheat and barley. Despite the assumption, and empirical demonstration, of a high degree of complementarity between livestock numbers and feed demand, it does not seem realistic to assume no response of cereal demand to a general increase in cereal prices. Indeed, the aggregate feed demand equation, (6.21), predicts that a 1 per cent increase in 1967-8 feeding cereal prices (operating through the variable for the price of high-energy feed) would cause a reduction in cereal feed demand of approximately 40,000 tons. This does not seem infeasible and it suggests that the feed demand equations for individual cereals require the inclusion of price variables which would provide for a reduction in demand if all cereal prices rise simultaneously by the same amount. However, it should be stated that, in estimating the various demand equations a number of simple (as opposed to relative) cereal price variables were tried, but with remarkable lack of success in generating coefficients of appropriate sign. Thus it has not proved possible to estimate functions possessing all the desired properties.

(2) *The indirect effects of cereal price increases on cereal demand via the annual livestock inventory equations*

The effects of cereal price increases upon livestock numbers have been calculated in the following manner. In the case of the annual livestock inventory equations the values of the explanatory variable for 1967-8 have been applied to the chosen equations, and with the exception of the lagged endogenous variables which change with time, these values of the explanatory variables have been assumed to hold in following years. (In the case of the quarterly livestock inventory equations a comparable procedure is adopted using values of the explanatory variables in the second quarter of 1967.) When applied to these static values of the exogenous variables each equation traces out either an upward or a downward growth path—the only case of the latter type is for breeding pigs. The effect of increasing feed prices is to shift the system represented by each equation on to a lower growth path. The reasons for this will become evident below, and result from the negative coefficients of the feed price variables. The equations are all such that there is progressive divergence between the growth paths traced out for different feed prices, until stationarity is achieved for all the paths. Stationarity occurs when long-run equilibrium levels of inventories are achieved with respect to the prevailing (1967-8) prices, that is, when the adjustment processes are fully worked out.

All of the annual inventory equations for total livestock and breeding livestock (the response paths of these latter determine those for fattening livestock) are first-order difference equations of the basic form

(10.1) $$Y_t = bY_{t-1} + a$$

where $b < 1$, and a is a constant which is equal to the summed value of the coefficients of the explanatory variables (other than Y_{t-1}) multiplied by the values of these explanatory variables in 1967-8. If initially $a > (1 - b)Y_{t-1}$ then the equation promotes an upward growth path until the time is reached at which $a = (1 - b)Y_{t-1}$, when equilibrium is attained. Conversely if initially $a < (1 - b)Y_{t-1}$ the growth path will be downward, and equilibrium is achieved with the same condition as for the upward growth path. Whether the growth path is upward or downward is irrelevant to the general effect which a feed price increase has upon livestock numbers. With higher feed prices (or lower product prices) livestock numbers progressively fall below the numbers which would have existed had no price change occurred until both paths reach equilibrium, after which there is no further widening of the gap.

The implication for feed demand of these patterns of response in livestock numbers is that feed price increases will cause demand to fall progressively below the level which would have obtained at the old prices until livestock numbers are fully adjusted to their long-run optimum.

In none of the annual livestock inventory equations used to predict the effect of feed prices upon livestock numbers is the feed price variable coefficient statistically significant, and in the case of the cattle inventory equations the standard errors actually exceed the coefficients of the feed price variables. This lack of statistical significance must be borne in mind in evaluating the ensuing analysis, as at best the errors on the forecasts are large, and at worst the exercise is ill-conceived.

Another property of the feed price coefficients in the annual livestock equations apart from, but not necessarily unconnected with, that of non-significance, is the low elasticity of response that they indicate. In spite of this the predictions in Table 32 show that appreciable reductions in livestock numbers would have occurred in the years 1968-9 onward in response to a 1 per cent increase in cereal prices in 1967-8. It is interesting to note in these results that there is a strong relationship between the direct prediction of the reduction in total cattle numbers, and that obtained by summing the separate predicted effects upon breeding and fattening cattle. By contrast, the predicted fall in total pig numbers greatly exceeds the sum of the separately predicted reductions in breeding- and fattening-pig numbers. It is partially because of this latter result, but primarily because of the absence of suitable livestock unit coefficients for the aggregate livestock classes, that in converting the predicted reductions in livestock numbers to livestock units, breeding and fattening pigs and cattle are converted in preference to the aggregates of these classes, although this will lead to lower estimated reductions in cereal feed demand. (See the bottom half of Table 32.)

In order to estimate the effects of the predicted reduction in livestock numbers on the demand for individual cereals, the livestock units in the bottom half of Table 32 were weighted by cereal consumption weights—there is a different weight for each class of livestock dependent upon the cereal considered—and aggregated by cereal and year. These aggregates were then multiplied by the coefficients of the livestock variable in the appropriate demand equation to calculate the effects on cereal demand of the reduction in livestock numbers. In estimating the effect on total cereal demand by employing equation (6.21), the total reduction in livestock units obtained by summing the columns in the bottom half of the Table, was used without any consumption weights.

Unfortunately the predicted reduction in total cereal demand caused by the predicted decline in livestock numbers exceeds the sum of the separately predicted reductions in demand for individual cereals, although the discrepancy diminishes with time (see Table 33). Hence, in 1968-9 the predicted fall in total cereal demand is approximately twice the sum of the reduced demand for the three individual cereals, but by 1971-2 the forecast ratio is only approximately 5 : 4. However, as previously stated, the coefficient of the livestock variable in the total cereal demand equation (6.21) was large when viewed from a technical standpoint, and hence the forecast reduction in total cereal demand may well be over-estimated. It is more likely that the true effect of the reduction in livestock numbers on cereal demand is approximated by the sum of the predicted effects on the demand for the three individual cereals in Table 33, even though these fail to take account of oats and sorghum demand. Certainly, the coefficients of the livestock variable in the equations underlying these three sets of predictions are more feasible than those in equation (6.21), although even they are on the large side.

One highly acceptable aspect of the results in Table 33 is the proportions of the predicted changes in the demand for the three individual cereals. The proportions are roughly those in which the three cereals are utilised for animal feed—in 1967-8 feed utilisation of barley, wheat and maize was 6,077,000, 2,369,000 and 2,648,000 tons respectively. This similarity in the proportions lends some credence to the results.

On the basis of the results in Table 33 it appears that the 'indirect effect' of a general increase in cereal prices exceeds the 'direct effect'. This statement does however require some qualification.

The results in Table 33 are for a general increase in cereal prices, and thus can only be compared with other effects arising from a similar cause. This rules out direct comparison with the predicted direct effects on feed demand for cereals in the first row of Table 31. However, the food demand predictions in the second row of that table do hold for a general 1 per cent cereal price increase, and amount to a total reduction in demand of 7,273 tons. As far as feed demand for cereals is concerned, the only direct prediction is that from equation (6.21) that a 1 per cent increase in cereal prices causes a 40,000 ton reduction in demand. Thus the total predicted direct effect of a 1 per cent increase in cereal prices is of a cereal demand reduction of 47,273 tons. Given *ceteris paribus* conditions this effect would persist indefinitely. The 'indirect effect' occurs because *ceteris paribus*

Table 32: Effects of a 1 per cent increase in the price of feeding cereals in 1967-8 upon livestock inventories in later years—annual livestock inventory equations

	Total[a] Cattle (9.11)	Breeding[a] Cattle (9.13)	Fattening[a] Cattle (9.15)	Breeding[b] Pigs (9.19)
			(Change in numbers)	
1968-69	–10,195	–3,695	–3,886	–4,233
1969-70	–15,298	–5,597	–6,058	–5,580
1970-71	–17,852	–7,799	–7,271	–6,009
1971-72	–18,935	–8,819	–7,949	–6,146

	Fattening[b] Pigs (9.21)	Total[b] Pigs (9.17)	Fowls[b] (9.22)
		(Change in numbers)	
1968-69	–26,813	–69,887	–168,347
1969-70	–48,895	–105,970	–319,051
1970-71	–55,921	–124,599	–453,958
1971-72	–66,345	–134,218	–574,730

	Total[a] Cattle (9.11)	Breeding[a] Cattle (9.13)	Fattening[a] Cattle (9.15)	Breeding[b] Pigs (9.19)
	(Changes in terms of 1967-8 Livestock Units[c])			
			(Change in numbers)	
1968-69	*d*	−3,931	−2,720	−2,117
1969-70	*d*	−5,955	−4,241	−2,790
1970-71	*d*	−8,298	−5,090	−3,005
1971-72	*d*	−9,383	−5,564	−3,073

	Fattening[b] Pigs (9.21)	Total[b] Pigs (9.17)	Fowls[b] Pigs (9.22)
	(Changes in terms of 1967-8 Livestock Units[c])		
1968-69	−8,741	*d*	−1,683[e]
1969-70	−15,940	*d*	−3,191
1970-71	−18,230	*d*	−4,540
1971-72	−21,628	*d*	−5,747

[a] In these equations the feed price variable is *pF*, the price of all feedingstuffs. It is assumed that a 1 per cent increase in the prices of feeding cereals would cause a 0·6 per cent increase in *pF*.

[b] The price variable in the equation is *pE*, the price of high-energy feed. This was assumed to increase by 1 per cent.

[c] For details of the livestock unit statistics employed in the study, see Appendix II.

[d] No livestock unit coefficients have been employed for aggregate livestock classes, only for subclasses.

[e] The evidence of the quarterly model suggests that most of the change in fowl numbers will be due to broilers and table birds rather than laying fowls. Broilers (for reasons stated in Appendix II) are weighted in 1967-8 at 0·0072 livestock units per bird and laying fowls at 0·018 units. An arbitrary decision has been made to weight each unit in the total fowl aggregate at 0·01 livestock units.

conditions do not hold and cereal price increases cause a drop in livestock numbers with a consequent fall in cereal demand (in addition to the 47,273 tons). If one takes the sum of the predicted reductions in individual cereal feed demand in Table 33 to be the 'indirect effect'—this equals 103,982 tons in 1971-2—then by 1971-2 the forecast 'indirect effect' would be over twice as large as the 'direct effect'. Before accepting this conclusion it is necessary to pose the questions (a) has the 'indirect effect' been overestimated, and (b) has the 'direct effect' been under-estimated?

With respect to the first of these questions, there is on balance no reason to suspect overestimation of the indirect effect. It is true that (a) the livestock variable coefficients in the feed demand equations are high, and (b) that the coefficients of the feed price variables in the annual livestock inventory equations are statistically nonsignificant. Both of these facts might imply overestimation of the effects on feed demand which are transmitted via the livestock economy—the first point would certainly imply it. However, there is a counter to these, which rests on evidence presented in the next section. This is that the quarterly livestock

Table 33: Effects which the predicted reduction in livestock inventories in Table 32 would have upon cereal demand[a, b, c]

	Barley (8.12)	Wheat (8.17)	Maize (8.14)	Total cereals (8.21)
				(Changes in tons)
1968-69	–24,306	–9,202	–9,426	–90,000
1969-70	–41,399	–16,290	–15,129	–150,000
1970-71	–48,144	–20,547	–20,253	–150,000
1971-72	–55,860	–24,757	–23,365	–130,000

[a] It will be remembered that the oats feed demand equations were unsatisfactory and that they do not permit the effect of changes in livestock numbers upon the demand for oats to be calculated.

[b] The predictions of the changes in livestock numbers are for changes at the December census date. The livestock number variables entering the feed demand equations are crude averages produced according to the formula (the number of livestock at $June_t$ + 2(the number of livestock at $December_t$) + the number of livestock at $June_{t+1}$)/4. Thus there is no strict comparability between the annual predictions of livestock inventories and the variables in the feed demand equations; they have nevertheless been treated as comparable for the purposes of this exercise.

[c] The predicted changes in the inventories of breeding and fattening cattle, breeding and fattening pigs, and fowls (predicted in Table 32) were converted by the cereal consumption weights for livestock (see Appendix II), and the resultant changes in consumption weighted livestock units were multiplied by the appropriate coefficients in the feed demand equations.

inventory results indicate that the annual model underestimates the reduction in livestock numbers caused by cereal price increases, and in the main these results are based on coefficients of feed price variables which are statistically significant, which lends added weight to the results. If the annual livestock equations have underestimated the reduction in livestock inventories this would tend to counteract the effect of the large coefficients of the livestock variables in the cereal feed demand equations, and the predicted reductions in demand for individual cereals may be reasonable.

Turning to the second question; first consider the possibility of underestimating the 'direct' reduction in feed demand caused by a cereal price increase, given a fixed number of livestock: It is true that the high-energy feed price coefficient in equation (6.21) is not significantly different from zero, and its true value might therefore be higher. However, there is no reason to suppose that this is the case; for, in examining the feed demand for individual cereals, other than oats, it was not possible to establish a negative relationship between the demand for cereals and their prices expressed in absolute terms. Therefore lack of success in accomplishing this for the aggregate cereal demand equation is not so surprising. The major point, however, concerns the demonstrated complementarity between livestock numbers and feed demand. The strength of this relationship appears to be such that the aggregate amount of cereals required to feed a given number of livestock changes little in response to cereal price changes–in equation (6.21) the simple correlation between feed demand and the number of livestock units is 0·97. What is possible is substitution between different cereals, and the results of the individual cereal demand equations suggest that this happens fairly readily in response to changes in relative cereal prices. Therefore, it appears that a change in the price of one cereal will depress demand for that cereal but so increase the demand for other cereals that the reduction in total cereal feed demand is very small.

As far as underestimating the other component of the direct effect, the change in food demand for cereals, there is no reason to assume that this has been underestimated either. It is widely acknowledged that food demand for basic cereal products is 'highly inelastic to price' and it is not therefore surprising that relatively small changes in demand are estimated. However, it is true that with the exception of maize demand for food, these estimates are based on nonsignificant coefficients of the cereal price variables, but this in itself does not imply that the true coefficients should be larger–rather the contrary.

Thus it seems entirely consistent with the results of this study that the 'direct effect' of an overall cereal price increase on cereal demand is small, and that the more important effect is due to changes in livestock numbers.

(3) *The effects of cereal price increases upon livestock numbers–quarterly livestock inventory equations*

Further light is shed upon the feed-livestock interaction by examining the quarterly livestock inventory equations. In a similar exercise to that performed on the annual model, a 1 per cent increase in feeding cereal prices was assumed to have occurred in the second (June) quarter of 1967, and to have persisted thereafter. The effects of this price change upon livestock numbers were then estimated, the results being presented in Table 34.

In comparing the quarterly results in Table 34 with the annual ones in Table 32, it should be borne in mind that the former cover two harvest years, 1967-8 and 1968-9, while the latter cover four years. It should also be remembered that the annual inventory results are for U.K. livestock, whereas the quarterly results cover England and Wales, although clearly the vast majority of U.K. livestock are to be found in England and Wales.

Nevertheless, there are a number of similarities about the two sets of results which lend mutual support to one another. Consider, for example,

Table 34: Effects of a 1 per cent increase in the price of feeding cereals in the second quarter of 1967 upon livestock inventories in later quarters–quarterly livestock inventory equations

(Changes in numbers)

	Breeding[a] cattle (7.26)	Calves slaughtered (7.28)	Fat cattle: effect of breeding stock (7.29)	Fat cattle: effect of calf slaughter (7.29)	Fat Cattle: effect of fat cattle (7.29)
1967					
3rd qtr.	–5,455	–1,113			
4th qtr.	–9,765	–2,348			
1968					
1st qtr.	–13,171	–3,912			
2nd qtr.	–15,861	–5,427		+304	
3rd qtr.	–17,762	–6,640		+1,148	+227
4th qtr.	–19,489	–7,552	–830	+2,421	+1,060
1969					
1st qtr.	–20,854	–8,292	–1,486	+4,034	+1,972
2nd qtr.	–21,931	–8,888	–2,005	+5,596	+3,363

(Changes in numbers)

	Fat cattle: net effect (7.29)	Breeding pigs (7.32)	Fattening pigs (7.38)	Other sows (7.39)	Broiler & table fowls (7.41)
1967					
3rd qtr.		–1,180	–6,689	–291	–80,000
4th qtr.		–2,259	–6,689	–767	–150,000
1968					
1st qtr.		–3,245	–6,689	–1,203	–300,000
2nd qtr.	+304	–4,146	–19,134	–1,600	–310,000
3rd qtr.	+1,375	–4,971	–30,517	–1,964	–390,000
4th qtr.	+2,651	–5,724	–40,911	–2,296	–450,000
1969					
1st qtr.	+4,520	–6,413	–50,413	–2,601	–500,000
2nd qtr.	+6,954	–7,043	–59,114	–2,877	–650,000

(Changes in terms of 1967-8 livestock units)[b]

	Breeding[a] cattle (7.26)	Calves slaughtered (7.28)	Fat cattle: effect of breeding stock (7.29)	Fat cattle: effect of calf slaughter (7.29)	Fat cattle: effect of fat cattle (7.29)
1967					
3rd qtr.	−5,804	[c]			
4th qtr.	−10,390				
1968					
1st qtr.	−14,014				
2nd qtr.	−16,876			+213	
3rd qtr.	−18,899			+804	+159
4th qtr.	−20,736		−581	+1,695	+742
1969					
1st qtr.	−22,189		−1,040	+2,824	+1,380
2nd qtr.	−23,335		−1,404	+3,917	+2,354

(Changes in terms of 1967-9 livestock units)[b]

	Fat cattle net effect (7.29)	Breeding pigs (7.32)	Fattening pigs (7.38)	Other sows (7.39)	Broiler & table fowls (7.41)
1967					
3rd qtr.		−590	−2,181	−146	−576
4th qtr.		−1,130	−2,181	−384	−1,080
1968					
1st qtr.		−1,623	−2,181	−602	−2,160
2nd qtr.	+213	−2,073	−6,238	−800	−2,223
3rd qtr.	+963	−2,486	−10,275	−982	−2,808
4th qtr.	+1,856	−2,862	−13,337	−1,148	−3,240
1969					
1st qtr.	+3,164	−3,207	−16,435	−1,301	−3,600
2nd qtr.	+4,868	−3,522	−19,271	−1,439	−4,680

[a] The price variable in (7.26) was the price of compound feedingstuffs for cattle. This was assumed to increase by 0·6 per cent as a result of a 1 per cent increase in cereal feed prices.

[b] For details of the livestock unit statistics employed in the study, see Appendix II.

[c] Calf slaughter is not an inventory variable, it is a flow, and therefore cannot be assessed in terms of livestock units.

the predicted changes in breeding- and fattening-pig inventories. For both of these the level at which the difference in numbers, caused by a 1 per cent cereal price increase, arrives at stationarity appears likely to be similar whether predicted by the annual or the quarterly model. Additional support for the annual results by the quarterly ones with respect to the feed price effect, is afforded by the statistical properties of the coefficients of the feed price variables in the quarterly livestock inventory equations. In the breeding inventory equation (7.32) this coefficient is highly significant and in the fattening-pig inventory equation (7.38) it exceeds its standard error. Thus the size of the indirect effect predicted by the quarterly equations is of similar size to that obtained from the annual equations, but rests on coefficients which are more acceptable in a statistical sense. The feed price variable coefficient is also significant in the quarterly equation for the inventories of sows not in pig, equation (7.39).

Similarly, there is some agreement in the predicted change in fowl numbers obtained from the annual and quarterly models. In fact the quarterly prediction, which is for broiler and table fowls only in England and Wales, is of a somewhat larger change than that for total fowl numbers obtained from the annual equation, (7.22). It was this quarterly result which suggested that a large part of the annually predicted change in total fowl numbers might be in broiler numbers, and that a large weighting should be given to broilers in estimating a livestock unit coefficient for an average member of the total fowl aggregate.

In the case of cattle inventories there is considerable difference between the two models in their predictions of the impact of a cereal price increase. The peculiarities of the quarterly fat-cattle inventory prediction have already been explained in the previous chapter, and must be discounted because of the failure to satisfactorily identify the relationship between breeding cattle and fat-cattle numbers. However, comparison of the two forecasts of the change in breeding-cattle numbers is valid, and it is clear that the quarterly equation predicts a larger change than does the annual one. As the feed price coefficient in the quarterly equation (7.26) is statistically significant, whereas that in the annual equation (7.13) was not, it appears most likely that the annually predicted effects of a cereal feed price increase upon cattle numbers have been underestimated and that in consequence so have the 'indirect' effects upon cereal feed demand.

Because of the perversity of the fat-cattle inventory predictions in the quarterly model it has been decided not to perform the last stage of the exercise done with the annual livestock equations, that of calculating the effect of the reduction in livestock numbers upon cereal feed demand. However the evidence of the quarterly results is that, if anything, the effects on feed demand predicted by the annual livestock equations are under-estimates. This is so for the following reasons: (a) with the exception of fat cattle, the quarterly equations predict reductions in livestock numbers which are as large, and in a number of cases larger, than those obtained with the annual equations, (b) the quarterly livestock results cover only England and Wales, while the annual ones cover the whole U.K., and (c) the feed price coefficients in the quarterly equations are statistically more satisfactory than in the annual equations, thus lending more weight to the quarterly than to the annual results. This last point has the additional importance of signifying that the relationship between feed prices and livestock numbers is an important one, and should be studied in an examination of cereal price policy effects.

D. Implications for the application of the minimum import price policy

The principal objectives of the m.i.p. policy are to reduce exchequer costs in the payment of subsidies to cereal producers, and to reduce imports so as to save foreign exchange. The first objective is automatically achieved if the market prices of cereals are raised, although it will be offset to some extent by additional subsidies to livestock producers. These are likely to result from the fact that changes in costs, including those of feed, are taken into account in determining the guaranteed prices for pigs and eggs.

As far as the second objective is concerned, the ability to save foreign exchange, the answer is less clear. The annual model predicts that a 1 per cent increase in all cereal prices in 1967-8 (hypothetically caused by increased m.i.p.s) would have caused the demand for wheat, barley, maize and oats to fall below what it would otherwise have been by approximately 150,000 tons (47,273 + 103,982) by 1971-2. There would, however, be further reductions to come since the adjustment of livestock numbers to their long-run equilibrium levels would still not be fully accomplished by 1971-2. Demand for the four cereals in 1967-8 was 20,314,000 tons. Therefore after full adjustment of the livestock economy it appears that a 1 per cent overall cereal price increase might eventually cause demand for the four cereals to fall by about 1 per cent, or 200,000 tons. Taken on its own, and assuming that net imports were reduced by the full 200,000 tons, this implies that even if foreign cereal suppliers raised their prices to the m.i.p. levels there would eventually be no extra loss of foreign exchange—the unitary elasticity of demand case. But in the interim years, before full adjustment, when demand would be less than 1 per cent below what it would otherwise have been, there would be an increase of foreign exchange costs if the offer price of imported cereals were raised to the m.i.p. level. If overseas suppliers did not increase their offer prices for cereals, then the foreign exchange costs of cereal imports would decline, and the Exchequer would receive extra revenue.

However the principal cause of any reduction in cereal demand appears to be due to a fall in livestock numbers. This would cause a reduction in livestock output, which would necessitate addition livestock product imports at a foreign exchange cost which might well exceed that which ought to be saved on cereal imports. Hence, even if foreign suppliers do not increase the offer prices of their cereals there may well be no saving of foreign exchange.[5] If they do increase their offer price to m.i.p. levels then it seems inevitable that there will be an increase in foreign exchange outflows. It should be pointed out that the effects of increasing cereal prices upon the livestock sector are so large as to put the m.i.p. policy in serious conflict with other current major policies aimed at the livestock sector. These policies aim at increasing the output of beef and bacon, and of sustaining the growth of output of pork and eggs so as to meet the growth in demand.[6] The success of these policies could be severely restricted if feed prices are increased.

The implications just discussed are those of an equiproportional change in the prices of all cereals simultaneously. It does, however, also appear that manipulating minimum import prices so as to alter the relative prices of cereals could be done to some effect. Evidence provided by the cereal demand results suggests that feed demand for all of the cereals, except oats, depends upon the relative prices of cereals, as does barley demand for food and industrial purposes. The U.K. has in a number of recent years had a considerable surplus of feeding quality barley which had not been absorbed domestically at prevailing prices, and which was proving increasingly difficult to export. At the same time maize continued to be imported on a considerable scale; in 1967-8, 2,648,000 tons were used for animal feed and 1,008,000 tons for human and industrial purposes. Feed demand for maize and barley, and barley demand for food, all appear to be fairly sensitive to the relative prices of maize and barley. Thus it would seem to be possible to increase barley demand and decrease that for imported maize by raising the m.i.p. of maize so as to increase its market price relative to that of barley. Similar adjustments in minimum import prices could be made to encourage substitution between other cereals in animal feed uses. It does therefore appear that the m.i.p. policy could be used to solve the problems raised by the emergence of short-term surpluses of domestically produced cereals. These problems are that in a free market the surpluses could only be disposed of if prices fell to levels which might considerably reduce returns to farmers if target indicator price revisions are operative, or greatly increase Exchequer costs if they are not. Neither of these problems would arise if the supply of cereals from overseas was effectively reduced by the imposition of high import levies.

[5] It should be made clear that there are other economic costs imposed by the application of minimum import prices. For a full analysis of these see Josling, T. E., op. cit.

[6] See the Annual Price Review White Paper for 1969, Cmnd. 3965.

9

Perspective

An attempt has been made in this study to estimate a set of economic and technical relationships which provide insight into the manner and extent to which government cereal pricing policies influence the agricultural sector. To accomplish this, it has been deemed necessary to examine the determinants of livestock numbers in addition to cereal supply and demand. Because of the policy-oriented objectives it was felt to be necessary to employ a positive rather than a normative type of analysis; that is, it was decided to try and discover what agriculture's collective responses to certain economic stimuli actually would be as opposed to what these responses ought to be under certain assumed behavioural norms. Multiple regression analysis applied to industry level time-series data appeared to be the most appropriate methodology for this purpose, and has hence been employed throughout.

This type of methodology is not without its problems, and a number of these have been encountered during this study. One set of problems has arisen because of the rapid technological changes which have occurred in agriculture during the period 1954 to 1970. In consequence many relevant variables have exhibited either increasing or declining trends. This has posed problems in the use of distributed lag analysis, where the dependent, and hence also the lagged dependent variable, have moved in a strongly secular manner. Because these trends may be due, in part at least, to technological (or social) factors which are not quantifiable and cannot therefore be properly considered in analysis, it seems probable that their cause may have been credited to the lagged endogenous variable. This would cause the coefficients of such variables to be biased upward and distort the estimated long-run elasticities. Nevertheless, after a considerable amount of experimentation, estimates of long-run elasticities of cereal supply and livestock inventory adjustment were obtained which were adjudged to be satisfactory on *a priori* grounds.

Another problem arising from the existence of pronounced trends in many variables is that of multicollinearity, which may give rise to instability in the estimated coefficients and a tendency for these estimates to have large standard errors. This, plus the problem of absence of suitable data in some instances, led to the estimation of a large number of alternative formulations of some relationships (particularly of acreage responses) in an attempt to minimise the impact of these difficulties. This search for the most satisfactory set of equations, for the 'final model', has required the evaluation of a large amount of statistical information, and even at the end of this lengthy procedure it has been necessary in some cases to accept as a final best estimate an equation in which not all the coefficients are statistically significant. Statistical significance is however only one test of the acceptability of a result, and the lack of it is often insufficient grounds for rejecting an estimate of the influence of a particular variable. Where such a variable is considered to play an important role for theoretical or technical reasons it may be unwise to reject it solely on grounds of statistical significance. Similarly if an estimated coefficient is close to its expected value, or where alternative estimates of a coefficient show a high degree of consistency there may be sufficient grounds for accepting a statistically non-significant coefficient.

In spite of the various problems mentioned this study appears to have identified a number of interesting and important relationships. Detailed and lengthy statements have been made in the four preceding chapters concerning the attributes of those equations considered to have the most acceptable properties, and will not be fully reiterated again. However it does seem appropriate to restate the major empirical conclusions of the study.

The own and cross-price elasticities of supply for barley and oats appear to be elastic in the long-run and to be of moderate size, although inelastic, in the short-run. This suggests a much greater degree of responsiveness of cereal supply to producer prices than previous research has indicated, and implies that policies of controlling such prices may be employed to modify the composition of cereal supply with some hope of success. It should be recognised however that the full effects of such policy changes will not be felt within the space of a single year. This does not always appear to be recognised by the authors of the annual Price Review, and the language of these documents frequently conveys the impression that the results of policy changes are expected to be achieved quickly. Clearly the adoption of such an attitude, possibly allied to the use of incomplete models to explain short-run supply changes, may lead to over-frequent adjustment of guaranteed prices under the policy.

Wheat in contrast appears to have an inelastic supply response to price, and hence to be rather insensitive to changes in guaranteed price policy. In view of the fact that policy statements accompanying the annual Price Review frequently indicate that increased wheat price guarantees are offered in order to elicit more wheat output, this result is of considerable significance. It was also found that total cereal supply seems to be price inelastic even in the long-run. This result, which is corroborated by previous research,[1] indicates the limitations of cereal supply control by means of short-term adjustments of producer prices. Furthermore it has been indicated that there is a trade-off between the total cereal acreage and that of grassland. This suggests that expansion of cereal supply can, as should be expected on technical grounds, only be achieved at the cost

[1] See the previously cited works by B. Hill, G. T. Jones, and Rachel Dardis.

of reduced agricultural output elsewhere, probably in dairying. The existence of this trade-off suggests a conflict between policy objectives which does not appear to receive much explicit recognition in the announced policy statements.

Similar conflicts between policy objectives appear likely to arise in the application of the minimum import price (m.i.p.) policy. Where minimum import prices are employed to support producer prices, as may be the case in future, the remarks addressed to the guaranteed price policy in previous paragraphs will apply. A different set of conflicts emerge when, as at present, the m.i.p. policy is used to influence user prices paid for cereals—these will occur on the assumption that m.i.p. changes cause parallel adjustments of the floor prices for cereals in the U.K. market. Application of the m.i.p. policy to raise U.K. market prices for cereals in this way can be invested with two main objectives; one of these is to reduce and control the Exchequer's liability for deficiency payments to cereal growers; the other is to reduce the volume of cereal imports (and possibly also foreign exchange costs, although the current policy arrangements do not seem to assure this consequence). This latter objective requires that cereal demand as a whole should decline as minimum import prices for cereals are raised. The results obtained suggest that even in the long-run total cereal demand only has a price elasticity of approximately unity. Furthermore, the largest part of the change in cereal consumption implied by this elasticity results from induced changes in livestock numbers rather than from changes in feed and food consumption for given numbers of livestock and the human population. Hence any reduction in cereal demand caused by higher minimum import prices seems likely to be achieved at a cost of reduced livestock production of all types. The additional livestock imports which may result from this reduction of domestic livestock production may well cancel out any foreign exchange gains from reduced cereal imports. Alternatively, additional livestock price guarantees in order to maintain the level of U.K. livestock production may well offset any reduction in the value of deficiency payments to cereal growers.[2]

One interesting and noteworthy feature of the supply results concerns technical interdependence in the growing of cereals. This is manifest in the estimated model by a causal chain reaction in which later sown cereals compensate for the influence of weather fluctuations upon cereals sown earlier. This chain effect runs from winter wheat to spring wheat to barley, oats and mixed cereals. Previous econometric work on U.K. cereal supply has tended to overlook this technical interdependence between cereals, a circumstance which may have hindered previous attempts to uncover price elasticities of cereal supply. A similar type of interrelationship has

[2] For a detailed formal examination of the trade-offs between policy objectives when minimum import prices or guaranteed producer prices are imposed see Josling, T. E., op. cit.

been found between livestock of different ages and types in the course of estimating the livestock inventory equations. Clearly, technical interdependence between enterprises is an accepted feature of agriculture, and it is right that it should be reflected in supply equations which purport to have structural properties.

In conclusion it may be appropriate to attempt to answer questions about the usefulness of the work presented in this book. On the one hand the work may have instructive value to those who wish to study cereal pricing policies or who are interested in the construction of formal systems for the examination of such policies. On the other hand it is hoped that the work will become part of the basic stock of information drawn upon when policy decisions are being formulated. While there are reasons to suppose that the scholarly function may be fulfilled, nagging doubts persist that empirical studies with meaningful content for policy making fail to accomplish their mission in this regard. Such doubts stem from the judgement that the mechanisms are weak whereby U.K. agricultural policy-making organisations incorporate empirical information of econometric origin into their decision-making process. This may be due partially to misconceptions of the way in which this type of information can be used.

It is not, for example, appropriate to advocate that empirical relationships of the type which have been presented contain all the necessary information needed for decision making, usually they do not. These relationships may however be a source of some crucial information such as price elasticities which may be difficult to obtain by other means. This information should be treated along with information from other sources as part of the basic stock of *a priori* information.

One way in which a stock of information from diverse sources might be used is in the development of simulation models of the agricultural industry. In this context a simulation model is seen as a set of equations which are rendered consistent, where the structural form and parameter values are imposed (rather than directly estimated) to accord with *a priori* information from the various available sources. Implicitly such a model lies behind any policy decision, and there would seem to be virtue in trying to formalise it. Any such venture requires that new *a priori* information be generated in order that the simulation system can be adapted to the changing character of the economic system. This changing character often means that econometrically estimated parameters are not constant as assumed, but are continuously changing. Thus it is necessary for the econometric work to be continually updated and revised if it is to prove a satisfactory source of information for policy making.

Development of simulation systems along the lines suggested is only likely to be accomplished if the organisations responsible for policy formation, primarily the Ministries of Agriculture, Fisheries and Food, can be persuaded to express sufficient interest in such work. But more than this, the work required to develop these decision-making aids is wasted unless policy-making bodies are prepared to use such aids alongside their traditional methods in order to assess their worth. Only under these conditions can the efficacy of this type of work finally be assessed. Ideally, testing of this type would require the setting up of a specialised research department within the Ministry of Agriculture to accept responsibility for the testing and development of the formal models of the agricultural economy.[3] A number of other vital functions could then be performed by this research body. It would be able to perform the essential job of updating the content and form of the decision-making aids which had been developed. It would provide a two-way link between independent research and policy makers. In one direction this would involve the collection and sorting of the research of a number of scattered individuals in order to establish which results improve the stock of knowledge. In the other direction the research department would, because of its role in assessing empirical work, be in an ideal position to establish priorities for new research. As an adjunct to this, the organisation could act as assessor for the allocation of research patronage. Therefore, on a number of counts, it would appear desirable to establish a practicing central agricultural economic research organisation to help econometric and other empirical research in agriculture to achieve its declared aims. In particular, the creation of such a body would give greater relevance to the type of work which has been presented here, as well as providing the stimulus for fuller development of this kind of research.

[3] Organisations of this type are found for example within the United States Department of Agriculture.

Appendix I

Relationship between international and U.K. grain prices[1]

It is generally accepted that the market for cereals in the United Kingdom is an open one, and that the market prices which prevail are basically world prices.[2] The validity of this assumption is crucial in determining which are the appropriate structures to describe the working of the U.K. cereal economy. Thus an attempt is made in this Appendix to justify the assumption. The approach adopted is to demonstrate the existence of a relationship between the prices received by U.K. cereal producers net of subsidy and those paid for imported supplies of similar quality. The argument that the relationship which exists is not accidental but causal depends to a large extent upon the way in which prices of imported grains have behaved in international markets, and thus it seems appropriate to consider the movements in international cereal prices over the study period.

A. Movements in international cereals prices

A study of international cereals prices over the period 1955-1965 reveals a number of interesting features.[3] Firstly, the broad price trends have been similar for all grains, falling from 1955 to 1958, remaining at roughly the same level until 1961, and then showing a subsequent increase. Despite this broad correspondence of movement, there have been large differences in the degree of price variability between different grains; Figures 7a and 7b demonstrate this quite clearly. Hard wheat, maize, and sorghum prices have remained relatively stable and have shown a low degree of inter-year variability. Soft French wheat has shown a less stable pattern, its price movements being more closely allied to changes in the price of coarse grains than to those of hard wheat. In contrast, a high degree of variability has been exhibited by the prices of barley, oats and rye.

These differences in the stability of the international prices of cereals may be attributed to a number of factors. In the case of wheat the role of the International Wheat Agreement in stabilising wheat prices should be

[1] Much of the material in this section has been published in the author's contribution to Britton, D. K., *Cereals in the United Kingdom; Production, Marketing and Utilisation*, pp. 617-625. Pergamon Press, Feb. 1969. With permission of Pergamon Press Ltd.

[2] This view should be modified somewhat as a result of the imposition of minimum import prices for cereals from 1964 onwards, but in view of the lack of vigour with which these have been applied thus far the modification is not a serious one.

[3] This brief summary is based on an article by Mrs. A. K. Binder, 'Relationships in World Prices of Coarse Grains and Some Implications for an International Grains Agreement', Food and Agriculture Organisation of the U.N., *Monthly Bulletin of Agricultural Economics and Statistics*, Vol. 15, No. 9, Sept. 1966, pp. 1-15.

acknowledged. The Agreement, by effectively assuring the major wheat exporters of a large stable market with an announced price range, has created an environment in which the two largest exporters, Canada and the U.S.A., have been prepared to hold large stocks of wheat, and to control the size of these stocks in such a way that the realised price of Manitoba No. 1 wheat has remained within the established price range since 1953-4.[4]

Maize and sorghum price stability is largely due to the dominant role played by the U.S.A., in the markets for these two grains. In 1966 United States exports accounted for 64 per cent of the world maize exports and 81 per cent of world sorghum exports. During the same year, the U.S.A. as the only major holder of stocks, carried stocks of maize and sorghums equivalent to 88 and 109 per cent, respectively, of the volume of world trade in these grains, a reduction of more than half from the stock levels of 1961, when the U.S.A. carry-over of these grains was at its peak. As a result of this dominance the price of maize from other exporting nations has remained close to U.S.A. prices at all times, and the price of sorghum has maintained a steady relationship with–on average 10 per cent below–the price of maize.

The volatility of the international prices of barley, oats, and rye has been such, that not only have their relative prices changed with respect to the prices of other cereals, from year-to-year, but so also have their relative prices to one another. Reasons for this price instability may be attributed to the characteristics of the markets for these grains. Firstly, no country dominates the export market for these grains to the extent that the U.S.A. (and Canada in the case of wheat) does for the grains previously mentioned. Secondly, in contrast with the positions of hard wheat, maize and sorghums, the stocks of barley, oats and rye held by exporting countries are small relative to the total volume traded, and thus no buffer stock is available to insulate prices from the effects of changes in demand or supply. A third contrast arises with respect to the demand situation for barley, oats and rye. For, whereas hard wheat, maize and sorghum are exported mainly to countries which do not produce close substitutes themselves, some of the major importers of barley, oats and rye produce substantial proportions of their own requirements of these cereals. Thus fluctuations in the production of these crops by the importing countries may cause considerable variation in the level of trade.

It is interesting to note the implications of the observed price movements of cereals for the substitutability of cereals for one another in different uses. While milling wheat and high quality malting barley prices might be expected to have some independence of coarse grain prices, it would seem reasonable to expect coarse grains prices to move closely together. That the relative prices of coarse grains to one another change from year-to-year

[4] See: International Wheat Council, *International Wheat Prices.* Secretariat Paper No. 1, Dec. 1961, p. 35.

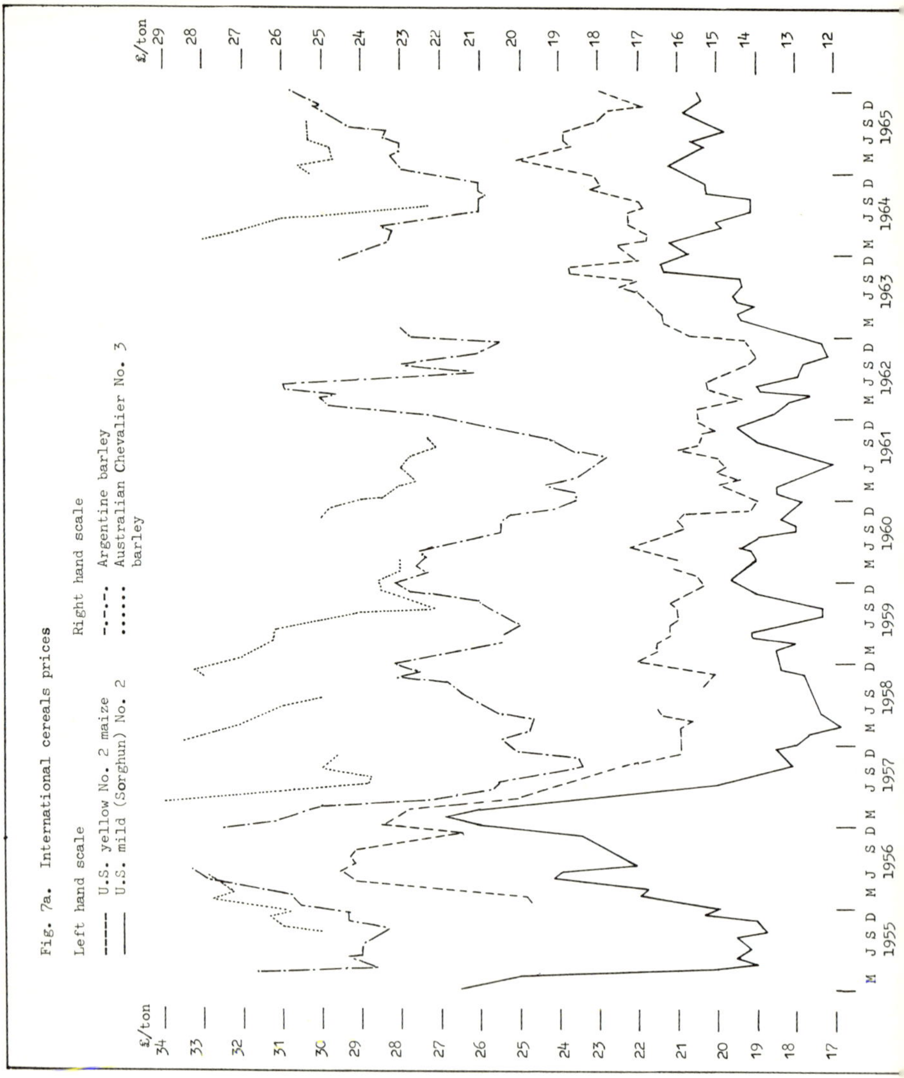

Fig. 7a. International cereals prices

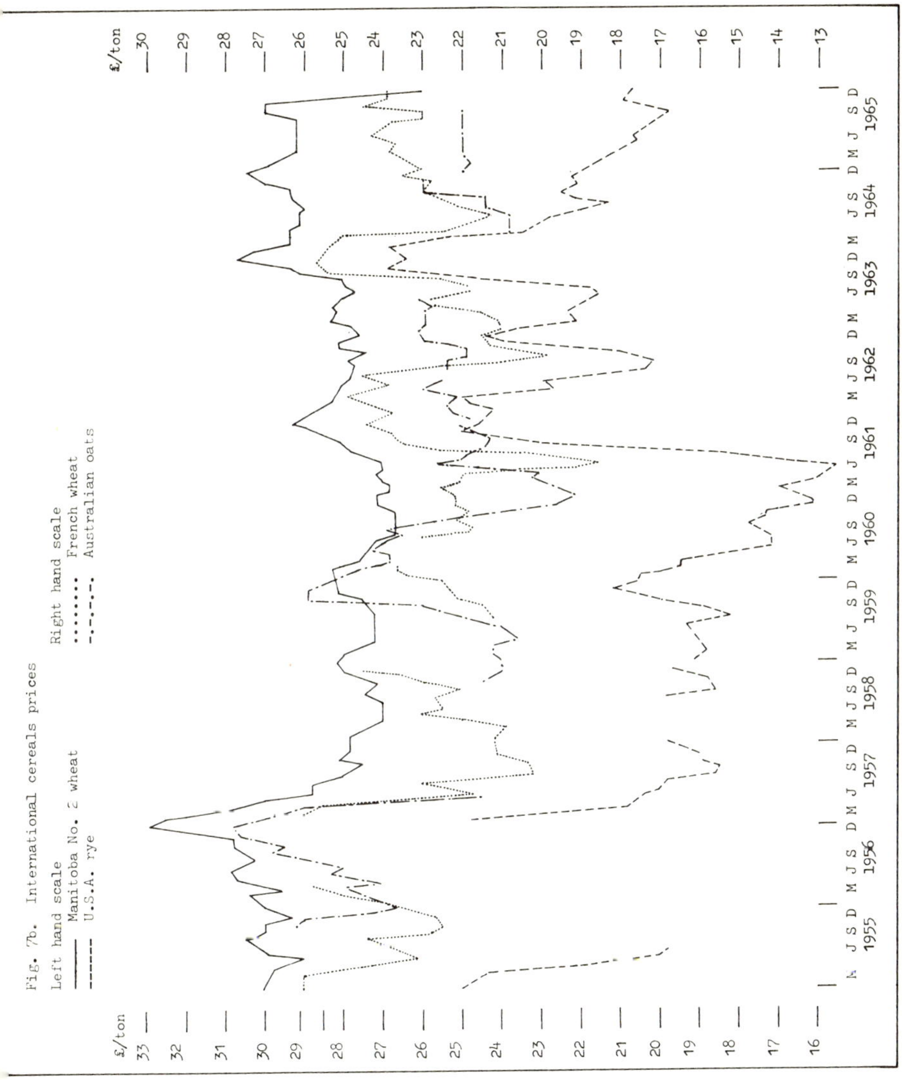

Fig. 7b. International cereals prices

suggests some limits to the substitutability between them. This is not wholly surprising in view of the inflexible nature of some demand for industrial uses, and of the large demand for compounding with its built-in resistance to changes in the composition of proprietary feeds.

B. Analysis of the difference between imported and home-produced cereal prices

The data used in this analysis are the following:

'Cereal Prices Paid to Growers' excluding cereals deficiency payments, as recorded at the ports of Bristol, Hull, Liverpool and London, have been used to represent the prices of all domestic cereals.[5] For the prices of imported wheat, barley and oats of feeding quality, the average market prices of ex-store lots of imported grain at the ports of Bristol, Hull, Liverpool and London have been used, and these are recorded on the same basis as the series used for domestic grains prices.[6] The price of Manitoba Northern No. 2 wheat c.i.f. U.K. ports, was used for the price of imported milling wheat, and Argentine Plate barley c.i.f. North Sea ports for the price of imported malting barley.[6] This latter series of prices is rather low for barley of malting quality, but as it can be shown that the prices of barley from all overseas sources move closely together it seems reasonable to accept it as an appropriate indicator.

The analysis, which has been performed on the difference between imported and domestic cereals prices, consists simply of subtracting the monthly U.K. price from the imported price, for the period January 1955 to December 1965, and studying the patterns of the differentials. The results are summarised in Figure 8, which presents the average differential in selected years for five types of domestically produced cereals.

A clear similarity in the pattern of the price differential is evident for all five classes of cereals. After the U.K. harvest of July, August and September, domestic cereal prices fall rapidly, and there is a large positive differential of prices of imported over domestic grains; in the case of malting barley U.K. prices fall rapidly after harvest so that the negative differential is eliminated (Figure 8d). A peak differential is rapidly reached, in August for both wheats, September for feeding barley, November for feeding oats, and in December for malting barley, after which domestic prices improve steadily relative to the prices of imported cereals so that the price differential declines–increases in the case of malting barley.

In the cases of milling wheat and malting barley there have been major differences in the seasonal pattern of the price differential in some years. Figure 8c indicates that, while six of the years exhibited the 'normal' seasonal pattern, in four years the prices of U.K. milling wheat fell relative to the prices of imported wheat in the later months of the harvest year. The

[5] The source of these data is M.A.F.F., *Agricultural Statistics, England and Wales.*

[6] The source of these data is Mrs. A. K. Binder, op. cit., pp. 12-15.

Fig. 8. Average price differences between imported and U.K. cereals prices
Jan, 1955 - Dec, 1965

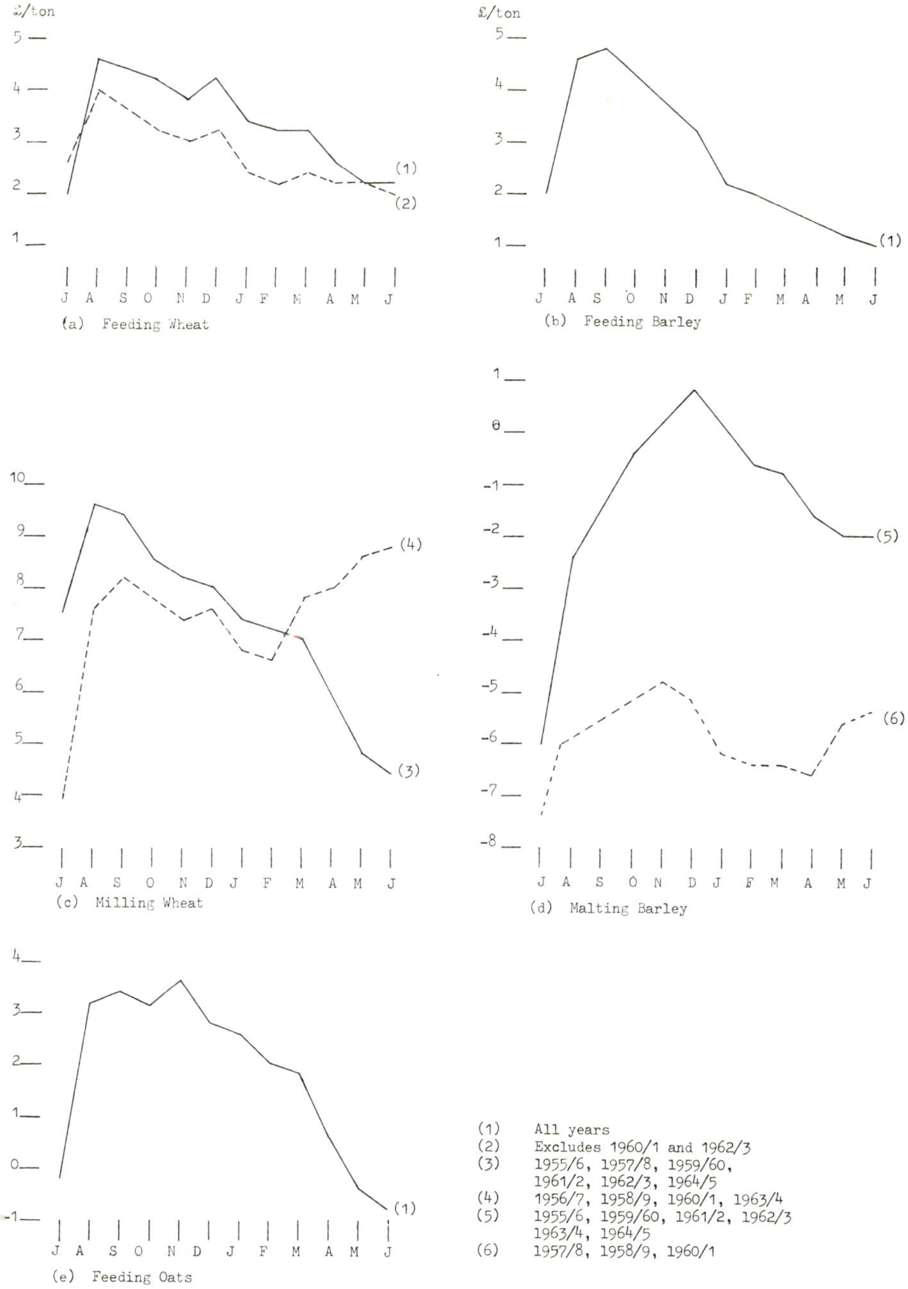

reason for this difference in these four years appears to be attributable to the high level of unsold stocks of wheat on farms at the end of those years. In the three years 1958-9, 1960-1 and 1963-4 (no data on unsold stocks are available for 1956-7), unsold wheat stocks on farms at the end of April were the equivalent of 15, 14 and 17 per cent of the year's crop respectively, as opposed to an average of 8 per cent in other years. In two of these years, 1956-7 and 1960-1, and to a lesser extent in 1958-9, the high levels of these unsold stocks may themselves be attributed to the relatively large wheat harvests, and in 1963-4, difficulty was experienced in selling the crop of domestic wheat, unsold wheat stocks were large, and prices fell in the latter part of the season in comparison with prices of imported wheat as farmers tried to reduce their holdings of wheat. With the malting barley price differential the case is different. It is not that the basic pattern of the price differential varied, but that in three years, 1957-8, 1958-9 and 1960-1, the amount by which the price of U.K. malting barley exceeded that of imported supplies was markedly greater than in other years (see Figure 8d). This major difference resulted from the extremely low prices which were

Table 35: Results of regressing the price difference between imported and U.K. grains upon monthly dummy variables–July as the base month*

	Milling wheat 1955-6, 1957-8, 1959-60, 1961-2, 1962-3 & 1964-5	Milling wheat 1956-7, 1958-9, 1960-1 & 1963-4	Feeding wheat 1954-1965	Malting barley 1955-6, 1959-60, 1961-2, 1962-3, 1963-4 & 1964-5
July-constant	7·4	3·9	2·3	–6·1
Aug.	+2·2	+3·6	+1·8	+2·7
Sep.	+2·1	+4·2	+1·6	+3·9
Oct.	+1·2	+3·8	+1·4	+5·4
Nov.	+0·8	+3·5	+1·9	+6·2
Dec.	+0·7	+3·6	+0·9	+6·8
Jan.	+0·1	+2·9	+0·3	+6·3
Feb.	0·2	+2·9	+0·2	+5·6
Mar.	–0·5	+3·9	+0·4	+5·2
Apr.	–1·6	+4·1	+0·5	+4·3
May	–2·7	+4·7	+0·6	+4·0
Jun.	–3·0	+4·9	+0·4	+4·1
R^2	0·62	0·60	0·20	0·71
$\overline{R}^2$	0·55	0·48	0·04	0·64
$\frac{d^2}{s^2}$	0·38	0·83	0·74	0·73

	Malting barley 1957-8, 1958-9 & 1960-1	Feeding barley 1954-1965	Feeding oats 1954-1965
July-constant	−7·5	2·2	4·9
Aug.	+1·4	+2·4	+3·2
Sep.	+1·8	+2·5	+3·6
Oct.	+2·3	+2·2	+3·2
Nov.	+2·7	+1·7	+3·5
Dec.	+2·3	+1·1	+2·8
Jan.	+1·3	+0·7	+2·5
Feb.	+1·2	+0·5	+2·4
Mar.	+1·2	+0·1	−1·9
Apr.	+1·0	−0·3	+0·5
May	+2·0	−0·6	−0·3
Jun.	+2·3	−0·7	−0·6
R^2	0·18	0·59	0·25
$\bar{R}^2$	−0·27	0·55	0·14
$\frac{d^2}{s^2}$	0·83	0·49	0·45

* The coefficient for July is the intercept term, and the values against the other months are the coefficients of the dummy variables for those months.

obtained for barley in international markets during the period from August 1957 to September 1961, and from the fact that prices for domestic malting barley held up well, except in 1958-9 when they dropped following a particularly large increase in the size of the barley crop over that of previous years.

Needless to say, the use of average relationships, as in Figure 8, obscures the degree of year-to-year variability in the seasonal price differential, and if this variability were high the conclusions drawn could be misleading. However, for milling wheat, malting barley and feeding barley the variability about the respective seasonal patterns is low. This is indicated in the multiple correlation coefficients (R^2 and R^{-2}) obtained by regressing the difference between the imported and domestic prices of these grains upon a set of monthly dummy variables (see Table 35). For both feeding wheat and feeding oats the seasonal price variability is large, and in the case of the former the removal of the price differentials for 1960-1 and 1962-3 causes a marked fall in the average price difference (see Figure 8a). The high degree of variability in the price differentials for these grains is manifest in the low multiple correlation coefficients obtained for the regressions of their monthly price differences (given in Table 35). However, the similarity in the shape of the average seasonal price differentials of feeding wheat and oats to those of the grains whose price patterns exhibit relative stability appears to justify both their presentation and the derivation of general conclusions about the prices of all grains.

It will be seen from Table 35 that the Von-Neumann ratios for all the regressions are low, indicating the existence of positive serial correlation in the residuals. This is due to the price differentials for sequences of months being either all greater or lower than the average values given by the coefficients of the dummy variables. This suggests that the price differentials between imported and domestic grain are influenced by factors other than the seasons of the year, but it has not been possible to isolate these. However in spite of reservations concerning the existence of serial correlation it is apparent that there exists a general pattern of price differences between U.K. and imported grains, and that this pattern exists in spite of large year-to-year variations in the pattern of international grain prices. It has been seen from Figures 8a and 8b that in some years international grain prices rise, and in other fall steadily throughout the year. But, nevertheless, U.K. grain prices differ from these in the systematic way of the 'normal' seasonal price differential.

C. Conclusions

It is possible to conclude, therefore, that there is a relationship between world and U.K. cereals prices, which causes them to differ from one another in a predetermined and relatively stable manner. The seasonal nature of this relationship between these two sets of prices may be explained by, what could be described as, the seasonal difference of interaction between the U.K. and international cereals markets. This can be explained as follows:

In the immediate post-U.K. harvest period, there are ample supplies of domestic grains, and these will substitute for imported grains of similar quality. The limits of substitution are however low, in, that, for example, soft domestic wheats cannot replace hard wheats in milling, and that maize is only replaceable to a small extent by barley or wheat. There will be room however for the replacement of some imported soft and filler wheats by domestic wheat, and in the years before the U.K. became a net exporter of barley there should have been a displacement of some imported barley. Both of these substitutions do appear to have occurred, so that imports of barley and French wheat in the months after harvest have in general been less than the monthly average—this for a period from 1955 to 1965.

As a general working hypothesis it appears reasonable to suggest that in the months following harvest the supply of domestic grains is high relative to the demand for them, and thus domestic cereals prices are generally depressed during this period. A 'floor price' will be imposed by producers' reluctance to sell grain at below certain prices, given that they expect prices to rise later in the season and that they are now eligible for storage incentive payments. The lower autumn cereal prices become the higher the inducement to improvise means of grain storage, a move which would reduce the excess of grain supply.[7]

During this post-harvest period the degree of interaction between the domestic and international cereals market will be low, since the only imported cereals will tend to be of types which are not directly competitive with U.K. grains. It is probable however that market expectations about cereals prices later in the season will depend upon international cereals prices, and therefore that the 'floor price' of domestic cereals will be a function of the international prices of grains.

As the cereal year proceeds there will be an increase in the interaction between the two markets. For, later in the year domestic cereals supplies decline relative to the demand for them, with the result that the prices of domestic grains harden progressively, so that at the end of the season they approach the international prices for comparable grains. During this period millers, compounders and other users will be purchasing grain of similar quality from both domestic and foreign sources, so that the prices paid for them will be much the same. A further factor contributing to the seasonal pattern of price differentials is the seasonal change in the quality of home-grown cereals marketed. Imported grains throughout the year must be clean and of a uniformly low moisture content for storage on the voyage, whilst marketings of domestic grains are liable to be of poorer quality immediately after harvest, but improve throughout the year as cereals of progressively better storing quality are sold. This should result in some hardening of home-grown cereals prices relative to those of imported grains as the cereal year proceeds. However it seems unlikely that quality improvement is a major factor in explaining the seasonal price differential pattern, for as the Cereal Survey results indicate,[8] millers and compounders establish minimum grain quality standards and generally do not pay premiums for grain deliveries of superior quality.

It is of interest to note that, despite much larger domestic crops of both wheat and barley, in recent years, the prices of domestic cereals in the period of post-harvest flush have not been lower relative to imported grain prices than they were in earlier years. A probable explanation for this is that the rapid development of on-farm storage facilities, and the operation of the seasonal incentive schemes for wheat and barley, have done much to reduce the relative excess of domestic cereals supply in the post-harvest period and have mitigated the effect of larger crops.

The discussion above has treated the U.K. cereals market as if it were uniform, and has analysed the market situation employing prices measured at the ports. In fact the market is not uniform and it is useful to distin-

[7] An additional factor helping to depress prices at this period will be the movement of non-storable qualities of grain into the market.

[8] Britton, D. K., op. cit., p. 414.

guish between country and port markets. Country markets are insulated from port markets by the costs incurred in transporting grain to and from the ports. The effect of this insulation will be to make country markets more self-reliant and to diminish the interaction with international grain markets. In consequence it should be expected that prices of domestic cereals in country areas will in the post-harvest period fall below prices at the ports and that they may well rise above port prices at the end of the cereal year.

Appendix II

The data

This Appendix is aimed at explaining the exact nature of all of the variables employed in this study. Firstly all the basic published data will be described and identified by source. Secondly the construction of those series derived from the basic data will be explained, and the assumptions involved in the construction will be stated.

A. Basic data series

The data will be presented according to the four basic parts of the analysis, cereal supply, cereal demand, annual livestock inventories, and quarterly livestock inventories. Any data series which is required in more than one of these sections will only be mentioned with respect to the first relevant section in order. Series will be numbered consecutively, ignoring sections, and these numbers will be used to refer to the different series in describing the construction of such variables as are derived.

In all the following discussions time-series data are being considered. Except where it is explicitly stated that a constant is involved, it should be assumed that all the discussion of the basic and constructed data concerns time series. The length of the time series discussed may be gleaned from the main text of the study and is not stated in this discussion of the data.

(I) *Data for supply analysis*

All data are annual, and for July-June except where otherwise stated.

1. *Acreage of cereals*

(a) U.K. Acreages of wheat (*aW*), barley (*aB*), oats (*aO*) and mixed cereals (*aMC*), at the June census. These were assumed to be equal to the acreages harvested in the following July-June year.

Source: Crop Utilisation (U.C.) statistics published by the Ministry of Agriculture, Fisheries and Food (M.A.F.F.).

(b) Acreage of wheat at the December census in England and Wales. This was assumed to be the U.K. winter wheat acreage (*aWW*).

Source: Press Notices published by M.A.F.F. The full series was obtained directly from the Ministry of Agriculture, Fisheries and Food.

2. *Yield of cereals*

U.K. average yields of wheat (*yW*), barley (*yB*), oats (*yO*) and mixed cereals (*yMC*).

Source: Crop Utilisation, statistics published by M.A.F.F.

3. *Cereal prices paid to farmers*
The average prices of British corn purchased in towns of England and Wales prescribed under the Corn Returns Act, 1882. These are the prices of wheat, barley and oats, and exclude deficiency payments.
Source: Agricultural Statistics, England and Wales, M.A.F.F., H.M.S.O.

4. *Deficiency payments to growers*
The deficiency payments per cwt of wheat, and per acre of barley and oats.
Source: Press Notices, M.A.F.F. The full series was provided directly by the Ministry.

5. *Average monthly rainfall*
Average monthly rainfall in England and Wales.
Source: Annual Abstract of Statistics, C.S.O.

6. *Average monthly temperature*
Daily mean air temperature at sea-level in England and Wales.
Source: Annual Abstract of Statistics, C.S.O.

7. *Fertiliser application*
Home deliveries of nitrogen fertiliser in thousand nutrient tons.
Source: Monthly Digest of Statistics, C.S.O.

8. *Price of milk*
Net price received for milk by wholesale producers in the United Kingdom.
Source: Dairy Facts and Figures, The Federation of U.K. Milk Marketing Boards.

9. *Yield of milk*
Weighted average yield per cow, United Kindgom.
Source: Dairy Facts and Figures, The Federation of U.K. Milk Marketing Boards.

10. *Forage acres per cow*
(a) The basic data were obtained from the *Farm Management Survey* sample of dairy farms in the north west region. Forage acres per livestock unit were calculated for those lowland dairy farms of over 100 acres which had less than ten livestock units of pigs and poultry.
(b) Additional information used was that at a national level average forage acres per cow were 1·59 in 1968-9.
Source: Costs of Milk Production in England and Wales, April 1968 to March 1969, M.M.B.

11. *Acreages of other crops*
Acreage of rotation grasses, clover, lucerne (in England and Wales), permanent grassland, fodder crops (beans, peas, turnips, mangolds, other), and potatoes.
Source: Agricultural Statistics, U.K., M.A.F.F.

(II) *Data for demand analysis*

12. *Quantities of wheat, barley, oats, maize and rye utilised for different purposes in the U.K.*

(a) Feed utilisation–wheat (*wFe*), barley (*bFe*), oats (*oFe*), maize (*mFe*), and rye.
(b) Food utilisation–including manufacturing, milling, brewing and malting–wheat (*wFo*), barley (*bFo*), oats (*oFo*), maize (*mFo*), and rye.
(c) Seed utilisation–wheat (*wS*), barley (*bS*), and oats (*oS*).
Source: Commonwealth Economic Committee, *Grain Crops: Review.*

13. *Quantity of sorghums utilised for feed*
All imported sorghums were assumed to be utilised for animal feed.
Source: Trade and Navigation Accounts, C.S.O.

14. *Quantity of mixed cereals utilised for feed*
All of the U.K. mixed cereal output was assumed to be consumed by livestock.
Source: Crop Utilisation, M.A.F.F.

15. *Quantities of other feedingstuffs for animals*
(a) Wheat milling offals, and oilcake and meal disposals (high plus medium protein, and low protein).
Source: Monthly Digest of Statistics, C.S.O.
(b) Brewers dried grains, fish meal, blood and bone meal, other cereals offals, dried sugar beet pulp, and molasses. All of these data were available on the basis of June-May years only. They were however treated as if for July-June years.
Source: Incomplete series can be found in *Economic Trends,* No. 130, C.S.O., Aug. 1964. The series were completed by data provided directly from M.A.F.F.
(c) Barley malt culms.
Source: Crop Utilisation, M.A.F.F.

16. *Quantity of preserved forage*
The variable used for this was 'total hay production in the U.K.'. Hence silage is overlooked.
Source: Crop Utilisation, M.A.F.F.

17. *Prices of cereals for livestock feed*
(a) For wheat, barley and maize prices, indices were used for whole wheat (*pIW*), whole barley (*pIB*) and maize meal (*pIM*) (1954-5 to 1956-7 = 100).
Source: Agricultural Statistics, U.K., M.A.F.F., H.M.S.O.
(b) The series used for the price of feeding oats, (*pIO*), was a straight twelve-month average of the monthly series of 'feeding oats prices paid to growers', converted into an index with 1954-5 to 1956-7 = 100.
Source: Ag. Stats., E. & W., M.A.F.F.

18. *Prices of other feedingstuffs*
Price indices of wheat offals, maize meal, white fish meal, and the price index of all feedingstuffs (*pF*).
Source: Ag. Stats., U.K., M.A.F.F.

19. *Prices of cereals for human and industrial consumption*
(a) (i) For the average retail price of bread (*pBr*) a four quarter average of the 'retail price of white bread: large loaves' , has been used.

(ii) For the retail price of oats and oatmeal products (*pO*) a four quarter average of the published quarterly data has been used.
Source: Domestic Food Consumption and Expenditure, National Food Survey.
(b) (i) For barley (*pBM*), a twelve-month average of the monthly series 'malting barley prices paid to growers' has been used.
(ii) For maize (*pM*), a twelve-month average of the monthly series 'price of imported maize' has been employed.
Source: Ag. Stats. E. & W., M.A.F.F.

20. *Personal disposable income*
Source: Monthly Dig. Stats., C.S.O.

21. *U.K. Population*
Source: Monthly Dig. Stats., C.S.O.

22. *Retail price index (all items)*
A series has been constructed using shorter linked series with a base of 100 in January 1956. The original data were on a calendar year basis and were transformed to a crop year basis by averaging the values for adjacent years.
Source: Annual Abstract of Stats., C.S.O.

(The following data were required for construction of indices of the number of livestock units on farms.)

23. *Livestock numbers on U.K. farms*
Data for the following classes of livestock at the June and December censuses were employed:
(a) *Cattle:*
Dairy cows, heifers in calf with first calf, bulls and bull calves for service, other cattle > 2 years, other cattle 1-2 years old, other cattle < 1 year old, and cows in calf but not in milk.
(b) *Pigs:*
Sows for breeding, boars for service, other pigs > 5 months old, other pigs 2-5 months old, and other pigs < 2 months old.
(c) *Poultry:* Laying fowls, and table birds or broilers.
Source: Ag. Stats. U.K., M.A.F.F.

24. *Livestock Unit Coefficients*
While the feed requirement of certain classes of animals have changed on a per animal basis with time this is less marked for some animals than others. Thus static coefficients were used for some livestock. These were (in livestock units):

Bulls and bull calves 0·7	Other cattle:
Heifers in calf 0·7	> 2 years 0·7
Cows in calf but not in milk 0·7	1-2 years 0·7
	< 1 year 0·5
	Sows 0·5
	Boars 0·3

(Where one standard livestock unit is equivalent to the feed requirement of a 9 cwt cow producing 700 gallons of milk. This is equivalent to 4,179 lb of starch equivalent or 5,805 lb of concentrates at 72 per cent starch equivalent. The 4,179 lb is comprised of 2,190 lb maintenance, 120 lb for calf before birth and 1,869 lb for 700 gallons at 2·67 lb per gallon).
Source: Hopkins, J. R., West Midland Region of N.A.A.S. Information, 'Woodthorne', Wolverhampton, April 1967.
For certain other classes of livestock it was considered necessary to construct livestock unit coefficients which shift with time. These were for dairy cows and laying fowls, which have exhibited considerable increases in output per animal, and fattening pigs and broilers (including table birds) which have been bred with considerably improved feed-conversion ability. The following data were required for these purposes.
(a) *Milk yield per dairy cow*
Average annual milk yield per dairy cow in England and wales. *Source: Dairy Facts and Figures.* The Federation of U.K. Milk Marketing Boards.
(b) *Average yield per laying hen–U.K.*
Source: Production and Utilisation of Eggs in the U.K., M.A.F.F.
(c) *Concentrate requirement per dozen eggs*
Source: Farm Management Handbook, University of Bristol.
Only two observations were employed, 7·6 lb/doz. eggs in 1958 and 5·8 lb/doz. eggs in 1967.
(d) *Fattening pigs–concentrate requirement per pound liveweight*
Only two figures were used in this case. They were that the food-conversion efficiency in pig production (including both breeding and fattening stock) rose from 5·13 lb of feed per pound liveweight in 1953 to 4·42 in 1963-5. Data from the Cambridge costings scheme. *Source:* Sturrock, F. G., and R. F. Ridgeon, *A Comparison of Pig Production in England, Denmark, and Holland.* Farm Econ. Branch. School of Agric., Cambridge U., Occasional Paper No. 11, Dec. 1966.
(e) *Broilers–concentrate requirement per pound liveweight*
Data for only two years were employed, 3·0 lb of feed per pound liveweight in 1959 for a 3 lb bird, and 2·3 lb per pound in 1967. *Source: Farm Management Handbook,* Dept. Econ., Bristol U., 1959 and 1967.

25. *Cereal consumption weights for livestock*
Static weights based on 1957-8 data were derived for cattle, pigs and poultry, with a different set of weights for the consumption of each cereal. Thus the weights used were (consumption weights):

	Wheat	Barley	Oats	Maize
Cattle	2·86	12·38	35·59	8·48
Pigs	10·49	47·50	8·54	0
Poultry	45·74	8·62	15·56	8·28

These weights were calculated according to the following formula:

$$\text{weight } ij = \frac{(\text{cereal } i \text{ as \% } B.I.S.j)\,(B.I.S.j \text{ as \% } T.C.F.j) + (\text{cereal } i \text{ as \% } H.G.S.j)\,(H.G.S.j \text{ as \% } T.C.F.j)}{(B.I.S.j \text{ as \% } T.C.F.j) + (H.G.S.j \text{ as \% } T.C.F.j)}$$

where *B.I.S.* = bought in straight feed
H.G.S. = home-grown straight feed
T.C.F. = total concentrate feed
i = wheat, barley, oats, maize
j = cattle, pigs, poultry

Source of *B.I.S.j, H.G.S.j* and *T.C.F.j*: *Feeding Stuffs Survey,* 1957-9, M.A.F.F.

(III) *Data for the annual livestock inventory analysis*
(The livestock data used were those under set 21 in the preceding section.)

26. *Gross prices of livestock and livestock products*
The following price indices are calculated so as to take account of the deficiency payments to producers:

(a) Gross price index of clean cattle
(b) Price index of milk
(c) Price index of total poultry U.K.
(d) Price index of eggs
(e) Gross price of other clean pigs
(f) Price index of sows

Source: Ag. Stats., U.K. M.A.F.F.

27. *Value of livestock and livestock product output from U.K. farms at constant prices*
The value of output of the following products at 1954-5 to 1956-7 prices have been used:
Calves and cattle, sheep and lambs, pigs; poultry, eggs, and milk and milk products.
Source: Output and Utilisation of Farm Produce in the U.K. M.A.F.F.

28. *Data to calculate yield of milk per cow*
In calculating returns of milk per cow a series for the yield of lowland dairy cows in the north-west region was employed. The following data taken from *North-west Region Farm Management Surveys* was employed.
(a) Gallons of milk per livestock acre, lowland dairy farms, north-west region.
(b) Number of cows per 100 livestock acres, lowland dairy farms, north-west region.
(The price index of all feedingstuffs (*pF*) was that presented under 16 above.)

(IV) *Data for the quarterly livestock inventory analysis*

29. *Livestock numbers*

Census data at March, June, September, and December for livestock in England and Wales for the following livestock were employed.

(a) Cattle: Cows and heifers in milk, cows in calf but not in milk, heifers in calf with first calf, and other cattle.

(b) Pigs: Sows in pig, gilts in pig, other sows, barren sows for fattening, other pigs > 5 months, other pigs 2-5 months, and other pigs < 2 months.

Source: Ag. Stats., England and Wales, M.A.F.F.

(c) Fowls: fowls < 6 months for broiler production, and fowls < 6 months for table other than broilers.

Source: Ag. Stats. U.K., M.A.F.F.

30. *Calves slaughtered*

Monthly data on calf slaughter (*cV*) in the U.K. Aggregated on three-month basis for use.

Source: Monthly Digest of Stats., C.S.O.

31. *Prices of livestock and livestock products*

The following monthly price indices were used. Where relevant they make allowance for the deficiency payments to producers. (All indices have 1954-5 to 1956-7 = 100.)

(a) Price index of milk
(b) Price index of cows
(c) Gross price index of clean cattle
(d) Gross price index of other clean pigs
(e) Price index of fowls, England and Wales
(f) Price of eggs

Source: Ag. Stats. U.K., M.A.F.F.

32. *Prices of feedingstuffs for livestock*

(a) Price of feeding barley (*pFB*)–price for feeding barley paid to growers in England and Wales. It is monthly data and straight three-month averages were used.

(b) Price of feeding wheat (*pFW*)–price for feeding wheat paid to growers in England and Wales. It is monthly data and straight three-month averages were used.

Source: Ag. Stats. England and Wales, M.A.F.F.

(c) Price of compound feedingstuffs for cattle (*pCOM*). Monthly price index of compound feedingstuffs for cattle in Great Britain, 1954-5 to 1956-7 = 100. A straight three-month average was used.

Source: Ag. Stats. U.K., M.A.F.F.

(The indices used for the price of cows (*pC*), clean cattle (*plC*), and sows (*pS*) are those under 24.)

B. Constructed data series

(Numbers in parentheses are the references of the basic series above.)

(I) *Data for the supply analysis*

33. *Total grain acreage* (*aG*)

This is the sum of the acreages of wheat (*aW*), barley (*aB*), oats (*aO*) and mixed cereals (*aMC*), (*la*).

34. *Spring wheat acreage* (*aSW*)

It was found necessary to define the December wheat acreage for England and Wales as the U.K. winter wheat acreage (*aWW*, (*lb*). The spring wheat acreage for the U.K. is defined as the U.K. June wheat acreage (*aW*), (*la*), minus the winter wheat acreage.

35. *Returns per acre to wheat, barley and oats*

(a) Average deficiency payment per cwt of wheat (4); adding this to the average price of wheat (3) produced the average gross price of wheat.
(b) Average deficiency payments per acre of oats and barley (4) divided by their average yields (2) produced the average deficiency payments per cwt. Adding these to the average oat and barley prices (4) produced gross price series.

In the case of barley, deficiency payments were only made for feeding barley up until 1957-8. It was therefore necessary to adjust the average deficiency payment per cwt of barley downward for the pre 1957-8 years by the ratio of feeding barley production to total barley production (12).
(c) Gross prices for the three cereals were multiplied by their average yields per acre to produce returns per acre of wheat (*rW*), barley (*rB*), and oats (*rO*).

36. *Returns per acre of* (*all*) *cereals*

(a) Returns per acre of the individual cereals (35), were multiplied by their June acreages (1) and summed.
(b) The June acreages of wheat, barley and oats were summed and divided into the product of step (a) to produce a weighted average return per acre of cereals (*rG*).

37. *Returns per acre from milk* (*rM*)

(a) Net price received for milk by wholesale producers in the U.K. (8) was multiplied by average yield per cow in the U.K. (9) to produce average return per cow.
(b) The series of forage acres per livestock unit for the sample of north-west dairy farms (10a) was used to construct an index of forage acres per livestock unit with a base of 100 in 1968-9.

Because the sample on which this calculation is based was chosen so that nearly all the livestock units were dairy cattle, the index of forage acres per livestock unit is assumed to represent forage acres per dairy cow.
(c) Multiplying the index obtained in (b) by the national average of forage acres per dairy cow in 1968-9 (10b) produces an estimate of the national average of forage acres per dairy cow on a time-series basis. This is on the assumption that changes in stocking density were the same in the north-west region as in the U.K. as a whole.

(d) Dividing the product of (a) by that of step (c) produces an estimate of average returns from milk per forage acre.

38. *Weather (aridity) indices*
All of the weather indices used, autumn weather (*W*), spring weather (*WS*), and summer weather (*Wr*), were calculated according to the following formula.

$$\text{Index} = \frac{\frac{12}{n} \sum_{i=1}^{n} (Pi)}{\frac{1}{n} \cdot \sum_{i=1}^{n} (Ti) + 10}$$

where the *Pi* are the monthly average rainfall figures (5), and the *Ti* are the monthly average temperature figures. This formula for the de Martonne aridity index is that presented by Oury (op. cit.) and the constants employed which seem to be discretionary, are the ones used by him.

39. *Acreage of permanent and temporary grassland plus fodder (aPTGF)*
This is defined to be the sum of the acreages of rotation grasses, clover, lucerne (in England and Wales), permanent grassland, and fodder crops (11).

(II) *Data for the demand analysis*

40. *Quantity of cereal feed (qCF)*
This is the sum of (a) wheat for feed, (*wFe*), (12); (b) barley for feed, (*bFe*), (12); (c) oats for feed (*oFe*), (12); (d) rye for feed, (12); maize for feed, (*mFe*), (12); sorghums for feed, (13); and mixed cereals for feed (14).

41. *Quantity of high-energy feed (qHF)*
This is the sum of series (40), wheat milling offals (15), dried sugar-beet pulp (15), and molasses (15).

42. *Quantity of protein feed (qP)*
This is the sum of brewers dried grains (15); barley malt culms (15); oilcake and meal disposals (high plus medium protein and low protein), (15); white fish meal (15); meat, blood and bone meal (15); and other cereals offals (15).
All feeds which provide more than 13·0 per cent digestible crude protein in the diets of ruminants (fresh weight basis) were defined as protein feeds, and all those with below this amount as high-energy feeds. The crude protein coefficients were taken from McDonald, P., R. A. Edwards and J. F. D. Greenhalgh, *Animal Nutrition.* Oliver and Boyd, 1966.

43. *Price of high-energy feed (pE)*
(a) The following series were multiplied

price index of whole barley (17) x quantity of barley for feed (12).
price index of whole wheat (17) x quantity of wheat for feed (12).
price index of wheat offals (18) x quantity of wheat milling offals (15).

(b) The products of (a) were summed.

(c) The quantities of barley for feed (12), wheat for feed (12), and wheat milling offals (15) were summed.
(d) The product of step (b) was divided by that of step (c) to provide a weighted price index of high-energy feed (*pE*).

44. *Price of protein feed* (*pP*)
The category of other cereals offals (15) excludes wheat and barley offals, and was assumed to be mainly maize offals.
(a) Thus the following series were multiplied

price index of maize meal (17) x quantity of other cereals offals (15).
price index of white fish meal x quantity of white fish meal (15).

(b) The products of (a) were summed.
(c) The quantities of other cereals offals (15) and of white fish meal (15) were summed.

(d) The product of step (b) was divided by that of step (c) to provide a weighted price index of protein feed (*pP*).

45. *Livestock unit series for dairy cows*
(a) Milk yield per cow (in each year) (24) was multiplied by a factor of 2·67 lb, which is the estimated starch equivalent requirement per gallon of milk (24).
(b) To the product of (a), the estimated starch equivalent requirement for the output of an average cow, was added 2,310 lb, which is the estimated maintenance and calf support requirement of the cow. This produced the estimated total starch equivalent need, in pounds, for the average cow.
(c) One livestock unit was defined to require 4,179 lb starch equivalent (or 5,805 lb concentrate feed), (24). Thus dividing the product of step (b) by 4,179 gave the feed requirements of the average cow in terms of livestock units.

46. *Livestock unit series for fattening pigs*
(a) By a process of linear interpolation and extrapolation, using values of 5·13 and 4·42 lb of concentrates per pound liveweight of fattening pigs in 1953-4 and 1964-5 respectively (24), a series was constructed for the feed requirement per pound liveweight of fattening pigs.
(b) It was assumed that the average liveweight of fat pigs remained at 220 lb over the period. Thus the series formed in step (a) was multiplied by 220 to obtain a series of the concentrate requirements per fat pig in terms of pounds of concentrates.
(c) Dividing the series produced in step (b) by 5,805 expressed the feed requirements per fat pig in terms of livestock units.

47. *Livestock unit series for laying hens*
(a) Using the two observations that laying hens used 7·6 lb of concentrates per dozen eggs in 1958-9 and 5·8 lb in 1967-8 (24), an index of concentrate requirement per dozen eggs for the period 1954-5 to 1967-8 was obtained by linear interpolation and extrapolation.

(b) The index produced in (a) was multiplied by the series for the average yield per laying hen (24) expressed in dozens, and this yielded a series for the concentrate requirement per layer.
(c) Dividing the series produced in (b) by 5,805 produced expresses feed requirement per layer in terms of livestock units.

48. *Livestock unit series for broilers*
(a) Using the two observations that to produce 1 lb liveweight on a broiler required 3·0 lb of concentrate feed in 1958-9 and 2·30 lb in 1967-8 (24), an index of feed required per pound liveweight of a broiler was obtained by linear interpolation and extrapolation.
(b) It was assumed that the average liveweight of broilers slaughtered remained at 2·98 lb throughout the period (2·24 lb carcass weight at 75 per cent killing out). Thus multiplying the index in (a) by 2·98 produced a series for the food requirement per broiler.
(c) Dividing the series in (b) by 5,805 expressed the feed requirement per broiler in terms of livestock units.

49. *Total livestock units on farms–centred on the December census* (*b*)
The numbers of livestock, by class, at the June and December censuses for the U.K. were converted to livestock units by multiplying them by appropriate static coefficients or by one of the series of livestock unit values derived above (45-48). Thus the following multiplications were performed.
(a) Cattle:
(i) Dairy cows x series 45 (livestock units per average dairy cow).
(ii) Heifers in calf with first calf, cows in calf but not in milk, bulls and bull calves for service, other cattle > 2 years old, and other cattle 1-2 years old were all multiplied by 0·7 (24).
(iii) Other cattle < 1 year old x 0·5 (24).
(b) Pigs:
(i) Sows for breeding x 0·5 (24).
(ii) Boars for service x 0·3 (24).
(iii) Other pigs > 5 months, other pigs 2-5 months, and other pigs < 2 months were multiplied by two times the series for the livestock unit equivalence of fattening pigs (46). Twice the value of series 46 was employed, because as the life of the average fattening pig is about 6 months two fattening pigs per year will be required for every one measured at a point in time to maintain inventories at a constant level throughout the year.
(c) Poultry:
(i) Laying and breeding hens were multiplied by the series for the livestock unit equivalence of a laying hen (47).
(ii) Table birds or broilers were multiplied by six times the livestock unit equivalence for broilers series (45). Six times the value of this series was used because broilers have a life of somewhat less than two months and hence six batches of broilers could be assumed to pass through broiler houses in twelve months.

(d) By summing the numbers of livestock units in each subclass of livestock, total livestock unit numbers were calculated for cattle, pigs and poultry at the December and June censuses.
(e) The total livestock unit number variable was to be constructed to explain feed demand occurring over an annual period. Hence an average value for livestock unit numbers over the year was required, rather than a measure of numbers at one point in time. In order to accomplish this the class totals of livestock units calculated in step (d) were transformed according to the formula.

$$\frac{\text{(L.U. numbers) June}_t + 2\text{(L.U. numbers) Dec.}_t + \text{(L.U. numbers) June}_{t+1}}{4}$$

where $t = 1, 2, \ldots, n$ years, and L.U. = livestock unit. This device of giving a double weighting to the December livestock unit numbers effectively centres the average on the middle of each harvest year, which happens to be the time when feed demand is highest due to the non-availability of fresh forage.
(f) The December centred total numbers of livestock units by class, produced by step (e), were summed to produce a variable for the December centred total of all livestock units on U.K. farms (1).

50. *Total number of cereal consumption weighted livestock units on farms–centred on December* (*lw*)
In studying the demand for feed of the four different cereals considered, different classes of livestock (cattle, poultry, and pigs) were weighted according to the importance of the particular cereal in their diet. Hence the December centred totals of livestock units by class of livestock, produced in 48 (e), were multiplied by the four sets of weights presented in 25, to produce a cereal consumption weighted total of livestock unit numbers on farms (*lw*) for each of the four major cereals considered.

(III) *Data for the annual livestock inventory analysis*

51. *An index of milk returns per cow* (*rM*)
(a) The number of gallons of milk per livestock acre (28) was multiplied by 100 and divided by the number of cows per 100 livestock acres on lowland dairy farms in the north west. This produced a series for yield per cow.
(b) The series in part (a) was converted to an index of milk yield per cow with a base of 1954-5 = 100.
(c) The index of yield per cow was multiplied by the price index of milk (26) to obtain an index of milk returns per cow (*rM*)

52. *Returns index to cattle and milk* (*rICM*)
(a) The value of milk sales and of cattle sales were expressed as percentages of the total value of sales of livestock and livestock products (27).
(b) The gross price index of clean cattle (26) was multiplied by the value of cattle sales as a percentage of the total value of livestock and livestock

product sales and added to the returns index to milk (*rM*), (51), which had previously been multiplied by milk sales as a percentage of the value of all livestock and livestock product sales.
(c) The product of step (b) was then divided by the sum of the two percentages for milk and cattle as a proportion of the value of total livestock and livestock product sales to produce an index of returns to cattle and milk (*rICM*).

53. *Returns index to pigs* (*rH*)
(a) The series expressing the feed requirement per pound liveweight of a fattening pig (46) was converted into an index of feed efficiency with the base 1953-4 = 1·00.
(b) The result of step (a) was then multiplied by the price index of other clean pigs (26) to produce an index of returns to pigs.

54. *Index of returns to fowls* (*rF*)
(a) The series for average yield per laying hen (24) was converted to an index, with 1954-5 = 1·00.
(b) The series for the concentrate requirement per dozen eggs (47) was converted to an index with base 1953-4 = 100.
(c) The indices produced in (a) and (b) were multiplied together.
(d) The index produced in (c) was then multiplied by the price index of eggs (26) to produce a returns index to eggs.
(e) The series of feed requirement per pound liveweight of broilers was converted to index with 1953-4 = 1·00.
(f) Index (e) was multiplied by the price index of table poultry to produce a returns index to table poultry.
(g) The two returns indices for eggs and table poultry were multiplied by weights expressing the values of egg production and of poultry sales as percentages of total livestock and livestock product sales.
(h) The sum of the two weighted series in (g) divided by the sum of the weights produced a weighted returns index to fowls.

(IV) *Data for the quarterly livestock inventory analysis*

55. *An index of milk returns per cow* (*rM*)
(a) Reading the annual milk yield per cow figures in series (24a) as being for December, a quarterly yield series was constructed by interpolation. (This is a different basis to that used in deriving the annual *rM* variables.)
(b) Using March 1958 as the base equal to 1·00 an index of yield per cow was constructed from series (a).
(c) The index in (b) was multiplied by three-month averages of the price index of milk (31) to produce a returns index to milk (*rM*).

56. *An Index of returns to pigs* (*rH*)
(a) The values of the annual feed-efficiency index for pigs derived in 53a were interpreted as applying to December and a quarterly feed-efficiency index was produced by interpolation.
(b) The values of the index in (a) were multiplied by three-month averages

of the price index of other clean pigs to produce an index of returns to pigs (*rH*). (This is merely a quarterly version of the annual *rH* variable.)

57. *Returns to fowls* (*rF*)

The procedure adopted (and the variables) was identical to that in constructing the annual variable *rF*.

Steps (a), (b), (c), (e), (g), and (h) were performed on quarterly series derived from the annual ones by means of interpolation—the values of the annual series were interpreted as applying to the December quarter in each year.

Three-monthly averages of the egg and fowl price indices (32) were employed in steps (d) and (f) respectively.

Bibliography

Allen, R. G. D., *Mathematical Economics* (2nd Ed.). Macmillan 1964.

Binder, Mrs. A. K., 'Relationships in World Prices of Coarse Grains and some Implications for an International Grains Agreement', *F.A.O. Monthly Bul. of Ag. Econ. and Stat.*, Vol. 15, No. 9.

Britton, D. K., *Cereals in the United Kingdom*. Pergamon, 1969.

Chandler, A. I., 'An Analysis of the Econometric Problems Involved in Misspecifying the Unit Time Period of an Economic Model'. Unpublished M.A. dissertation, Manchester University, 1969.

Cochrane, D., and G. H. Orcutt, 'Application of Least-Squares Regression to Relationships containing Autocorrelated Error Terms', *J. Am. Statist. Ass.*, Vol. 44.

Colman, D. R., 'A New Study of United Kingdom Cereal Supply', *J. Agric. Econ.*, Vol. 21, 1970.

Coppock, J. T., *An Agricultural Atlas of England and Wales*. Faber, 1964.

Cowling, K., 'The Estimation of Supply Response at the Farm-Firm Level. A Comparison Among Programming and Regression Models'. Ph.D. Thesis, University of Illinois, 1962.

Cromarty, W. A., 'An Econometric Model for United States Agriculture', *J. Am. statist. Ass.*, Vol. 54, 1969.

Cromarty, W. A., *Predicting the Impact of Alternative Government Programs on the Wheat and Feed–Livestock Economies*. Michigan State Univ. Tech. Bul. 286, 1962.

Dardis, R., 'The Welfare Cost of Grain Protection in the United Kingdom', *J. Fm Econ.*, Vol. 49, No. 3, Aug. 1967.

Day, R. H., 'An Approach to Production Response', *Agric. Econ. Res.*, Vol. 14, No. 4, U.S.D.A., 1962.

Edwards, C., 'Resource Fixity and Farm Organisation', *J. Fm Econ.*, Vol. 41, 1959.

Feltner, R. L., 'Alternative Models of Feed-Livestock Economy'. Unpublished Ph.D. Thesis, North Carolina State University, 1964.

Foote, R. J., *Statistical Analyses Relating to the Feed-Livestock Economy*, U.S.D.A., Tech. Bul. No. 1070, June 1953.

Fuller, W. A. and J. E. Martin, 'The Effects of Autocorrelated Errors on the Statistical Estimation of Distributed Lag Models', *J. Fm Econ.*, Vol. 43, 1961.

Gardner, T. W., 'A Note on Cereal Prices and Acreages', *J. Agric. Econ.*, Vol. 12, No. 3, June 1957.

Greer, E. N., 'The Wheat Variety, Maris Widgeon', *Ceres*, No. 1, 1968.

Griliches, Z., 'A Note on "Serial Correlation Bias in Estimates of Distributed Lags,"' *Econometrica*, Vol. 29, 1961.

Griliches, Z., 'Demand for Inputs and Supply Elasticity', *J. Fm Econ.*, Vol. 44, 1959.

Griliches, Z., 'Distributed Lags: A Survey', *Econometrica*, Vol. 35, 1967.

Guise, J. W. B., 'Factors Associated with Variations in the Aggregate Average Yield of New-Zealand Wheat (1918-1967)', *Am. J. Ag. Econ.*, Vol. 51, 1969.

Heady, E. O., *Economics of Agricultural Production and Resource Use.* Prentice-Hall, 1952.

Heady, E. O. and L. G. Tweeten, *Resource Demand and Structure of the Agriculture Industry.* Iowa State University Press, 1963.

Henderson, R. M., 'The Utilization of Agricultural Land: A Theoretical and Empirical Enquiry', *Rev. Econ. and Stats.*, Vol. 14, No. 3, 1959.

Hildreth, C. and F. G. Jarrett, *A Statistical Study of Livestock Production and Marketing,* Cowles Commission Monograph, No. 15, 1955.

Hill, B., 'Supply Responses in Grain Production in England and Wales 1952-1963', *J. agric. Econ.*, Vol. 16, No. 3, June 1965.

Johnston, J., *Econometric Methods.* McGraw-Hill, 1963.

Jones, G. T., 'The Influence of Price on Livestock Production over the Last Decade', *J. agric. Econ.*, Vol. 16, Dec. 1965.

Jones, G. T., 'The Response of the Supply of Agricultural Products in the United Kindgom to Price, Part II', *Fm Economist,* Vol. 10, No. 1, 1962.

Josling, T. E., *The United Kingdom Grains Agreement (1964): An Economic Analysis,* Institute of International Agriculture, Michigan State University, 1968.

Leviatan, N., 'Consistent Estimation of Distributed Lags', *Int. Econ. Review,* Vol. 4., 1963.

Lipson, E., *The Economic History of England, Vol. II.* A. & C. Black Ltd., 1934.

Lord Ernle, *English Farming, Past and Present.* Longmans, Green & Co., *1922.*

Malinvaud, E., *Statistical Methods of Econometrics.* North-Holland Publishing Co., 1966.

McClements, L. D., *A Quarterly Model of Pig Supply,* Manchester University Department of Ag. Econ., Bul. No. 123, 1968.

McClements, L. D., 'A Model of Pig Supply', *J. Agric. Econ.*, Vol. 20, May, 1969.

McDonald, P., R. A. Ewards, J. F. D. Greenhalgh, *Animal Nutrition.* Oliver and Boyd, 1966.

Nerlove, M., 'Elasticities of Selected Agricultural Commodities', *J. Fm Econ.*, Vol. 38, 1956.

Nerlove, M., *Estimation and Identification of Cobb Douglas Functions.* North-Holland Publishing Co., 1965.

Nerlove, M., *The Dynamics of Supply.* Johns Hopkins Press, 1958.

Nerlove, M., and Wallis, K. F., 'Use of the Durbin-Watson Statistic in Inappropriate Situations', *Econometrica,* Vol. 34, 1966.

Oury, B. R. P., *A Production Model for Wheat and Feedgrains in France,* (1956-61). North-Holland Publishing Co., 1966.

Rayner, A. J., 'The Demand for Inputs and the Aggregate Supply Function for Agriculture', *J. Agric. Econ.,* Vol. 21, 1970.

Shaw, L. H., 'The Effects of Weather on Agricultural Output: A Look at Methodology', *J. Fm Econ.,* Vol. 64, 1964.

Strotz, R. H., 'Interdependence as a Specification Error', *Econometrica,* Vol. 28, 1960.

Telser, L., 'Discrete Sample and Moving Sums in a Stationary Stochastic Process', *J. Am. Statist. Ass.,* Vol. 62, 1967.

Thomas, W. J., The section concerning the U.K. in *'The Stabilisation of World Trade in Coarse Grains', A Consideration of the Underlying Economic Issues,* F.A.O., Commodity Policy Studies No. 14, 1963.

Trevelyan, G. M., *British History in the Nineteenth Century.* Longmans Green and Co., 1922.

Wallace, D. B., 'Cereal Production in the U.K. and Cereal Imports Over the Years', *Ceres,* No. 1, 1968.

Walters, A. A., *An Introduction to Econometrics.* MacMillan, 1968.

Waud, R. N., 'Small Sample Bias Due to Misspecification in the "Partial Adjustment" and "Adaptive Expectations" Models', *J. Am. Statist. Ass.,* Vol. 61, 1966.

Working, E. J., *Demand for Meat,* Institute of Meat Packing, University of Chicago, 1954.